Dr. John Pugh, in The Dynamics of Change in the Human Race: The Spirit's work (formerly Christian Formation Counseling) has written a wonderful book about the Spirit's intimate involvement throughout the process of counseling. Some books on Christian counseling baptize basically secular counseling with a sprinkling of Christian thoughts. Pugh's approach, though, integrates the Spirit throughout counseling and shows the central role of God in even the most serious human problems. This book will bless your spirit and enrich your Christian practice."

Everett L. Worthington, Jr. Author of Forgiving and Reconciling: Bridges to Wholeness and Hope.

"As the director of the Biblical Counseling and Spiritual Formation Network (BCSFN), I'm often asked, 'Why connect biblical counseling and spiritual formation?' My friend, John Pugh, in his work The Dynamics of Change (formerly Christian Formation Counseling) proves that spiritual formation and Christian counseling should and can be seamlessly united.

In the great tradition of Christian soul physicians, John shows that a truly biblical model of counseling offers a comprehensive portrait of human nature designed by God, disordered by sin, and most importantly, changed by grace. Connecting the Spirit's work and the daily faith experience of the Christian, The Dynamics of Change (formerly Christian Formation Couselin) develops a deeply relational approach to counseling—the relationship of the client to God and of the counselor and client to each other.

Astutely, John understands the myriad complexities of the change process. His model addresses these by exposing typical response patterns, both healthy and unhealthy, to the Spirit's work, and how these responses relate to our spiritual, relational, mental, volitional, and emotional capacities as image bearers. The end result of The Dynamics of Change is a fresh perspective on personality theory that is at once biblical and practical.

Readers longing to integrate historic spiritual formation into the very fabric of their counseling, pastoring, and spiritual friendship will find John's work invaluable."

Robert W. Kellemen, Ph.D., Founder, RPM Ministries; Director Biblical Counseling and Spiritual Formation Network; Author of Soul Physicians, Spiritual Friends, and Beyond the Suffering; and Chair of the MA in Christian Counseling and Discipleship Department at Capital Bible Seminary in Lanham, MD.

THE DYNAMICS OF CHANGE IN THE HUMAN RACE

THE SPIRIT'S WORK CHRISTIAN
FORMATION COUNSELING: THE WORK
OF THE SPIRIT IN THE HUMAN RACE

JOHN E PUGH

ISBN: 979-8-89419-167-6 (sc)
ISBN: 979-8-89419-168-3 (hc)
ISBN: 979-8-89419-169-0 (e)

Because of the dynamic nature of the Internet, any web addresses or links contained in this book may have changed since publication and may no longer be valid. The views expressed in this work are solely those of the author and do not necessarily reflect the views of the publisher, and the publisher hereby disclaims any responsibility for them.

THE EWINGS
PUBLISHING

One Galleria Blvd., Suite 1900, Metairie, LA 70001
(504) 702-6708

I want to dedicate this manuscript to my wife, Sally, who has endured many solitary hours while I was researching and writing this important work. I owe her a debt of gratitude for her enduring love and constant intercession on my behalf.

I want to thank my colleagues and brothers in the faith for your trust and patience with me! You know who you are.

CONTENTS

FOREWORD

There is growing evidence that the counseling needs of our society are increasing in complexity with a parallel abundance of self help solutions. Those engaged in the mental health professions often need resources by which to help those in their care. Unfortunately, for those in Christian counseling ministry, this abundance of self help, pop-psychology materials complicate ministry efforts to those facing such complex emotional, cognitive, relational, and spiritual difficulties. At one level, pop psychology offers quick and easy solutions, often yielding short-lived relief; yet at another level, such simplistic approaches offer false hope and increased disillusionment to those seeking professional counseling support.

In response to this crisis, many Christian thinkers have worked diligently to create resources for equipping lay and professional therapists in the enterprise of helping address the increasingly complex problems experienced by those seeking counseling and support. Some endeavors by well-meaning Christian authors inadvertently polarize those good seeking resources; that is, some demonize psychological principles as wholly worldly, whereas others enshrine so-called secular methodologies as the only authoritative way to understand the human dilemma and perhaps the only solution to our collective emotional ills. It is for these reasons that I feel honored to introduce my colleague, Dr. John Pugh's text: The Dynamics of Change in the Human Race: The Spirit's work formerly Christian Formation Counseling: The work of the Spirit in the Human Race.

Dr. Pugh provides an exegetically sound description of the human condition. In the same effort, he provides a well-integrated understanding and review of key systems in understanding.

This book provides simple and practical resources for lay and professional workers alike. Students and practitioners of Christian formation will find this book an indispensable aid to their work and a reliable reference for information on a wide range of topics related to Christian counseling. My only regret is that this book was not available sooner!

—Freeman Chakara, Psy.D.

SECTION ONE

INTRODUCTION TO CONCEPTS

The purpose of this written work is to identify the work of Christ manifest by the Holy Spirit's work in any given person's life and to use this information in a manner that it will successfully advance these individuals through the change process. While some might regard the idea of Christian or spiritual formation as too narrow of a focus by the variety of observed dysfunctional human behavior, on the contrary, a Christian formation perspective for the changing human behavior more dynamically actually involves a much broader, more focused view of human beings than traditional secular theories would propose. The perspective that judiciously employs Christian formation ideology would involve a more rounded and comprehensive description of how human beings respond and change. Formation perspectives may extend not only to counseling theory, but well beyond the concepts that describe human pathology. It more comprehensively lays the foundation and purpose for change in all human beings even those that never needed to see a psychiatrist, psychologist or professional counselor. Christian formation concepts do not just modify existing personality theory to know the heart mind of every individual, it creates a whole new foundation for the life-change process that might be used to truly help any person that is fully motivated to apply it.

The Christian Formation concept has been used to describe the Spirit's work within the life of a human being to change from their former selves into a more Christ-centered being beyond that of becoming a member of some institutionalized religion. This makes Christian formation a more personal form of experience that a person may have with God. It focuses on human beings who are in a living synthesis of their faith, through their everyday life experiences.

Christian Formation is especially relevant to counseling practice in light of this definition because spirituality is seen in terms of its practical manifestations of personal struggles that human beings face in themselves and in their relationships. This written work will outline major themes that bear relevance to the concept of Christian formation in the counseling context. First, there is the preconditioning of the Spirit evidenced through these personal struggles and in their troubled relationships—issuing concepts of conscience, guilt, and conviction. Second, there is the polar issue of control for human beings—the fear of being controlled at one end of the spectrum and controlling others as a defense against the fear of being controlled on the other end. By this study on the issue of control, the reader may more fully understand the biblical concept of self-control. Also, there is the issue of the proverbial "inner conflict" that will be viewed in a socio-spiritual nuance that will determine how human beings may cycle and recycle their experiences between interpersonal and intra-personal conflict.

The ultimate objective is to review the Spirit's work in the daily life of any person by looking for patterns that start with the typical responses that human beings give to the Holy Spirit's work and how those responses may impact the person's self-concept, behavior, and social and emotional functioning more dynamically. Primarily the human response to the work of the Spirit that convicts the world is to minimize that impact, but even through that minimization of the Spirit's impact, that person is dynamically changed for the worse. The Spirit's work may be observed in any individual, and would certainly be useful in the counseling practice as well. As the practical manifestations of the Spirit's work are considered, certain response patterns based on that initial response (self-critical, blame-shifting, denial or pleasure-seeking) will emerge. Formation strategies also focus on human beings who are in a living synthesis of their faith, or the lack thereof, In the following chapters, we will continue to describe these patterns and how they might impact our traditional theories and also how that modified point of view might also reformulate our strategies for change.

While the study of theological pneumatology traditionally carries the study of the Holy Spirit to higher-level theological explanations that involve a greater understanding of human experiences are transformed by the work of God, this text will observe these transformations by the practical evidence of the Spirit's work on the level of human experience. As well, when a spiritual formation model is developed for the purpose of establishing a personality construct, it will also create a methodology for counseling practice. This study will comply with the views of theological anthropology in a very real and practical way that involve a greater understanding of how human experiences are transformed by the work of the Spirit of God. This text will observe these transformations by the practical evidence of the Spirit's work on the level of human experience. As well, when a spiritual formation model for personality theory is understood from this point of view, a counseling methodology will also be realized, so that the work and study of integrating spiritual issues and values into counseling practice might be more effectively accomplished.

To be clear on how to use the concepts of this written work effectively, one must recognize that the Spirit has all of the same attributes of the triune God of whom he is a member. Such attributes as omnipresence and omniscience are attributes that the Spirit exercises actively to provide evidence of his consistent revelation about God himself to the entire human race, regardless of the individual's response to that revealed truth about God. While the Spirit's ministry to the believer is distinctively more intimate, there may be little observed difference in the response style of any given human being.

What is so reassuring to the follower of Christ is that these varied responses that human beings give the Spirit's preconditioning work do evidence spiritual activity even if they are not a follower of Christ by means of how they must minimize the Spirit's impact.

The ideas set forth in this written work may also have varied responses from those who consider themselves to be Christian counselors. Some may respond in a way to indicate that the specific concepts set forth in this work would amount to an over spiritualization or an over moralization of the typical problems that people face. This reaction may be due to the desire to separate that which is spiritual from professional therapy. There is little comfort to be found in such a distinction because the same objection reveals that within this perspective that there is an inadequate understanding of what Christian spiritual formation brings to the subject of defining human personality. A true psychology and accurate perspective on human personal theory would not rule out such what human beings generally experience with God. The Christian spiritual formation perspective on human beings embraces an important feature that would give a more comprehensive view of the realm of what could be the true psychology of the human being rather than being distinct from it.

At the same time, others will critique this written work as not being "biblical" enough. That perspective might disparage any reference to professional counseling or secular psychology as having nothing valid to offer. It is true that the counselor in training needs to have more than a psychological training to be effective, but the truly competent counselor should utilize everything that could help the counselor gain a greater understanding of people, placing every item of information about human beings into the arsenal of understanding including social science research. But a more comprehensive understanding of the human personality generated from theological perspective is essential for an effective spiritual formation strategy to be implemented. It appears that the present human need, and especially the future prospects for helping others in counseling, demands more training broadly rather than less training to be effective. Ultimately our learning must be from God, regardless of the source of information as Proverbs 1:7 admonishes, **"… the fear of Lord is the beginning of knowledge"** (NIV).

CHAPTER ONE

PRINCIPLES AND PRACTICES

Human beings have often encountered the troubled person that has been wounded by another person—usually the significant other—the person's wife, husband, father, mother, son, daughter, sister or brother. In this age of the individual, the rescue and remedy for such a hurting person would be in the attempt to make this person stronger, more independent and wiser in order to make that person immune to the blows from that "loved one," who shows little or no sign of offering any relief to that suffering person. With all of this, an opportunity for a more comprehensive intervention could be missed if the intervention does not include this person's response to the Spirit's work or if the strategy to overcome fails to recognize how the troubled person might be in the midst of a spiritual awakening through those difficult experiences. As well, this person might bring positive impact on those from whom the injury upon themselves had originally come. By heeding these possibilities, suffering people might not only build on the foundation of spiritual developments of the past already laid in their lives, but also through this spiritual formation or Christian Formation, not only may their personal needs be met, but their relational needs might also be met.

It is, after all, from such wounds from others that virtuous character might be formulated as indicated in scripture (James 1:1–2), but without the aid and comfort of the Spirit, chronic wounds from others would usually infect the human psyche to become deeply damaged and stigmatized to relationships throughout life so that a person's perception of self, others, and external events are distorted from what would be their natural reality. Beyond that, counselors have recognized that these hurtful responses do not have solely an external source, but when human beings are offended, the recipients of these blows respond with their own depraved resources making themselves nearly as culpable as others from whom these offenses originally came. What the Christian Formation gives to us is more than the influence of another sympathetic human being giving a listening ear to another troubled human being. Christian Formation can bring a spiritual influence that can neutralize the blows from others, establish the person in integrity, and bring hope of redemption to the person and to his relationships. But the conflict that can make one person respond positively to the message of redemption can make most human beings to become reliant on their own means to overcome their sense of culpability. And it is true that it is during times of relational altercation and conflict that it is difficult for most to acknowledge God and his Spirit because human beings mostly respond to relational conflict by drawing on their own fallible resources to make things worse.

The truth of redemption could free this person from these fallible methods, but for most people conflict often leads them to respond with more than a simple avoidance of the redemptive truth with self-made responses. This chapter will introduce three elements of spiritual formation that can give a deeper understanding of the typically tragic circumstances of the typical human experiences, so that a more effective strategy for change may be utilized.

The first element is the ever - present *preconditioning of the Spirit* that exists prior to any person's response to conflict. The second and third elements are viewed as subcategories of the first element. The second element is the ever-present failure of human beings to recognize that there is a better alternative for self-determination than to make *faulty attempts to control* their immediate circumstances. They typically feel that when they are compelled and/or oppressed by others, that may instigate within them the tendency to overstep the boundaries of their personal responsibility by attempting futilely o control situations that are beyond their ability to control. The third element involves the proverbial and ever-present internalized conflict that also projects to interpersonal conflict that will, in turn, recycle as an internal conflict once again.

The Preconditioning of the Spirit

Faiver, O'Brien, and Ingersoll (2000) indicate that by understanding the dynamic of guilt, counselors will have the benefit of a superior understanding of their clients. The previous comment is surprisingly a recommendation that does not come from an evangelical perspective and neither are the following classic views of the concept of guilt. Even Freud (1917/1966) understood the significance of guilt to understanding human beings describing it as a tension between societal pressures and personal desires for self-gratification, making guilt nearly synonymous with shame. The theory of personality that he proposed explained that societal demands and pressures reside internal to the human being in what he called the "super-ego" and desires for self-gratification reside within the "id." The "ego," as proposed by Freud's theory, negotiates a peace settlement between the "super-ego" and the "id" to maintain order within the human being. So much of what Freud proposes sounds much like the two natures that are present in the theology of the adherent to the Christian faith, the "sinful nature" and the "spiritual nature," but in contrast to Freud's idea, these two natures described in scripture do not directly conflict or negotiate with each other, but simply describe a state of condition in which the person lives. One more, the contrast of Biblical Theology to that of Freud's ideas is that the "id" works according to the "pleasure principle." According to Freud, the life-giving force for the person is to satisfy the "id" with pleasure, and that, if frustrated, will result in personality stagnation or strangulation minimally and ultimately in physical death (Rychlak, 1981).

And when, according to an evangelical view of Spirit Theology, there is a real but distinct person within the person that is both external and internal to the human being, namely the Holy Spirit, who is the true life-giving force in contrast to the Freudian idea of pleasure. According to scripture, conviction does not come from within the person (Freud's "superego") but from the same person who also gives life, the Spirit of God. Rather, it is the human being bereft of such spiritual comfort that foolishly substitutes pleasure for the solace that can be found in fellowship with the Spirit of God. So, while Freud loses a huge part of the equation in his analysis, namely God, he does recognize the significance of the guilt dynamic to the psychological makeup of human beings. Therefore, he personifies certain aspects of the human being to make them entities all of their own, virtual persons within the person.

Erickson (1963) understood guilt as developmental phenomena where at a certain adolescent stage of development, a young person would automatically feel the compulsion or urge to reach for his/ her very high ideal that the same person initially fails to believe is possible and consequently, loses the initiative. The consequence for this lost initiative is guilt, according to Erickson. The implication for Erickson's definition of guilt is one that indicates that guilt is merely a psychosocial phenomenon and not the product of any personal moral culpability. In addition to Erickson, existential therapists found guilt to be a failure to live up to one's "potentialities," making guilt purely humanistic (Arbuckle, 1975).

Further, biological behaviorism would indicate that guilt is the result of a lack of positive reinforcement of particular reward pathways in the brain as it relates to the external reality of one's positive affect and one's control over one's environment (Derlega, Winstead & Jones, 1999).1 As interesting and inviting as these concepts seem, what they lack is an understanding of guilt as an objective reality that has to do with the continuing revelation of God to human beings by the sovereign act of the Spirit who validates the truth contained in the written Word within the struggles of each person's life, yielding the common result of a constant experience with guilt mitigated only when redemptive truth is found and applied.

Natural revelation needs to be redefined, if not renamed. While the source of this revelation may be assumed to be nature or creation, nature is merely the context of this type of revelation that finds its source in God who is also the ultimate source of all revelation. Theology texts often downplay this source of revelation that otherwise adequately reveals the truth about God to human beings (see Romans 1:20–21). Compared to the source of knowledge about God through scripture, traditional theology seems to consider natural revelation a source of knowledge about God to be too subjective to be significant and/or the basis of officious personal claims of a private audience with God.[2] However, scriptures such as Romans chapters 1–8 and I Corinthians chapters 2 and 4 seem to clarify its role (We will explain how these passages indicate the significant role of natural revelation later in this chapter). Milton Erickson (1998) lists three categories of natural revelation as namely history, the constitution of humanity, and nature. He also indicates that special revelation (scriptures) is God's revelation of himself to humanity, as do many of the traditional theologies. And yet, Erickson (1998, 1989) does take the topic to a higher level:

There is a common ground or a point of contact between the believer and the nonbeliever, or between the gospel and the thinking of the non-Christian. All persons have knowledge of God. Although it may be suppressed to the extent of being unconscious or unrecognizable, it is nonetheless there, and there will be areas of sensitivity to which the message may be effectively directed as a starting point. These areas of sensitivity will vary from one person to another, but they will be there.

The following study will attempt to clarify and specify how this natural revelation might be observed in both the Christian and the non-Christian. It is also important to know the difference between natural revelation and the special revelation that is recorded in scripture, truly the only authoritative body of revealed truth. For the purpose of this text, the more personal type of natural revelation will be defined as the experience of humanity with God's revelation and his truth concerning himself and his relationship to the human race as evidenced through each person's life experience. For example, the passage of I John 1:9 tells the followers of Christ to confess their sins. Do human beings only know about their sins that they have committed that need to be confessed through the special revelation of scripture alone or do they have some residual connection with God as his creatures that enables them to recognize, with some degree of accuracy, what is wrong in their lives without finding chapter and verse? This perspective indicates the main function of natural revelation. It coordinates with the work of the Holy Spirit to give meaningful application of the written Word, giving individualized attention to the personalized application of biblical truth—albeit initiated through natural revelation. Thus, rather than compete with written revelation, natural revelation confirms the essential meaning of scriptures in a more personal, relevant, and significant way. This definition of natural revelation also raises the importance of natural revelation itself as an integral part of God's communication with his creatures for the purpose of personal redemption, improving the believer's spiritual discernment and assuring the follower of knowing the certainty of the application of scripture to his/her life.

Illumination is the work of the Holy Spirit defined in the same basic way as it is used outside any reference to the work of the Holy Spirit, as the light of the sun illuminates the moon. However, the illumination work of the Holy Spirit is reserved for the believer in Christ. It also follows that illumination is the working arm of natural revelation for the believer, whereas natural revelation is available to everyone in the world at large. Therefore, there are several distinctions to make between natural revelation and illumination. As it was indicated, natural revelation is universally applied to all human beings "so that they are without excuse" (Romans 1:20, niv. And natural revelation draws from human experiences, leading the person to the truth of scripture, whereas illumination accurately interprets and applies the truth of scripture to human experience. Natural revelation alone produces guilt and condemnation, but combined with illumination, it produces repentance and faith, as it has been traditionally understood (Berkhof,

1941; Bancroft, 1949). The Spirit, who Jesus named the Comforter, carries out his task of consolation with the parallel and yet not so obvious function of convicting (John 16:8).3 Some type of response to this work of convicting is inevitable during relational conflict, but human beings do not always develop a positive formulation of character from it. Edward Stein (1968, 25), long ago, had recognized that "guilt," like "light," is one of those phenomena everybody knows about it from direct experience yet few can explain in theoretical ways." However, the encouraging aspect to this doctrine is that every person will evidence this work of the Holy Spirit even when the heart of the person becomes ever more insulted by it and hardened to it. It is somewhat encouraging by this means in the various displays of human rebellion and resistance to the opposite side of the resolutions to their problems. Cornelius Plantinga Jr. (1997, 247) agrees with this perspective, "All sin has first and finally a Godward force." And David Powlison" (2001, 46) concurs that human motivational dynamics related to the human experience with guilt "have to do with God."

There are two basic responses that human beings give to the Spirit, just as Jesus also described these same two alternative responses,

> "... gather with me or scatter abroad" (Luke 11:23, NIV). One response shows how the comforting and the convicting functions of the Spirit combine as stated by Paul when he said, "knowing that the kindness of God leads you to repentance" (Romans 2:4, NIV). However, conviction creates in most people a negative self-esteem that is called guilt that could be turned into comfort for the person who regards the source and intent of the Spirit's work as it relates to the gospel that would bring redemption to the truly responsive individual. Robert Roberts (1993, 77) says that the "point of denying oneself, of losing one's psyche, seems to be to gain one's true self." Roberts is indicating the first principle of life by explaining that in human

beings' resistance to conviction, they often lose what they were hoping to preserve that is their sense of autonomy and identity, as Jesus conversely described, **"Whosoever loses his life for my sake will find it"** *(Mark 10:39, NIV).*

The alternative response is the most common and the only remaining choice when the first response is not chosen. This is the response of those **"who suppress the truth in unrighteousness"** (Romans 1:18, NIV. While the conscience might be the more personal vehicle of the conveyed truth as the Holy Spirit engages within the human mind, it is often from the feedback that is received from others that is the presumed source of guilt. Also, some of those that the guilty one might think would be the most unlikely person often conveys the most convicting message. By such means, the truth is often often out of focus, distorted, and magnified in its impact on the person through these relational conflicts. By this means, guilt can instigate within these hurting people is the explosion of raw spiritual nerves because the Spirit has inevitably already prompted the individual by the very same perspective on the matter so that the person is sensitive yet these matters are what others are not so careful in pointing out. What personal messages one might not take from God in conviction, one certainly will not receive from a mere mortal being who often brandishes the truth at the other person without a regard for his personal feelings about it.

Researchers Boster, Mitchell, and Lapinski (1999) summarized their experimental results in comparison of those confronted by others about something of which they were truly guilty would more frequently return a greater negative reaction than those accused of an inaccurate accusation of misbehavior. The recipients of this type of feedback (i.e. where the person was truly guilty seldom reacted to these confrontations or reflections from others without becoming primarily self-interested, hurt, and defensive so that what might not have been a problem prior to the confrontation for that same person, now becomes one. The perception of condemnation that is offered from another might also be at least partially the real truth, even when it is not wholly true. The Spirit may be revealing a personal need to a person through another person who is giving this person negative feedback in a way that may not be based on the other person's particular knowledge of the counselee's culpability or is not by any means completely accurate. And from this exchange, suffering people would most often attribute that sense of guilt as an unfair insult from these other people rather than seeing it for what is—that God is using others to confirm his Word.

In scripture, there are two identifiable methods that human beings use to suppress the truth that may be further defined as the natural-adaptive means that human beings use to reduce the impact of the Spirit. In Romans 2: 14–15, Paul is speaking about the Gentiles who had not had the privilege of knowing or receiving the law, that they, **"were a law unto themselves,"** noting that they avoid the brunt of the message of internal **natural revelation in their conscience by either** *accusing or defending.* The problem with determining the meaning of this passage involves the interpretation of the two participles cited here (**"accusing"** and **"defending"**). The question is what might be the subject of these active participles. The process of elimination may suggest that the answer is simply that the subjects of each participle might be the "Gentiles", avoiding the conviction of the law that "written in their hearts." As C.S. Lewis (1943/1980, 20) described, "We feel the rule of law pressing on us so."

To avoid conviction would be egregious enough but in the avoiding of it is found the greater complication of sin. Most of what the observer of human tragedy will see in human beings are not primarily that they plot revenge and avoid blame, but their counter to aggression is mostly a defensive reaction and at times, automatically enacted like a reflex that is intended to reduce the pressure of guilt on themselves. As John MacArthur (1994, 19) states, "Guilt is not conducive to dignity and self-esteem." Further corroboration of these categories related to accusing and defending, taken from Ephesians 4: 18–19, indicates that there may be indeed two factors for each of these methods of accusing and defending intended to reduce conviction.

They are darkened in their understanding and separated from the life of God because of the ignorance that is in them due to the hardness of their hearts. Having lost all sensitivity, they have given themselves over to sensuality.

Terms like *ignorance and hardness may suggest the accusing functions of self-effacing and blame shifting,* whereas lost sensitivity and sensuality may suggest the excusing functions of *denial* and *pleasure seeking*. Earl Wilson (1987, 84–86) indicates that these types of responses represent "motivation by guilt" that attempt to accomplish a noble goal but have an even more negative result by this means. It is understandable that the human being who faces the Spirit's truth must find a way to reduce its impact or be more miserable than a human being could possibly withstand by living with it unresolved. But counselees may not attribute this state of being as due any particular fault of their own because they perceive a greater benefit for themselves in depersonalizing the conviction of the Spirit that they presume to be wholly from a human source. Thomas Oden (1980, 180) indicates a similar notion when he says, "The stress now is upon God's action toward our guilt, and not our frail attempts to atone for or cancel out our own guilt."

Figure 1.1.1

Style of Relief	Pleasure-seeking	Denial	Self-effacing	Blame-shifting
Self-concept	Helpless	Autonomous	Inferior	Justified
Social Interaction	Selfish	Shallow	Avoidant	Aggressive
Behaviors	Addictive	Rationalizing	Blaming	Controlling
Emotions	Despair	Worry	Fear	Anger

O'Connor, Berry, & Weiss (1999) recognize that interpersonal guilt is adaptive and may be responsible for a wide range of psychological problems. Mark McMinn (1996) also recognizes that spirituality cannot be the attained adaptive nature of human beings. Human nature produces the opposite from what the human being intends so that by attempting to reduce guilt on his own, he complicates it further. In the end, his culpability creates such blame and shame so that he regularly *tends to find natural and adaptive means of his own to minimize the impact of his own conscience by using mostly self-righteous denial and pleasure seeking to compensate for the unpleasant sense of guilt* that he would otherwise experience in his conscious mind, self-effacing self-punishment to remove the need to be punished, and/or blame shifting to place the burden of his guilty conscience on another. From life examples and the scripture, it seems that there are basically two accusing factors and two excusing factors: blame shifting and self-effacing styles, denial and pleasure-seeking styles respectively. These styles hold further implication for the plastic state of a person's self-concept, social interaction, typical behaviors, and primary emotional responses as indicated above.

To explain this figure above, one might focus on the four columns to the right of the heavy vertical line. These categories do not represent mutually exclusive categories for any given individual. In other words, one may use denial as well as blame shifting, moving from one to another in succession. Pleasure-seeking develops into addiction because it provides and substitutes a temporary sensational relief for the pain of guilt experienced that only creates a need for more sensational relief. While addicted people may recognize the poverty of their behavior, they become helpless to stop their dependence, issuing a persona of selfishness to others and placing them into an emotional state of despair. The response of denial attempts to rationalize guilt into ambivalence, but in *rationalizing*, they soon create a torturous path into a life of worry. People using denial carry a persona of autonomy so that they appear to have everything under control, but this only makes them more impervious to the truth of their relationships with others that others may be described as *shallow*. People using the *self-effacing* response have an affinity for the inferiority complex because of their tendency to self-blame. Feeling *inferior*, they tend to avoid *social relationships* out of embarrassment and *fear* that an intimate relationship would expose their most negative attributes. This response to conviction may be the source of many of the affective difficulties that appear among human population. The blame-shifter fears control of others, but offsets that fear by aggressively attempting to control every situation in order to preempt any potential for personal culpability and loss of control by placing blame on another. His determination to avoid blame builds to the crescendo of *anger* and rage as he attempts, against any real hope, to *justify* himself at another's expense.

Two of the responses are identified as excusing strategies that are also involved with the problem of the unresolved inner conflict. The pleasure seeker attempts to increase relief from his/her inner conflict (both the product and the cause of interpersonal conflict by a superficial means rather than by dealing with the specific issues of conscience directly. The application of this superficial, stimulus seeking solution for life change is so quick and easy that it is used with impunity, while conviction related to the true need is usually suppressed. This inner conflict, along with other consequent liabilities of sensational relief, is gradually and tragically deepened to the point creating within the person the opposite sensation, an undesirable sensation of despair that is the result of lost prospects for change in the course of seeking pleasure to offset guilt. The pleasure seeker soon becomes locked into the pattern of addiction despite the d*iminishing returns for sensational relief* that *renders* him to feel more and more hopeless over time.

The person who uses denial is also attempting, perhaps unintentionally, to minimize the impact of the Spirit's work of conviction and the conflict within self, but by this approach, this person ultimately creates more inner conflict and conviction of guilt. This person is gratified to experience a temporary sense of relief through the assumption of personal autonomy that is a deceptive misrepresentation of the person's true state. This person will, out of necessity, consistently maintain denial regardless of the lack of evidence of the person acquiring any realistic autonomy by rationalizing away any evidence to the contrary.

But rationalization will never completely resolve the major issues that this person continues to face in life so that the practice of denial will result in the person taking a torturous path through worry and tension. Those in denial will then tend to increase their focus on themselves in order to alleviate the pain within, and while greater aspirations for stronger relationships persist, this increasing self-focus will tend to make their relationships shallow and superficial.

The third and fourth category of self-effacing and blame shifting responses involve the phenomenal dynamic of control. Fearing the loss of control relates both to the self-effacing approach, as well as the blame-shifting strategy. Both are involved with the paradoxical issue of control. On one hand, the self-effacing person possesses a foreboding feeling of inferiority, but on the other hand, the person using the self-critical response has not fully surrendered to this sense of inferiority and thus resists the connotation. While those who are self-effacing are highly suspicious about their personal culpability, they avoid significantly intimate relationships that might expose their suspicion, but at the same time, they yearn for greater intimacy in their relationships. People of this response mostly live in fear that, one day, they will be denied the respect that they think they need to sufficiently feel worthy enough to have relationships with others. Self-effacing responders mostly avoid relationships in order to hide their suspected personal liabilities and yet in their isolation, they yearn to be regarded with significance. Whereas, blame-shifters presume that others will exert their controlling influences over them so that blame-shifters will prevent others' controlling influences by controlling others as a defense against their future attempts. Their determination is often so hard-nosed that they are the last to notice how angrily determined or self-centered they have become. They do not observe readily how controlling they have become because they have willfully distorted heir circumstances in life in order to feel justified with their controlling behavior. They also believe others will control them if they do not control others first—reinforcing their motivation for control.

A community youth worker had recently graduated from Christian college and struggled in his role as a youth worker, especially through the week when there was little or no accountability for his work. He began to reflect on his life and how he had come to this point—his long-awaited dream of being in ministry. It was not always this way growing up in his home in a small mid-western town. His parents were not fit to raise children (as he would tell the story) and seemed to pawn him and his sister off to the neighbors and to nearby relatives as often as they could. He spent most of his summer days at an elderly neighbor's home and the couple at this home often fought with each other so violently that he often would hide under the kitchen table to escape the turmoil. He recalled one occasion of the woman chasing her husband with a meat cleaver in her hand. But at his parents' home, he was even more dispirited by his mother's constant yelling at him—feeling that he should be invisible so that she would not need to feel any obligation to his care.

The only nurturing adult that he had found in his growing up years was a youth pastor who had taught him about Christ and introduced him to a Christian fellowship that provided an escape from the hopelessness of his home life. He was sincere with his new faith, but even during his new adventures at a Christian college some of the old demons brought an inescapable sense of despair. It was there at college that he met and later married a young woman who also had hopes of marrying someone who wanted to enter into the ministry. He was thrilled that being with her was moving him closer to the realization of his ultimate aspiration. Her friends were more cautious about him than she—observing that he didn't seem to show her much respect and would ask her out for a date and then would complain about her behavior when he would feel embarrassed about his own lack of financial means to take her anywhere for the evening. As she told the story much later in life, the suspicions that her friends raised were only small omens to the greater atrocities of their future married life.

He had finally realized his dream of becoming youth worker himself in a para-church ministry agency where he could rescue young hearts and minds, like his youth pastor had done for him earlier in life, but it all seemed like a hollow victory. He presumed that he could reenact the same kind of successful ministry of which he had been the recipient, having learned from the master himself, but he obsessed about his failures to do so and was reenacting the sense of what his life was like prior to his contact with the youth pastor more than he was the life that he had since that time. During his first youth ministry, his contact with the youth was minimal and his supervisor was too busy to hear about his problems so he pretended to be okay, but beneath it all he suffered.

However, his anger and frustration would boil over and only his wife could tell of his tirades during that time in his life, and she only began to manage that after many years of blaming herself for these incidents. He would come home at lunch in such a foul mood during the week that he would not want to eat, and then would criticize her cooking. If she would protest his mistreatment, he would toss the plate of food across the kitchen, falling short of the trashcan and then would yell at her to clean it up, as he would go to a restaurant to eat. He often lamented that he could do better if he had a wife who would support him instead of her being so self-centered that she would demand so much of his attention. Decimated from his onslaught, she would try to work harder to please him. Seeing her gracious response, in Napoleonic fashion, he would start to take greater advantage of her, making requests for acts that she would later describe as sadistic sexual behavior. He moved to another youth ministry, hoping that it would improve matters, but each position came to an end when she sought the help for their marriage for the problems that they were having. Soon after he left his last position, he also separated from his wife, developed an alcohol problem, and cohabited with a number of different women. His wife was not ready to give up on their marriage as easily as he did. She came to counseling to see if there was any way to avoid a divorce. When he became aroused by her imperturbability for the marriage, he wanted to defend his lifestyle and so he came to counseling as well.

They were counseled separately, upon his request, to which the counselor also agreed because the counselor wanted to prevent more of the same manipulation with which he had so decimated his wife in the past. When he proceeded with counseling, he seemed willing to reconcile with her, but he insisted on his own terms exacting more concessions from her. At moments in counseling, he became angry and started to enlist all of the alleged indiscretions that he believed she had committed against him in the past. The counselor became familiar enough with the circumstance and believing in the model described above, began to confront his anger with her with something like the following question: "What is making you feel this level of insignificance, culpability, and offense that you would attempt to pass on such ridicule to your estranged wife when you know what you did in this relationship?" (Presumably, he was confusing the convicting work of the Spirit with his own notions about her failures, making him feel inept as a youth worker attempting to negatively contrast her alleged failures with his own failures.) He would attempt to attribute the cause of his guilt to her again and again, but the counselor would refuse to hear it that way by saying, "No, it is not her that causes you to feel this way about yourself; it is much more personal than that!" With that, his argumentation gave way to a moment of clarity and he would start to explain many of his personal experiences, internal motivations, and images and how they had been formed, confessing how wrong he was. However, he often found it difficult to persist with that approach and would quickly revert to his former self.

Reviewing and reinterpreting events as a gracious God and comforting Spirit would do, counseling sessions with him would recapture his attention to this new mindset from time to time. However, the marriage was not to be repaired. It was not to be repaired because he had already promised himself to another without telling anyone else and was living with this other woman for over a year before he started counseling. Many years later, he did mellow and became the captive of this other woman whom he had married and at that time he gave greater sacrifice to her than he did his first wife, but with whom he faced a similar form of unhappiness that his first wife had faced with him. At this point in his life, he often lamented that he had ruined his life and was going through what his first wife had gone through with him. Later on, his first wife did very well as a single mom of a teenage son and daughter working at a good-paying job, but it took many years of counsel to repair her spirit after internalizing many years of hardship and abuse from her former husband. From this one example, denial initially prevented this man from an opportunity to realize his dream of ministry and agonizing over his imminent failure further deepened his self-deprecation. Blaming his wife only temporarily lifted part of the burden but in the end deepened his guilt and ruined his marriage. Finally, his response to increase the volume of his carnal appetite for women and alcohol were only futile attempts to drown out the still small voice of God that had plagued his conscience for years.

The Tension Over Control

The accusing factors of blame shifting and self-effacing responses align with another major concern, namely the issue of controlling behavior. Reality therapists have spoken of human beings basic problem as their faulty attempts to control the world around them (Glasser, 1981), but then these same reality therapists seem to return to their clients a more bonafide attempt to control the world around them. As well, the behaviorists' assertive training model suggests that some control is necessary as long as it is not too extreme. Assertive training views the issue of anger in a polar manner. At one end, a person should avoid the extreme of becoming so incredibly angry to dominate all others, and on the other end the person should avoid retreating into the submission by becoming the proverbial doormat (Jones & Butman, 1991). As it was in the beginning, God did give Adam and Eve dominion over the earth, but that sense of creaturehood has gone awry. It may seem that world threatens to consume and control so that the politics of moral equivalence indicate that the most egregious responses to this controlling world are also justified. The threat of control so drives human beings into their own personal defenses that they lose context of their creaturehood and attempt to take upon themselves the role of God to sit in the judgment seat to judge these alleged injustices. In so doing, the blame-shifting response removes the person from what he was meant to be and makes his bad situation worse.

The assertive training model describes the two opposing facets of the world in which we live, one side that dominates and the other side that is submissive. The assertive trainee must take the prerogative to find some middle ground that places him in a flux between two extremes: one extreme is to live in fear of being controlled by the power of other controlling people and the other is controlling others as a defense. Both extremes represent the human being's fallen capacity to have a right relationship with the outside world: one is a failed dominion and the other is a failed submission. The one extreme fears control of others that would reflect the response of the self-critical approach to minimize the Spirit's impact by overcompensating for a human being's inherent identity for submission. The other extreme controls others as a defense against the fear of being controlled. Thus, the response of the blame shifter also minimizes the Spirit's impact by subverting the human being's appropriate role of dominion with self-centered power over others.

Psalm 1 also teaches us that most people live in a flux between the two extremes, vacillating between **"walking in the counsel of the ungodly,"** stuck in the middle with **"standing in the way of sinners,"** and to the other extreme of **"sitting in the seat of the scornful."** To accept the counsel of the ungodly may be the moral equivalent of selling one's soul, but at least, as the passage suggests, by accepting the counsel of the ungodly this person has freedom of movement in this world as he **"walks."** In contrast to this, the **"sinner"** has consciousness of the question about the appropriate path that he or she should take in life but wants the best of both worlds and, therefore, is stuck to "stand" between the two extremes. Further, the scornful person is one who pretends that he is not engaged in this problem at all and so becomes cynical of both extremes and is given the active role of **"sitting in the seat of the**

scornful." The escape from the power of control in the world according to Psalm 1 is to live apart from this world—that is to live as a **"blessed man meditating on the Word."** Personal prospects for one's progress in life are better assessed through the meditation of scriptures than they are predicted by the world's philosophy of life, as stated in the following verses of Psalm 1. The blessed man is sustained **"like a tree"** by the rivers of water—progress that is neither evident to the world nor predicted by this world. In contrast, the ungodly are **"like the chaff"** driven by the wind—that represents a paradox to the world's predicted outcome as one who has complete freedom of movement. While the tree, representing the follow of the godly philosophy, appears to be unmovable, it is by this immovableness that the tree is sustained through the life-giving sustenance of the river by which the tree stands.

The passage of II Peter 1:4 indicates this blessedness, as it is also described in Psalm 1, is for the one that is made a **"partaker of the divine nature."** The rounded description includes the virtue of self-control that is in keeping with this power and control construct. The representing the follower of the godly philosophy, appears to be unmovable, it is by this immovableness that the tree is sustained through the life-giving sustenance of the river by which the tree stands model for the overcomer of the world's control would look like figure below. It is similar to the assertive training model, but it obviously lacks the aspect of the third alternative at the top of the model that is indicated by the term "self-control:"

Figure 1.1.2

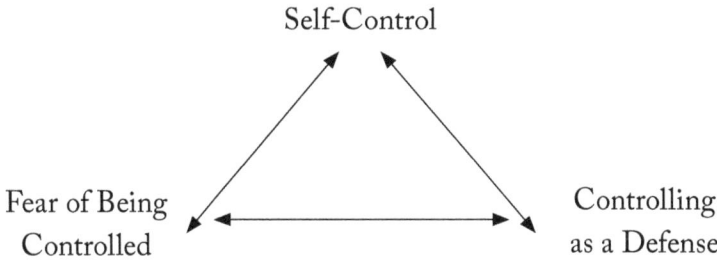

Most assume that self-control is a virtue that prohibits excessive eating, drinking, anger, and other such embarrassing behaviors. While all of that may be partially true, self-control has a much more positive thrust than it has for the avoidance of excessive negative traits, as the theoretical study of Baumeister & Exline (2000) also seems to indicate. Self-control, according the passage in II Peter 1, reconstitutes the person's relationships so that this person can truly live above the strife of the world and its controlling influences. Self-control is a spiritual freedom or *"Christian liberty."* One could describe the person possessing self-control as a *fully functioning human being in possession of his/her mind, emotion, and motivation.*

This stated definition is evident but also truly a paradox because the virtue of self-control is ultimately from God and not self-controlling at all. The only way that self-control could exist is through God's assistance. In addition, this virtue is not a once and done act of God in the person's life on which he can rest, but it is the quintessential struggle of life for every human being.

If one wants control of an uncontrollable situation, he must find self-control by letting God have control. The human paradox is that a person will most often try to gain control of an uncontrollable situation by losing control over self, first. As Oden (1980, 104–105) indicates, "The kernel of much biblical psychology could be reduced to this: as the human problem in relation to the future is the anxious attempt to control the uncontrollable." Consider a little boy who is oblivious to his mother's screaming at him, and in the end, she despises herself for screaming at him as well. However, she finds it is impossible to stop yelling because her son has conditioned her by being so impervious to her wishes to control his behavior unless she does. He now only responds to the highest decibel that she can accomplish. If the child were able to process the circumstance like an adult, he might respond with this comment, "So, Mom, you would like me to control my behavior because I am out of control and you convey this to me by going out of control yourself. Now let's see, I am out of control, you are going out of control to gain control of me, so nobody is in control!"

A young minister of counseling many years ago received a phone call from an older woman that he had known from a former church that was to be the first of a series of phone calls. Each phone call would last over an hour. She knew that her son-in-law was formerly his young disciple, and she thought that he might have influence over her son-in-law concerning the ordeal that she was having with her son-in-law. She explained over and over again in-law forbade her to have contact with the grandchildren without their presence. Apparently, the grandchildren had repeated a critical comment that she had made how her son-in-law had been rude beyond what anyone could tolerate and continued to emphasize how much he had mistreated her daughter. Little was said about the main purpose for these lengthy, one-way conversations. The woman had never approved of her daughter's marriage, and recently, her daughter and son-about their father while they were visiting her home without their parents' presence. This event was the culmination of years of tension between them and induced the new policy that she was now protesting. She alleged that she had not said what the children had said that they had heard her say. She made her protest by means of finding even greater fault with the person of whom she denied that she had ever criticized to her grandchildren.

The young minister thought after some reasoning with he r that he could avoid becoming entangled, but she went to another mutual friend who called for a meeting of all parties. The young minister arrived at this meeting thinking that he would observe this event, but his friend who had called the meeting decided that this young minister would actually chair this meeting. As a young and inexperienced counselor, he tried to think of a good question to ask. Envision that sitting before him are these two couples—mother and daughter in the center of the four, the son-in-law on the left and his father-in-law on the right. The latter of the four had no idea what he was doing there. He presumably came to keep peace at home, as was later learned. And so, the young minister asked his big counselor question, "What is the problem?" It was apparently a profound question because for at least five minutes no one knew how to answer it. But wouldn't you have guessed it! The son-in-law was first to speak. "Well, it is as plain as this! She does not at all like me as her son-in-law," as he nodded in the direction of his mother-in-law. From this, his mother-in-law grew white as the blood drained from her face. She blurted out, "I never expressed anything unkind about him," – other than what she perceived to be true of him, of course.

For a moment, the young minister sat there a little puzzled. Wasn't this the same woman who had worn out his listening skills by a constant litany of complaints about her son-in-law's character? He mused that she must have thought that she had so spiritualized her persecution at his hands that the young minister would be obliged to keep his observation to himself. But he didn't. "I remember a number of conversations on the phone with you and if I were to sum up what you were saying, it would be just that." She became even more ashen and mumbled that she was sorry for mistreating her children. Another pause during his contemplation about what this woman was doing made him consider a number of possible explanations for the immediate circumstance. Was she deliberately and cunningly deceiving all of them knowing all along about what she was perpetrating or was she herself caught up in something that in her mind justified her actions? He asked her about her intentions when she had spoken to him on the phone—if she had thought that she was being critical of her son-in-law or defending herself. She indicated the latter of the two was the more valid of the two optional answers. He also asked her what it was that she thought she was defending herself when she said "something" to the grandchildren that had led to the policy of being restricted her from their care. She said, "I thought that I was defending myself to the grandchildren because he would be so rude to me when I came to visit them." Many more discussions broke out that led to the discovery that the basis for much of the treachery back and forth between parties was due to a fear that the other would gain the greater advantage and limit the other. Their fears were true to the other's prediction because that is exactly what happened. Excessive controlling behavior is often the resort for those who fear being controlled by another. The example cited here also indicates how conflict is first internal before it is realized externally, introducing the next element.

The Internalized Conflict

The excusing factors of denial and pleasure seeking align with this third element of spiritual formation labeled the internalized conflict because the source of this internalized conflict is assumed to be the unresolved conviction of the Spirit that is the residual experience for each person. Denial is an attempt to hide one's hostility toward others or to avoid the appearance of being primarily self-interested so that the person misrepresents himself as being without much personal culpability. By using denial and pleasure seeking, one might attempt to ignore the internal conflict that serves as the basis for these responses, but in doing so these responses take a more personal toll on that person's relationships and emotional state. Pleasure seeking blocks the initial sense of conviction by overpowering the person's affective function with pleasurable stimuli. No wonder this is the response category that leads to addiction. The following model of explanation demonstrates how internal conflict becomes interpersonal conflict and how interpersonal conflict becomes inner conflict:

Figure 1.1.3

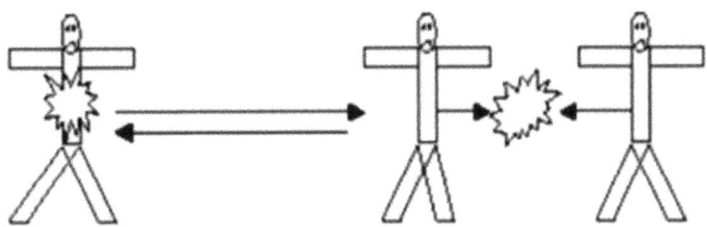

Illumination indicates that inner conflict can precede, follow, or even cycle back and forth with interpersonal conflict. And Malony (1995) observes that conflict is personal before becoming interpersonal.

As well, aggression and conflict never happen in a vacuum or without some interpersonal context. Conflict is preceded by the perceptions of others mistreating or rejecting so that one or both persons may react aggressively toward each other, as Powlison (2001, 47) states, "Self-evaluation is not intrinsically an autonomous, intrapsychic function." There is always some personal motivation behind conflict that involves our perception of how others perceive us. But Powlison (47) adds, "Inside any emotional reaction, behavioral choice or habit, any cognitive content, any reaction pattern to suffering, you ought to hear and see active verbs at work." For example, Nazis had to paint the Jews as mongrels preying upon the markets and people of Germany before they could justify hating the Jews to the extent of herding them into boxcars, branding them with a number, and eventually exterminating them in concentration camps. Even where there is no history of conflict between people, some stigmatized personality types initiate conflict over some perceived past injustice, even when the present circumstance does not support that perception. Jesus also indicated this to his disciples, **"If the world hates you, it hated me before it hated you"** (John 15:18, NIV).

The term προτον *or proton*, translated "before," indicates first in order rather than first in time, the latter of the two nuances would be indicated by a different Greek term that would be conducive to the temporal definition of the English term. People hate and despise others for reasons more inherent to their own self-concept than for reasons inherent to others. Middelberg (2001, 341–354) concurs that there is a "projective identification sequence" in conflict. Therefore, it is inappropriate to take any insult too personally, but that is also easier said than done!

Inner conflict is also a topic of both secular and Christian psychology. Gestalt concepts, as do existentialists' (Kellogg, 2004),warn that the introjection of impersonal material from others into self or the projection of one's own material onto others produces internal conflict called "disturbances of the contact boundary" (Perls, 1959). Cloud and Townsend (1992) indicate that the observances of appropriate boundaries are important for one's personal psychological growth and for the psychological growth of families. However, it is important to cite in the context of the discussion of spiritual formation that there should be a boundary of influence set between the influence of the **"still small voice"** of the Spirit and the perception of self that internalizes the feedback from others.

A summary of what many counselees are saying to counselors about their struggles in relationships might be expressed in this manner, "Even though it is true that Christ has given his life for me and the Spirit through the Word of God supplies all my need for life, it not enough to restrain my sadness and disappointment over what I am going through now with this significant person in my life." It is as if what Christ has done and is still doing is so insignificant in comparison to the more recent events with a significant other. This amounts to a practical atheism (see Welch, "When people are big and God is small," 1997). The Spirit's influence counters the influence of an enemy of the faith known as the "world." The voice of the Spirit is evident and distinct from the world and does not leave the world with an ambivalent response so that any response: good, bad or indifferent, is evidence of his presence in the person's life.

Paul had a similar conflict with the Corinthian church where he spent an abnormally longer period of time helping its establishment—estimated at eighteen months. After he had crossed the Aegean to winter in Ephesus, the problems began when he had the brilliant idea that he would advance the Jewish believer (They never fully accepted Gentile believers into the church) by these Christian Jews receiving vital material help from these same Gentile Christians whom they had virtually rejected. And the Gentile support him because a growing family might become too costly, and that he should not get married if they were going to support him because a growing family might become too costly, and that he had no right to ask to ask them for money in the first place because his apostleship was also in question.

The focus of Paul's discussion in I Corinthians chapters 2 was placed on how he learned to deal with their disparaging comments. He knew that there was a selfish motive behind their accusations against him and their self-justifications for not giving help to the Jewish church, but he also would not respond to their criticism with the same self-focus that was apparent in their comments. It is uncertain how long that it took for Paul to answer these complaints, but we know his answer was effective according the second epistle – II Corinthians 7:11-13 **"At every point you have proved yourselves to be innocent in this matter** [12] **So even though i wrote to you, it was not on account if the one party that did the wrong or the injured party but that you could see before God, you could see yourselves how devoted to us you are.** [13] **By all this we are encouraged."** Paul's focus was on as I Corinthians 2:16 indicates, as a result of having the Spirit indwell us,"**so that we have the mind of Christ."** In chapter 4, he defends his record very simply a without listing all of his own efforts. In a very personal way, he reveals his humble purpose and did not make his own assessment of how well he thinks he is doing as a **"faithful steward"**. Further, he shows his spiritual maturity by writing, **"I care very little if I be judged by you or by any man's judgment or by any human court, it is the Lord who judges me."** I Corinthians 4:3-4.

Putting the two concepts together from chapter 2 and chapter4, (chapter 2 we can use the Spirits work as opposed to those who in the human race that play God with their criticism and those that are responding to criticism can be confident even when they are at fault. Paul recognizes the agony of guilt seems to be entirely firm the source of conviction that is human and that the conviction of the Spirit has entirely different and unexpected outcome. When God convicts, he points us to what we can improve and to what our next step would be. When we allow the conviction of human beings become greater in significance than the conviction of the Spirit of God, our soul hears the dreaded voice of condemnation, "I want you to feel really bad about what you have dome, n but there is not a blessed thing that you can do to improve your reputation with us." Instead in thus case, Paul asked God if there was any truth in what they were alleging about him. What does Paul say about God's answer? He said, **"I know nothing against myself...my conscience is clear."**

Paul chose the higher power and refused to be convicted by the lower court ruling. His conscience was clear, regarding the "no condemnation" from God within himself. He also reasoned that he did not assume he was innocent from that time forward because God would show him at some future date another perspective on his role, but for now, his self-concept regarding their resistance to him. It is uncertain how long Paul waited after this incident with Titus to send this letter, but it was right to ask them for money in the first place because his apostleship was also in question. om God within himself rather than the opinion of the Corinthian critique. He also reasoned that he did not assume that he was innocent from that time forward because God could show him at some future date another perspective on his role, but for now God had not spoken to him about what he should do or could do to correct the concerns raised by the Corinthians. How did Paul know that he was innocent of all charges? There is a distinctive means through which the Spirit does his convicting work. He convicts by means of comforting with the hope for change by pointing the person who is responsive to this means of correction, renewal, reconciliation, and redemption in any circumstance of conflict. It is the confidence that God can sufficiently reveal himself and his will through personal failures and failed motivations in the person's own conscious mind in a way that produces solutions that give hope and separate the voice of the Spirit from the voice of people. When other people's opinions are the sole source of conviction, it could be summed up this way, "I want you to feel very bad about what you've done, but there is nothing that you can do to improve your relationship or reputation with us." Conflict with people is better resolved by a vertical movement rather than by a horizontal one. As I John 1:7 corroborates, **"Walk in the light as he is in the light, and you will have fellowship with one another"** (NIV). This verse recognizes the best means of getting along with the most difficult person or with those who would make little or no attempt to be accommodating is to develop a better relationship with God.

A couple that came for counseling, who I will call the "Internalized Couple," serves as an example of how this element of spiritual formation can be used in the helping relationship of counseling. To describe them briefly, he was a dominant, task-oriented successful engineer and businessman who could show emotions when he reflected on his perception of his lost hopes and dreams for his family and marriage. She was a weak person with physical problems, carried her feelings on her sleeve, she took things personally, and made negative comparisons of her life to other people's lives. In her eyes, he was cruel to her and to the children; she felt no compassion or love from him; he was too concerned about money; and he was, worst of all, critical of her role as the wife, mother, and housekeeper. In his eyes, she was always on his case about what she wanted him to do in repairing their old-but-stately home, she never appreciated what he thought they should do, she insisted on her way, and if he objected, he was labeled as cruel and heartless by her. He retreated and she would sulk. What was so ironic was that when either of them was treated graciously and kindly, they were mostly very nice people to be around. It was when they started to predict negative reactions and feedback about themselves coming from the other that would reduce them to such bitter despair! It was a long arduous task to pry away that tendency to prejudge each other from their minds and see how they were fulfilling their own prophecy of doom upon each other by these negative predictions.

Summary

The Spirit of God is at work in people's lives long before they come take any steps toward changing and the major focus problem-solving is upon the person's failed attempts to silence the voice of the Spirit, not recognizing there is hope by embracing his message. Second, people will often overlook those matters that they have created by their failed attempts to resolve on their own not believing that they could resolve those problems that they believe to from an outside source by recognizing how the Spirit is using this adversity to resolve their own personal struggles. A person's attempt to control people and circumstances that they cannot control as faulty substitutes for the benefit of self-control is an example of this work of the Spirit. Third, conflict begins long before people make contact and it is often based in the prediction of negative feedback from the person with whom the conflict is involved. Developing an outlook that is based on a redemptive view of others not only brings the spirit of hope to the individual, but it also brings improvement to those relationships. By using the chart at the end of this chapter or Figure 1.1.1 may utilized for a rapid assessment may conducted an individual. The remainder of this written work will look at the above categories of responses and some attempt will be to correlate the more classic diagnoses with these spiritual assessment categories. The following figure illustrates the connections between various categories of coping responses to their presentation of problems. Connections between character assessment and their affective intensity are also shown in the following figure 1.1.4.

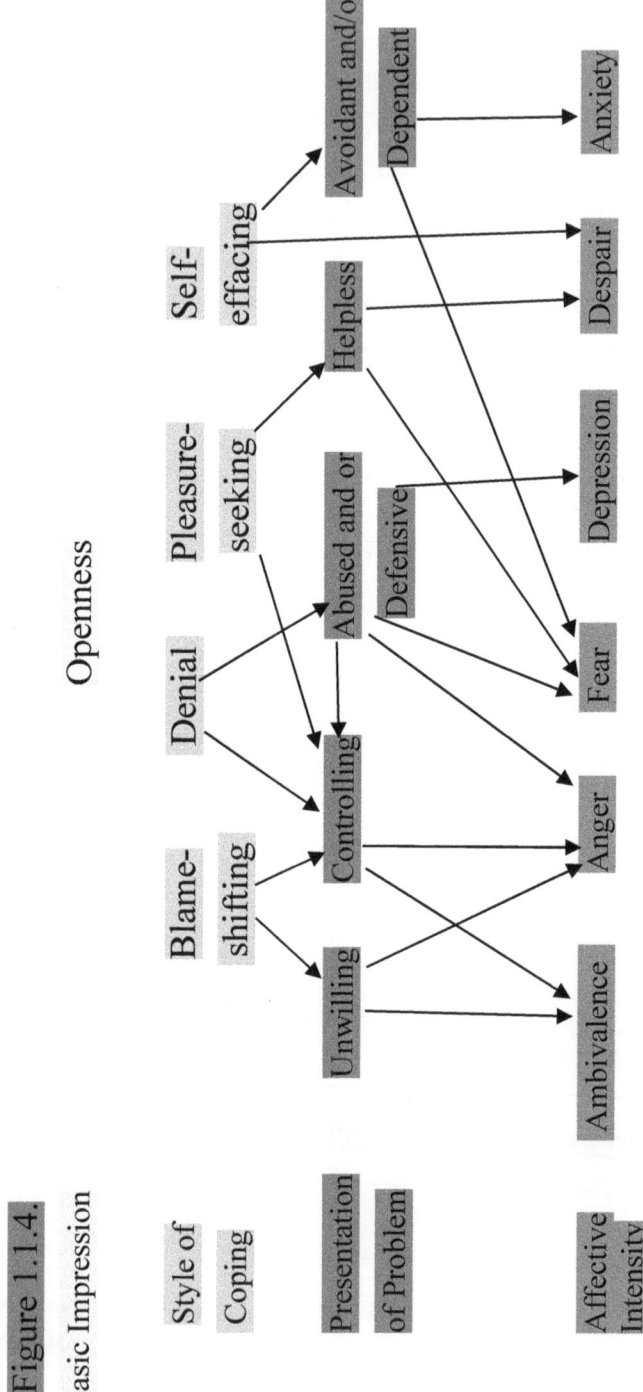

Figure 1.1.4.
Basic Impression

SECTION TWO

ACCUSING FACTORS

As in the case of the excusing factors, the accusing factors are also those natural and adaptive means that human beings use to minimize the impact of the Spirit's work of convicting or convincing. Accusing responses are the result of human beings experiencing some form of guilt. Any guilt experience is likely followed by one of these 2 factors (excusing and accusing factors) that are referred to in chapter 1. However, the initial guilt response usually does not consistently express itself with guilt feelings, and when these guilt feelings are expressed by the person, it does so for a very short time until the individual person deflects this sense of guilt into some other form of response, such as in the case of accusing factors of self-effacing and/or blame-shifting responses that are covered in this section. The issue of control is also significant to the discussion about these accusing factors, and in this accusing category of responses, some individuals respond to the work of the Spirit in a timid, self-effacing way and others in a more blame-shifting way. The timid, self-effacing person more prominently fears the control of others and other outside influences, while the blame-shifting person appears to be determined to control others and outside influences as a defense against this fear of being controlled. Both responses fear the control of others and other outside influences. However, with one response, blame shifting, this fear is not very evident and is underlying the controlling behavior, and with the other, the self-critical response, characterized as fear or anger, that rules the person's life. Of these responses, the blame-shifting response is the more ostentatious controlling behavior but even with the self-effacing responses, it appears to be controlling at times in a more passive-aggressive way.

Figure 2.0.1

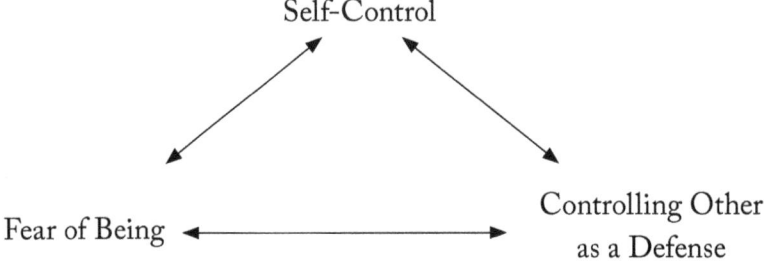

Accusing factors are the most utilized by clients in the initial forging of the counseling relationship, particularly self-effacing and blame-shifting. For that reason, counselors need to assess the openness of the client to understand to what degree that client may be non-compliant in regard to revealing the essential truth with the necessary details that the fear of control and shame would prevent. Just because a person seeks help does not mean that they will comply to getting the help that they need.

Non-compliant clients are typically depressed and anxious and that are of the self-effacing category of responders or they are manipulative or passive aggressive in the blame-shifting category of responders. Gary Oliver (1997) enlists several possible strategies that prospective clients may use when seeking their initial contact with a counselor. According to Oliver, only a fraction of those seeking counseling in the initial stages are genuinely interested in placing themselves in a bona fide effort of counseling. Compassionate and candid communication regarding the counselor's assessment on the part of the non-compliant person's commitment early in the process could provide the best outcome for the remediation of problems and would secure the client's initial commitment or reveal the client's lack thereof for successful completion of the process. Certain ethical questions also need to be resolved in order for the process to go forward that has to do with a focus on the counselor's character and conduct, more than it does the client. Ethical problems often issue from the challenges where the counselors perceive they have too little control over counseling outcomes.

When Paul the apostle admonished the church leadership to restore believers that overtaken by hypocritical immoral behavior in Galatians 6:1, he indicates that spiritual people should take heed to their own spiritual issues to be effective in their counsel with others. The passage continues to render excellent instruction for the counselor. Verse 2 indicates that the spiritual person should bear the burdens of the person that is overwhelmed by his own burden of mistakes, misjudgments and trespasses and in so doing, that spiritual person fulfills the law of Christ when help this person bear the load. To fulfill the law of Christ is to have compassion for that person regardless of how they respond initially. The spiritual person should make a clear commitment to the helping process using the benchmark of Christ's compassion on Calvary where he died for those who had not committed to him but rather opposed him and that had mocked, hated, tortured, and abandoned him. The law of Christ is reflective of the John 13 passage where Jesus indicates that one should love others as he has loved them. From this, it is understood that helping has as much to do with the spiritual person's self-analysis as it does with a careful analysis of the person whom they are helping.

When a person begins to confide in a friend, parent, teacher or in their counselor about their personal problems, the one that has taken this sacred duty to help others should realize that this person would naturally feel vulnerable about the loss of control inherent to that counseling relationship. Also, if the counselor has not resolved his fear of those that control among other important personal and spiritual matters, the opportunity for the counselor to develop the counselee's trust might be lost because such fear cannot remain hidden forever. Any person seeking counsel would be, at minimum, on guard with this concern that may not represent a person seeking to control his counselor or the counseling sessions.

The person that seeks help for a problem would have a natural fear for that the person in whom they are confiding will think that the helping person will require that person to change in a way that they do not agree. This produces a natural barrier to the formation of the helping relationship. To reduce the barriers that this sense of a loss of control produces for the person seeking help is found in Romans 2:4, **"God's kindness leads you to repentance"** (NIV). What works for the Almighty in bringing constructive change to a person's life should also be the standard approach of the counselor when the same objective is in mind. In order to remove this fear from the client about revealing very personal matters to the counselor, the counselor should also remove any personal bias about the counselee, especially one that regards any resistance as disqualifying the suffering person from having a successful result. The counselor should rather expect resistance as a part of the drill. Cowan and Presbury (2000) do not attempt to bring a biblical point of view to the topic, but they rightly indicate that major resistance is found in the context where counselors have practiced a closed system that means that the counselor continues to maintain the preponderant amount of control of counseling sessions. God's method for changing people is to use kindness, patience, and compassion, and likewise the counselor should not become overly conditional and suspicious of the client in regard to the counselee's initial lack of cooperation or even in the case where more flagrant resistance is observe.

Openness to Change

A counselor might expect that openness could be evaluated by how much information the counselee verbalizes to the counselor. However, measuring the quantity of verbiage is not a sufficient evaluation of the client's openness. A talkative counselee may not be adequately and sufficiently disclosing the essential information for a successful process, and an untalkative client may not be necessarily unwilling to enter the process openly. To be adequately prepared to know how to accurately evaluate the client's openness, the counseling process would be much more effective when the counselor considers some possible reasons for and the possible circumstances where the client expresses little in their communication.

There are at least five possible reasons for the circumstance of the untalkative client. First, untalkative clients may anticipate how the counselor would respond to them before they ever meet with the counselor. This may be a circumstance where the solution is apparent even to the client, but the client finds it difficult to accept the anticipated responsibility to resolve the matter. A client in this circumstance may assume that the counselor will evaluate the difficulty in the same manner as the client has already thought to address it, and the client would then be reluctant to verbalize this same perspective, fearing that the counselor would make a compelling argument for the client to accept what the client already suspects as being true and has not successfully applied. Second, untalkative clients may not have a high regard for professional counseling as a forum that would really help. Frankly, it has been a genuine concern of the profession itself for many years so that this perspective may not be altogether unmerited (Truax & Carkhuff, 1972). This may be evident in a circumstance where clients feel it is an embarrassment that they could not solve their own problems and regret the waste of time and expense in going to professional counseling. The third reason that some clients may counseling process that have not been completely listed here, cognitive ability could be less formerly addressed than by giving a lengthy intelligence inventory when used for therapeutic purposes, and counselors should not always presume negligible results from person who possess low cognitive ability.

Methods for gaining meaningful information from the person would involve the following approaches. First, questions should be used to create consistency in the information gathered from the counselor's consistency. Consistency is essential with the talkative clients because of the phenomenon of cognitive dissonance that is inherent to the very talkative person. A comment that could be used to compare the statements of the client when there is an observed agreement in comments: "Yes, I remember that you said that before." These comments of this person where there is an observed is also a comment that the helping person could use to compare state, "But you said something that sounded differently about this matter on a prior occasion." The important aspect is to maintain compassion and to speak honestly to your client. This will also lay the foundation for the person seeking help in regard to matters that may require their courage to address (e.g. Ephesians 4:15).

CHAPTER TWO

THE TIMID, SELF-EFFACING RESPONSE

The timid, self-effacing response is ordinarily thought be a problem that others have caused the timid person to have because the timid person is thought to have lived in an environment where others have been threatening and were aggressive toward this individual. This might be a true in the description of the timid person's early environment, but the scriptures also indicate that timid people are far more active than passive in their response symptomatic traits. Perhaps blaming oneself has the function of offering atonement or making oneself a sacrifice for one's own shortcomings or to become overly accepting of responsibility for wrongdoing to prevent further blame for oneself or a loved one, and by this, the person mollifies his own sense of guilt or unworthiness. However, timid and fearful people consistently and globally exhibit a lack of trust in others and have little self confidence that not only emotionally impacts them, but also negatively impacts others in a way that depreciates their relationships. Not all timid, self-effacing responses to the work of the Holy Spirit result in a clinical diagnosis, let alone with an anxiety or mood disorder, but all human beings may ultimately respond in this manner at some time in their lives. The careful counselor might have the opportunity to identify and successfully counsel others with affective difficulty when the counselor understands these concepts. Minimally, the timid, self-effacing response is an inadequate means to respond to the work of the Holy Spirit that follows certain universal patterns of behavior involving social interaction, self-concept, and affective disposition as it was previously described. Their social interaction is avoidant, their self-concept is predisposed to inferiority, and they feel that they are blamed more than necessary, and therefore they experiment. It is uncertain how long that it took for Paul to answer these complaints but we know his a

Answer was effective according the second epi....le – II Corinthians a great.

Background Information to Fear and Anxiety

Fear and anxiety are responsible for a wide range of health and emotional issues and may accompany many other mental health diagnostic conditions. A study involving patients in a clinic for internal medicine provided a report that almost two thirds of patients that were scheduled for office visits in a given time frame had serious anxiety symptoms and a high percentage of these patients were likely experiencing a type of anxiety disorder (Sansone et. al. 2004). Anxiety often acts as a trigger to the acute phase for a number of profound mental health conditions that were formerly in a state of remission. Such is the case for schizophrenia (Naeem et. al. 2006). Another important issue regarding the counselee presenting a phobia or anxiety condition is what may be understood as the "suddenness" phenomenon (Hunt et. al. 2006). The onset of anxiety symptoms that seem to be "out of the blue" that means the person experiencing any given, form of anxiety has a sudden start of symptoms especially with the experience of panic anxiety. Anxiety itself interrupts cognitive process, as in the case of test anxiety where the student studies all night and enters the exam room on high alert, opens the exam book and cannot remember anything that he studied. Anxiety also interrupts and distorts cognitive abilities, as in the case of more severe forms of anxiety conditions such as Post-Traumatic Stress Disorder (PTSD) and obsessive-compulsive disorder (OCD). PTSD is often characterized by delusions of persecution and OCD is often characterized by (Obsessive) overuse of thinking and planning and a (Compulsive) behavioral response to those distortions as indicated by its name Obsessive-Compulsive Disorder. Also, when person has a psychotic break from reality, it is usually triggered by the onset of anxiety. This is the reason that when a schizophrenic is taken to the ER for having a period of peak hallucinations that but with anti-anxiety medications they are not **typically medicated with antipsychotics**.

There also seems to be a dual processing of anxiety in the brain that may account for the reason that the onset of anxiety seems to occur without warning or reason. It was theorized by early behaviorists that anxiety resides mainly in the autonomic nervous system (Wolpe, 1973). The autonomic nervous system is responsible for the body functions involved in anxiety conditions such as heartbeat and respiration.

Autonomic functions do not require the mental process of deliberation, planning, and executive function. This is the bottom-up pathway for anxiety through the Amygdala and cognitive interventions are not as effective. The autonomic nervous system may be the reason for the person's lack of awareness to anticipate the current anxiety state, why mental processes are seemingly reduced or blocked when acute anxiety occurs, and why anxiety symptoms are mostly related to difficulties with breathing, the blood's circulation, and other autonomic functions. The fact that it is an acute emotional experience creates within human beings the tendency to assign some other meaning or cause to the experience, regardless of the accuracy of that explanation. This tendency to use rational powers to understand the cause and meaning of an emotional condition is probably how many superstitions and phobias are manufactured. Avoidance reinforces the autonomic response so that the person is not aware of the source of the problem, but when the person proceeds in life without avoiding the anxiety invoking stimuli, the person tends to become more conscious of the source of anxiety.

As an example of the way that the autonomic nervous system works, a professor in college might come into one of his classes with a boa constrictor wrapped around his body and ask his students if they would like to take turns holding his pet. While he may assure each of them that the snake has been recently fed and no harm will assuredly come to them for holding this snake, he will probably have very few students who will take him up on his offer. This result is due to the fact that fear and anxiety are not processed primarily on the higher cortical levels of the brain where complex thought takes place. Can you imagine a student casually indicating, "Oh well, if you have fed the snake this morning, I should like to add this intellectual experience to my repertoire of academic opportunities?" Likewise, fearful and anxious people can be aware of the irrationality of their feelings and yet be unable to change their anxiety responses.

Figure 2.2.1

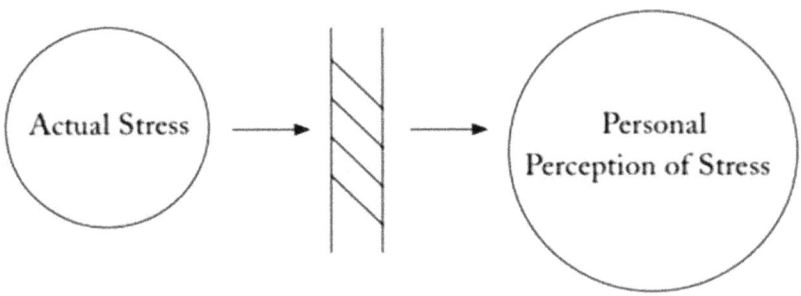

Anxiety is based on the perception of one's inability to cope with life situations as indicated in Matthew 6:25–33. The magnitude of the actual stressor may not be as great as it is feared, transformed by the person to be larger than life. Richard Ecker (1985, 30) used a model that looked like the one shown above.

Ecker based his model on the concepts of Hans Seyle and believed that distorted perceptions regarding the magnitude of stressors were the basis of anxiety. These flawed cognitive processes are major source of neuroses, according to Ecker. He also believed that the anxiety experience involves the autonomic nervous system and more specifically, that anxiety could be remedied by an adjustment on the higher cortical level of complex thought, especially in regard to the magnitude of the stressor. What may be overlooked here is the more personal aspect of anxiety that would also modify this model, specifically, the person's self-perception and one's perceived capacity to manage stress that may be a more dynamic basis for acute anxiety than the misperception of the magnitude of the stressor.

One principle of spiritual formation that addresses the issue of anxiety from this perspective and poses a potential solution to one's perceived lack of personal capacity to handle stressful circumstances is found in I John 4:4 that states, **"Greater is he that is in you than he that is in the world"** (NIV). This instruction considers one's personal capacity to manage the stress posed by one's social environment through a relationship with a great and powerful God. The perception of one's personal capacity to manage any level of stress that may seem overwhelming is improved when the person's attributes are supplemented with the presence of God's attributes. So, Ecker's model may be true insofar as it goes, but there is also this dual action of both the perception of personal coping capacity along with the misperception of the stressor.

Figure 2.2.2

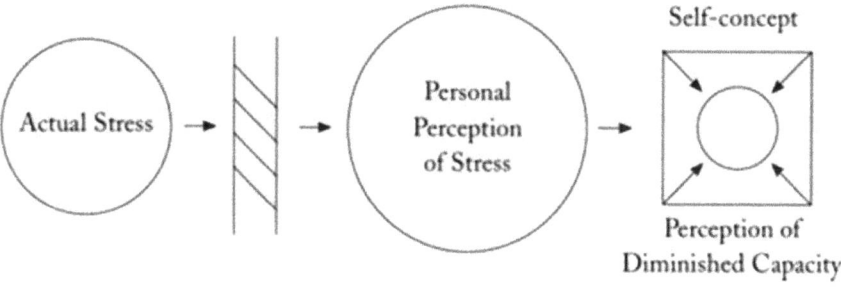

The perception of the magnitude of the stressor is inflated with the anxiety experience, and as well the perception of one's personal capacity is greatly diminished for the person who experiences acute anxiety. To illustrate, if you were a mouse who made your home in the barn for elephants at the local city zoo and you were aware of the fact that the large figure towering above you might innocently pick up one of its large appendages and step on you and not even notice that you were under its large frame, you would be terrified at the very thought. However, if you would, on the other hand, imagine that you, as the mouse, were the elephant's equal—transformed into the size of an elephant in your mind, you might be much less terrified. If you bump into that large significant other, you could say, "Excuse me!" and move about your own business.

While some people may contract one form of anxiety as opposed to another based on biological and genetic factors, there may be something learned from the mean age of onset regarding the different diagnoses of various anxiety disorders. For example, if the mean age of onset for one category occurs later in development than another, it may suggest that the person was able to compensate sufficiently for stress until a certain threshold of stress for a particular anxiety condition would occur. The statistics regarding the mean age of onset of these anxiety conditions do suggest an ascendancy of order. For Panic Disorder the mean age of onset is twenty-seven, for Agoraphobia, it is age twenty-six, for OCD it is the mean age of twenty-four, for Generalized Anxiety Disorder (GAD) it is the mean age of twenty-one, for Social Phobia, it is age fifteen, and for Simple Phobia it is age twelve (Thyer et. al 1985).

The median age of onset was also researched for seven selected mental disorders, including three anxiety conditions: Phobias, Panic Disorder, and Obsessive-Compulsive Disorder with medians of thirteen, twenty-four, and twenty-three respectively (Burke, et. al. 1990). (While the mean is the average based on the sum of all ages divided by the number of people with that given condition, a median represents the fiftieth percentile with half of the population of a certain condition above and below that age.) The more profound anxiety conditions seem to have a delayed development. This would indicate that there is a buildup of stress that activates an underlying action potential for a given anxiety condition. It is as if various anxiety conditions have a certain threshold that, like a trap door, is subtly ready to spring open under the weight of certain amount of stress load that is equivalent to a given anxiety condition. Stress load concepts may also explain why there is a sudden onset of such anxiety states such as panic. The Diagnostic

Interview Schedule (DIS) asks four questions to diagnose panic attacks for experimental purposes:

1. Do you ever have sudden episodes of rapid heartbeat or feeling like your heart is pounding?
2. Do you ever have sudden episodes of lightheadedness or feeling faint?
3. Do you ever have sudden episodes of sweating, hot flashes, or trembling?
4. Do you ever have sudden episodes of chest tightness or smothering or not being able to get enough air? (Diagnostic Interview Schedule, 1981)

All four questions contain the word "sudden" that indicate that the physiological disturbance occurs in a manner as though it were "out of the blue." The analogy of the delivery truck that crosses the same bridge with a weight limit may help to elucidate the relationship between stress load and the suddenness factor. The truck picks up cargo from stop to stop and in the early going nothing happens when it crosses the bridge. Anxiety-laden counselees, when they are younger, are more tolerant of stress and none of the symptoms now experienced by the slightest provocation occurred earlier in life as they do later. However, when stress—the kind that threatens the human being's identity in a personal way—remains unresolved, it will take its toll with the passing of time. As the truck accumulates cargo, the threshold capacity for the bridge that it crosses will be eventually approached, and without much warning, other than the warning of the sign on the bridge, peril draws near in a silent approach.

At the last stop, a tiny parcel may be loaded that is relatively insignificant compared to the weight of the entire load of cargo picked up prior to this one, but with this last tiny parcel it places the entirety of the cargo over the weight limit. The bridge caves in like a trapdoor and the whole truck falls into the water at the last crossing of the bridge. The truck driver would likely assume that it was the last shipment that was responsible in order to consider what might be the best explanation for this catastrophe—leaving him with only theories about how this had happened. This also closely exemplifies the failed cognitive appraisal of the anxiety sufferer.

The model proposed by this author has some similarities but some very real differences with the humanistic alternative explanation for what this author categorizes as the accusing factors (later this author will also consider the excusing factors). Instead of focusing on guilt as a real objective culpability, attributional theory prefers to use the term blame, whether or not there is any objective culpability on the part of the suffering person. One point to make in contrast to this, the person suffering from anxiety and depression could either blame others or blame themselves to avoid true objective guilt. What difference does it make? If the stress is reduced for whatever pathology the person is suffering by an exoneration of that person no matter how real their culpability, how could we not fear that the anxiety and depression would reoccur? The secular helping profession does not want to deal with rightness and wrongness of their clients, but would it not be wrong if in helping the person their real culpability was either ignored or superficially exonerated when to do so would only create more suffering? It is this author's contention that the sufferers of anxiety and depression are neither exclusively and totally exonerated in lieu of others' guilt nor are they ever exclusively or to totally culpable. The one and perhaps the main reason that secular attribution theory is effective is that methods based on attributional theories are not so focused on the person's fault or culpability for their problems so that it would convey to the client that they must fix their own culpability, whatever it may be, by their own means and strength of character. It is equally true that when and if anyone realizes what is their own culpability, they should also realize that they are dependent on the Spirit to make this change according to the grace of God that works in them. It is important to note that the attributional literature does link what they call self-blame to significantly higher levels of distress like depression and anxiety (Glinder & Compass, 1999; McGraw, 1987). Blanchard-Fields and Irion (1988) also indicate that the upside for the negative attribution of self-blame is allegedly self-control that could also counter the adverse effects of anxiety distress. One study indicated that in the context of the aftermath of serious automobile accidents self-blame had some benefit for the development of learning to drive more defensively and more responsibly (Delahanty et. al., 1997). As the thesis of this written work has already pointed out, there is some personal short-term relief derived from the use of self-blame or more precisely from the self-effacing response that is posed by the respondent as a solution for any perceived wrong that may be deemed as a social misqueue or act of aggression, but the use of self-blame will at the same time produce longer-term complications to one person's life. Their affective state may be also negatively impacted if the experience with guilt is not utilized in a spiritually constructive manner. Glinder & Compass (1999) did make the distinction between characterological and behavioral (circumstantial) self-blame. Their regression analysis of variables relating anxiety to self-blame measured these variables with women who were informed of their diagnosis of breast cancer and showed a strong correlation between anxiety and depression with both characterological and behavioral self-blame.

Characterological self-blame predicted distress prospectively, whereas behavioral self-blame predicted distress consistently or circumstantially. This means that the person who characteristically processes stress by means of self-blame invariably ends up in the anxiety state, no matter what the circumstance. The source of the emotional distress in the case of characterological self-blame is found in the person's self-concept. On the other hand, behavioral self-blame is found in the stressful circumstance and a natural human response to the environmental threat, a circumstance like the case of the announcement of a cancer diagnosis, that would naturally cause any human being to circumstantially react with anxiety. It is the natural starting point for all human beings to react to major threats with anxiety, but many people are predisposed to react with self-blame when stress occurs, as it is their character to react this way regardless of the level of the threat. This is consistent with the idea of the modified Ecker model that shows that the major component of the anxiety experience is the diminished capacity to engage with stress. While we cannot always control the level of distress that is elicited from the environment, at least we may learn to have some leverage with how we will manage our stress.

The Spirit can teach us a more perfect way that gives us assurance in the face of threats to our well-being, People are generally to many possible sources of stress. However, the Spirit teaches us what to believe and how to behave under any threat of crisis that can set us apart from that of being mere mortals in our reaction to stress. Certainly, the central point to make about any guilt experienced during a crisis is in the distraction that we have with our guilt that either is irrelevant to the stressful situation or it interferes with the finding the solving the problem at hand. The Spirit can bring to one's personal realization that stressful situations are conduits to personal growth and spiritual development. At best, self-criticism amounts to repentance without faith, an attempt to acquire goodness by doing something. This indicates that one cannot reach one's ideal goal by personal determination. Another good principle is found in Philippians 2: 5–6 that indicates that believers should "**have the same mind that Christ**," In this context, the passage provides the exemplary attitude that Christ had: "**being in very nature God did not consider equality with God something to be grasped**" (NIV). In other words, Christ did not have to work in order to become God. It was his nature. He did not need to convince his Father in heaven, his disciples on earth, or himself by conducting acts of deity to prove to himself that he was God. Likewise, by following his passion, human beings cannot produce the desired result unless they have the spiritual foundation to provide for that result, even if they are convinced that this is the result that should occur in the end.

Medical treatment for anxiety is very effective, especially in the short-term, but medical treatment provides an interesting caveat because of the problems associated with the use of benzodiazepines medications have what is called a rebound effect, meaning that patients rebound with the symptoms as the drug is eliminated from the person's system so that the symptoms of anxiety for which they had taken the medication increase. When the patient stops taking the medication or when the patient tolerates the medication biologically, a rebound of symptoms can occur with greater intensity than the original symptoms. When going off of benzodiazepines, the patient should reduce the medication, slowly attenuating its use over several months. For this reason and other reasons, some anxiety conditions are better helped with antidepressant medications. In fact, a Selective Serotonin Reuptake Inhibitor (SSRI) is often prescribed at maximum dose for PTSD, OCD, and PD. Despite the efforts to find better medications, the use of prescription medications is not always successful, especially when medication is used without concurrent counseling.[1] Some blame is placed on the non-compliance of patients to consistently take their medications, others point to the side effects that complicate their use as a reason for their limited efficacy (Gutierrez-Lobos et. al., 2000). Counselors and psychologists should learn more about the human body and especially about the central nervous system as it relates to psychotropic medications so that they might be competent to monitor the effects and benefits of their use. Medical interventions are generally helpful and should not be avoided, but the counselor should recognize that medical treatment does not solve people's life issues and problems. Those suffering from anxiety and other conditions are facing a battle on two fronts: physiological and psychological and both are under the umbrella of what one might call the spiritual foundations of the person. Spiritual formation principles embrace both the biological and psychological explanations of human suffering and behavior when they are appropriately and accurately applied. This is in direct contrast to the common assumption that spiritual matters are only associated with all that is of no real consequence or significance to what the human brain can do, rather than to do anything to the physical state. Medical interventions may help the person on one front of the battle when used and monitored carefully. The psychological front of these personal battles may be best addressed through counseling, especially when spiritual formation strategies are at its foundation.

Anxiety Conditions

While there are many formal diagnoses that could serve as examples of the self-effacing nature of this class of diagnostic conditions, the following descriptions of the formal anxiety diagnoses are used to demonstrate how the issue of self-effacing self-criticism is related to the sense of personal culpability experienced by these anxiety sufferers:

1. *Obsessive-Compulsive Disorder* (OCD): Obsessions pertain to intense mental processing associated with anxiety and compulsions pertain to repetitive behaviors that are futilely applied to quell the mental anguish that anxiety-laden obsessions create. Obsessions may be characterized as the attempt to change something by means of mental gymnastics with little hope of being successful at changing anything at all. The despair related to their obsessions requires other measures that relate to the development of compulsions. Compulsions represent the failed attempts to relieve anxiety that is produced by these obsessions. The hyphenated condition connects the pain of repetitive and cyclical thought patterns or obsessions with the temporary relief obtained by repetitive behaviors called compulsions. These behaviors have been varied from matching every threatening thought with a counter thought measure, to countless checking the stove and the light switch to avoid some hypothetical danger, and to that of vain attempts to avoid contamination of disease or infection through some peculiar and inadequate means of protection. Some OCD sufferers have deteriorated in their condition to the extent of being unable to maintain the order of their former compulsions. In the end, their homes are piled up with unopened mail, unwashed clothes, and dishes in the sink and they often refuse to allow anyone to help them with the condition of the house because to do so would mean a greater sense of culpability. Some men and women with OCD may have had wonderful potential careers, but they decided not to risk mistakes by not making certain essential decisions, hiding in their offices, delegating all executive

responsibility to their secretaries, and spending their time with trivial matters that may temporarily yield to them some sense of meaningful purpose. Compulsions, the attempted remedy for the agony of obsessions, leave the person with an even more difficult pattern to change and greater despair and hopelessness in regard to personal prospects for change. The desired effect and object of all of these compulsive endeavors become more and more elusive to the experience of the person with the OCD condition. The OCD sufferer often, for this reason, suffers from a comorbid depression.[3]

2. *Agoraphobia*: Two Greek terms combine to make a diagnostic one that means literally "fear of the market place," but the fear of agoraphobia is not isolated to the market. It is a generalized fear of going outside of the security of one's home or familiar environment. Agoraphobia is usually a progressive condition that may start with the avoidance of travel to certain place, but the boundaries of the safe zone around the person become enclosed by each new sense of personal inadequacy to deal with the outside environment. The experience of agoraphobia may have varied levels of anxiety from panic attacks to a less apparent feeling of insecurity that serve to tighten the boundaries that become this person's self-made prison. The term agoraphobia is probably a misnomer because the fear of agoraphobia is not so specific as in other phobias, such as arachnophobia.[4]

3. Social Phobia: Social phobia may be very selective in terms of the social circumstances in which it is observed. Not all social situations create the symptoms for the person with social phobia and the symptoms within the social context will vary for any given person of this diagnosis. Its onset may come at a time when the person is actually undergoing some stress of conducting public speaking or holding a conference with business associates or leading small groups. Typically, there is a rationale as to why the person of this diagnosis would become anxious in a given social circumstance and not in another.[5]

Such was the case for a pastor who had been a senior pastor for several congregations and never had a problem with social phobia, known by some as "stage fright," until he came to his current congregation. The counselor asked if he had the same high esteem for this congregation as he had for past congregations. His response indicated that he was less than enthusiastic about this one, and upon further inquiry it is was evident that he did not like this situation at all. Anger and anxiety are closely associated when it comes to understanding the reason for their occurrence. One way to understand anxiety in contrast to anger might be to define anxiety as a form of anger that the person forbids her/himself to express. Such was the case for this pastor.

4. *Panic Disorder (PD)*: To understand panic disorder, one must understand the basic element of panic attacks. Panic attacks may be due to a general medical condition such as mitral valve prolapse, a form of heart arrhythmia. However, there are many medical and physical conditions that can serve as the source for any of the anxiety or depression conditions. Typically, causes for panic symptom, such as these, disqualify the resultant condition from the diagnosis, in which case the person receives an alternative diagnosis. However, treatment may not vary greatly from conditions that seem to have no physical basis. Panic attack symptoms number thirteen in all and a panic attack must have minimally four symptoms to qualify as a panic attack (<u>Diagnostic</u> <u>Statistical</u> <u>Manual</u> 4th edition published by the American Psychiatric Association that moving forward will be expressed as the DSM-IV-TR 2000, 209–210):

1. Palpitations, pounding heart, or accelerated heart rate (tachycardia).
2. Sweating
3. Trembling or shaking
4. Sensations of shortness of breath or smothering
5. Feeling of choking
6. Chest pain or discomfort

7. Nausea or abdominal distress (Nervous bowel)
8. Feeling dizzy, unsteady, lightheaded, or faint
9. Derealization (feelings of unreality) or depersonalization (Being detached from one's body)
10. Fear of losing control or going crazy
11. Fear of dying
12. Paresthesia (numbness or tingling sensations)
13. Chills or hot flashes

Explanations for these symptoms may be delineated in the following manner: fear of dying, trembling, sweating, and a sense of unreality may have a natural and logical relationship of sensation patterns for any given person. Faintness and hot flashes may also be experientially connected. However, all symptoms seem to result from the involuntary the reaction of the autonomic nervous system, causing the heart to pump high-oxygen blood to the extremities. The lungs have greater demand for oxygen, constituting the smothering sensation, and anticipatory anxiety at onset creates a drop in CO^2 blood gas, constituting the feeling of choking or hyperventilation. This is the reason that relaxation exercises seem to give some temporary relief to anxiety symptoms. Relaxation exercises are also used in systematic desensitization and focus on the extremities for initial tensing and relaxing of muscles and then move to muscles of the abdomen and head, literally forcing the high oxygen blood back to the trunk of the body. Biederman et. al (2005) state that depression is frequently associated with panic disorder and suspects that there is a developmental relationship between them. Dannon et. al (2002) recognize that both the norepinephrine and serotonin neurotransmitter systems may be involved with panic that are also the neurotransmitter systems involved in depression. Neurons are under-active with these two systems for both depression and panic. Blocking reuptake1 is what a number of antidepressant medications do that are used to medicate both of these conditions. By blocking reuptake, medications up-regulate these neurotransmitter systems, making more neurotransmitter substance available at the receptor sites. The Dannon et. al. (2002) study also indicated that depletion of norepinephrine was considered a source of panic attacks and that the Selective Serotonin Re-uptake Inhibitor (SSRI) was a good alternative treatment for panic. Saddock & Saddock (1998) indicate a certain receptor subtype of norepinephrine, the α-2 receptor, has an affinity to panic symptoms when, in general, almost all types of norepinephrine receptors are associated with depression. Depletion of norepinephrine is also responsible for symptoms of low respiration, tachycardia, and inattentiveness.[5]

A policeman in a medium-sized city had been in treatment for panic disorder through major medical centers for a number of years that yielded little results in stemming the attacks that he was experiencing. He was fearful that he would experience an attack at his workplace, though this had not yet happened. He feared that the result would be that he would lose his job because he handled convicted criminals regularly and, therefore, could not afford to let this problem go unresolved. After many years of struggle, a Christian counselor asked him if anyone had inquired about his family background while attending the various treatment centers. He responded to this question by indicating that they had not focused on this issue very much and that there was no action that was taken on what he did reveal to them about his family background. He then spoke extensively of his mother with whom he had an extremely difficult relationship throughout his life. During his childhood, he remembered that he and his father would sleep occasionally in the family car while she was into one of her "tirades." He also indicated that he was not permitted to sleep in his bed or open his Christmas presents beyond the initial wrapping because his mother warned that if he would sleep in his bed or would open his presents, that he would ruin them. He also was more than admonished as a toddler for stepping on the frayed ends of the throw carpets placed throughout their home. He would be punished for causing them to go out of parallel by making him brush the ends for hours with a small brush to separate the strands.

When inquiry was made about his current relationship with his mother, he indicated that his mother had basically ruined his first marriage and that his current wife was about to leave him over his mother's interference in their home. It seemed that his mother would drop by the house and would start to criticize what they were doing in their home's décor and he would be obliged to say nothing about her comments. This was causing him emotional turmoil and playing havoc with his marriage. The counselor instructed him to prepare himself to communicate with his mother about her interference and establish some boundaries. The prospective exchange was role played several times to ensure that he would not create any new problems by this exchange. Also, he was instructed to call the counselor after he had attempted to confront his mother. One Saturday afternoon, the counselor received a phone call. His mother had just dropped in and began her routine criticism. He asked her to stop and requested of her to establish a better type of relationship with them. She objected to what she assumed to be his insult of her. He communicated that he would not give into her objection and would not return to the former status of their relationship. At this, she left his home in a huff, stating that she would never return. In the phone conversation, the counselor asked him how he was doing after this had happened. He said, "I always feared making my mother angry, but it felt really great to stand up for myself and resist her manipulation to do as she pleased in my home and standing up to her without losing control of myself." Counseling continued to maintain this order in the mother-son relationship and for him to make his relationship with his wife a priority. Somewhat ironically, he never had another panic attack after he had confronted his mother on that fateful day.

1. *Generalized Anxiety Disorder (GAD)*: This condition may be understood as constant intense worry. It is not as much of a polar condition as panic disorder that is characterized by peaks of panic and valleys of despair, but a person with GAD may have some anxiety attacks (less than four of the above panic symptoms) or even a less frequent panic attack. It is called "Generalized Anxiety Disorder" because it is anxiety in a steady state and the object of fear is global. It is apparent that the basis for this condition is

one's diminished self-concept for coping with life in general. One counselee diagnosed with GAD revealed that her brother who was also her neighbor joked that he could hear her arrive home at the dark of night and she would be in her front door before he could hear her car door close. She also had a history of an abusive father and that information was a key to helping her through her difficulty. Many clients with GAD have learned to disguise their anxiety by mannerisms such as a short laugh after each statement. This does not mean that everyone who laughs has an anxiety difficulty, but in some cases, it may be a learned behavior of those with a legitimate difficulty that is meant to disarm an acquaintance from thinking that the person has a serious problem.[6]

2. *Post-Traumatic Stress Disorder* (PTSD): Two major subcategories of PTSD exist. One is the result of military action and the other is the result of trauma experienced in civilian life. The distinction may not be so profound when it comes to treatment other than the fact that the military trains the person to be engaged in traumatic events. However, the simulated event of military battle may not be an adequate representation of the reality of one. Symptoms that are most noticeable are not so much the primary symptoms, but the secondary ones, such as alcohol and drug abuse and the inability to maintain long-term relationships. However, these secondary symptoms find their origin in the primary symptoms. The primary symptoms involve the phenomena that persons of this diagnosis often find their life after trauma unreal and cannot readily adjust to ordinary life. Flashbacks, nightmares and panic attacks of the previous trauma often occur through various means. They often experience irritability and depression, apparently unable to bring closure to the life events of the past trauma. Research on PTSD finds that there is usually a precipitating event of trauma prior to the trauma that serves as source of the initial onset of symptoms (Davison et. al. 2004).[7]

One Viet Nam veteran and his wife came to counseling for the purpose of resolving their marital difficulty. However, she was the one who had initiated the process and he was content to attend group therapy at the local Veteran's hospital to handle the difficulty he had with PTSD, not seeing at all the need for additional counseling for his marriage. However, he did come, and as reluctant as he was, and he did tell of how he had gone fishing with his father when he was eight years old. All that he can remember after arriving at the lake was that he was sitting on the shoreline soaking wet and looking out on the lake searching with his eyes for his father. Somehow, he had made it to shore when the boat over-turned, but his father never made it to safety. He presumed that his father had helped him because he was not as good of a swimmer as his father was, but he could not remember what actually happened. This early experience of trauma apparently predisposed this man to become victim to a more severe form of PTSD after experiencing military conflict overseas. As far as it could be understood, his childhood experience was not a topic at the hospital and he refused to discuss this matter in counseling with his wife as well.

Formation Intervention for Fear and Anxiety

When devising an effective treatment protocol for the counselee that presents any form of anxiety, the counselor must first start with an accurate interpretation of the counselee. An accurate interpretation about the counselee and his problem in any case should drive the counselor's methodology. Understanding the individual person apart from a formal diagnosis may be accomplished by focusing more on the field of information around that specific person, especially as it relates to matters of spiritual formation. As well, a sound personality theory that accounts for all aspects of human motivation in general from any possible source of information, including principles of spiritual formation, will assist the counsel- or to make appropriate therapeutic decisions. When this is accomplished to the highest possible level, the counselor can begin by gaining essential data considering all of the possible paradigms of explanation and then carefully listening to the client, the counselor may discern pertinent data to be used. Once the counselor has arrived at some tentative conclusions regarding how this person is to be understood, the concepts of explanation need to be tested for validity. The counselor may look for the manifestation of an anxiety related condition and may consider at least six areas of a formation intervention:

1. The very nature of this anxiety experience is one where the onset of difficulty seems to come out of the blue. Therefore, the counselor should help the person differentiate the symptoms and current anxiety evoking circumstances from the cause of the condition. Clients will tend to insist that their main problem is the anxiety experience itself when, but with the delayed impact between cause and effect, the counseling process should focus on the person's development of self-concept. While the anxiety sufferer may experience extreme emotional upheavals when they are in an anxiety state, the physiological apparatus involved in the anxiety experience is working appropriately in the context of the person's outlook on life. Also, the cause may not be apparent because of the delayed physiological response to the anxiety-inducing causes.

    The illustration of the truck picking up cargo demonstrates this circumstance of how stress builds up over time and then how anxiety symptoms are far removed in time from the initial trend toward a downward spiral of their self-confidence. The orientation of the clients to think of anxiety as their problem rather than the underlying deficit in self-concept predisposes this person to desire symptomatic relief from their own personal attempts of remediation. Also, the counselee's past efforts to help themselves involved two possible approaches to the problem. One way is to run from the stress and another way is to fight with the stress. Of course, the fight and flight response theory has been around in secular psychology for many years, even though the terminology used may have changed over time (Folk-man & Lazarus, 1985). While the idea of fight and flight may be, in part valid and relevant to the anxiety phenomena, it does not recognize the forces from which anxious clients are running and with which they are fighting.

In general, it might be understood that the source of fight and flight is the counselee's poor self-concept or the circumstance in which it is sensed that way, but fight and flight alone does not identify the specific challenge waged against this person that a spiritual formation perspective could provide. To be more accurate, these fight and flight responses are ultimately the result of the Spirit's work that are intended to convince the person of the need for change, a need to modify person's course in vital areas necessary for life. Anxiety sufferers are not, however, cognizant to the work of the Spirit, and their focus is more on their personal culpability and vulnerability than to regard the experience for what the Spirit may be revealing to them. The element of personal suffering that follows the onset of anxiety comes from the natural and adaptive behaviors that human beings use to minimize this benevolent work of the Spirit. Through this failed reaction, needless suffering with anxiety is often created. While the client does not need to be convinced of the ultimate source of his anxiety initially and as the layers of difficulty are lifted from the person's life through the development of a coping strategy, the client may be finally enlightened about what God is ultimately revealing through those experiences. Anxious people may already be in some way blaming God for his lack of giving the adequate relief that is desired. For non-Christians, the counselor may increase the capacity of their self-concept by appealing to that person's desired self-concept except when that desire is self-centered or self-destructive.

2. The major perspectives for helping the person with an anxiety condition are the short-range coping strategy and the other is the longer range self-concept reinforcement. First, the short-range strategies may be characterized as "enduring hardness" strategy that involves a patient persistence of anxious clients to be in control of

their emotions rather than their emotions being in control of them. As indicated previously, the shorter-range coping strategy draws the counselor to consider effective symptom relief to their current bouts of anxiety. In progressive succession, continued episodes of anxiety can add additional stress that has already presented profound symptoms and can retroactively fuel future anxiety states. Anxious clients tend to react negatively to stress by awfulizing and stressing more than necessary due to their lack of control over these episodes that only maintain this vicious cycle of further self-depreciation and experiences with anxiety.

A positive image in regard to one's environment has a somewhat transforming impact on the person's self-image and thus improves the same person's emotional state (Vassilopoulos, 2005). The more personal the environmental images, the more transforming it is to the person. While positive imagery may produce a similar experience to that of faith experiences, imagery that is not based on reality may have little impact on the personal challenges on which anxiety is based. The journey of the spiritual formation experience is not always a pleasant and easy road, but the Spirit helps the person face his personal difficulties in life with a realistic hope, not an artificial one. There is both a physiological and a psychological disturbance with the anxiety experience that may be better endured with coping strategies that are aimed at the real-life issues that are the anxious person's actual circumstances and how that person typically responds to these circumstances. Positive biblical hope is the best short-range coping strategy that you can give a person that is in an acute state of anxiety. The major difficulty with the strategy of giving biblical hope may lie in how to effectively communicate it to any given client. Counseling in this manner would not be so much through a pure didactic means of communication, but as the giver of hope identifies the specific challenges that the person faces, the counselor will learn about the true nature of his difficulty and become more aware of a means to resolve it through the personal application of the principles of hope that are consistent with spiritual formation ideals.

Clair Weekes (1978), a therapist who dealt with panic disorder and agoraphobia, proposed to her clients that they confront their panic with doing all that they could do to cause themselves to have an attack. For her, anxiety was also an issue of having control of his emotional state. He surmised if they would try as much as they possibly could to have an attack, the client would be in control of panic rather than the other way around—theoretically plausible but experientially uncertain. More specifically, there are real life situations that are more foundational to these anxiety experiences than the anxiety experiences per se and that are far more dynamic to help the person find an appropriate sense of control of his entire life. In this vein, the counselor should investigate what is the significant relationship or circumstance in the counselee's life that has majorly contributed to this person's failed capacity for coping with stress and has served as the basis for the ensuing anxiety condition. As in the case of the policeman mentioned in this chapter, he resolved his anxiety by unburdening his life from his mother's manipulation and by believing that he could find contentment in life, even if that would result in displeasing and angering his mother. Also, the counselor should consider the person's ultimate aspirations in life that this may be person seems to have lost amidst the current fray of discouragements and disappointments that the person is facing.

3. Longer-range identity issues depend on the ideals and aspirations that the person uses to formulate an identity, but in relation to the principles of spiritual formation this process would direct any person to understand that his identity is connected to the image of God by which he was created and for the believer, identity is ultimately connected to the work of Christ. Success in overcoming anxiety will depend on how well any person might emulate this newly found bases for identity. Longer range identity issues run parallel to the short-range coping strategies and short range coping strategies

establish the longer-range identity concerns of this strategy. The process of realizing this newly founded identity through levels of spiritual maturity may take ultimately a lifetime to accomplish. The counselor may, at first foray in the direction of this objective, help that person establish a more substantial self-concept that assimilates the Spirit's work.

To accomplish this task, the counselor should carry out two strategies. One strategy is for the counselor to reveal his personal struggles or use the example of others in regard to how this new direction for identity is found. The other strategy involves listening to the counselee's narrative account and identifying the specific challenges to his self-concept followed by a recognition of the alternative directions and choices that would provide a means to realize that a new identity better copes with real life experiences. This can be accomplished to some degree even before the client completely understands or is even willing to accept the work of the Spirit. By putting the two main lines of strategy together, counselors might advance their clients through their own life experiences so that they might be successful in changing their direction in life by indicating to them how they might practically apply these short-range and longer-range strategies. Short-range strategies involve coping with the immediate challenges with real hope, long-range strategies involve a transformed identity.

Figure 2.2.3 Reaching the Anxiety Threshold

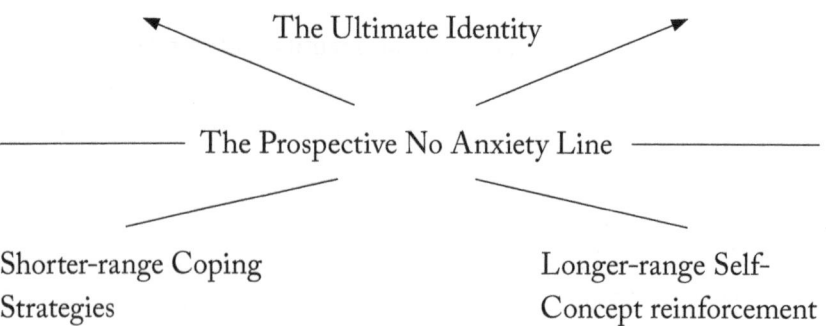

The Ultimate Identity

——————— The Prospective No Anxiety Line ———————

Shorter-range Coping
Strategies

Longer-range Self-
Concept reinforcement

4. Obviously in light of the general thesis of this written work, *guilt plays a major role in anxiety*, but it may not be the kind of guilt that most people typically understand it to be. Overt wrongdoing is not always the source of guilt, let alone the source of guilt for many other difficulties that human beings often experience. Romans 14:23 reminds us that sin, implied by the guilt experience, has another source that is in essence a lack of trust or confidence, as Jesus also indicates in John 16:8 when he said that the Spirit convicts the world of sin because of unbelief. This lack of faith creates a vacuum in the soul of the person that requires the presence of other forces and devises that further negatively impact the spiritual nature of the person. It is not as though people start out in life attempting to do wicked deeds. Having faith, even among children, is gradually discouraged early in life by the circumstances of life that cause them to eventually face their shortcomings that exist both within themselves and in the world around them. Furthermore, they naively start out assuming that finding contentment and goodness can be accomplished by personal willpower until they meet up with themselves along the way and find out as Paul had learned: he could not completely accomplish the good thing, and the evil deed he could not simply avoid (Romans 7:19–21). Human beings are all very aware of their failures, but to believe that God could provide for them sufficiently to accomplish feats to overcome their very personal struggles is typically an all too elusive idea. In response to their failed aspirations, they will tend to fight for autonomy rather than depend of God for his provision to begin the spiritual formation process, and they will tend to run from their problems to avoid the greater realization of their own personal need.

5. The use of *systematic relaxation* has been touted by behaviorist as a means to anxiety reduction to pair positive stimuli of relaxation with their awareness of physical tension in a way to reduce anxiety (Powell, 2004).8 Other behaviorists have coupled this idea with positive imagery as well to make the pairing both on the physical

level and on the self-concept level (Naeem, 2006). This would channel the hopelessness once felt in the past by some action in the present that help them to dispel that hopelessness by pairing it with a behavior that at least symbolically gives greater autonomy. Systematic relaxation may have some benefit for some clients that may give them a point of reference regarding the level of anxiety and tension that they are experiencing. Anxious individuals may not know how tense they are without relaxation to give them this point of reference or to realize how chronically tense they have been. On the scale of 1 to 10 with "1" being the least helpful and "10" being the most helpful technique, systematic relaxation is about a 1 or 2 as a stand-alone intervention. However, connected with other strategies recorded here, such as the real-life description of their personal need, they may only help the person to become aware of their building anxiety.

6. The remaining matters that should be covered by the counselor while counseling counselees in an anxiety state are twofold. One matter that the counselor should evaluate is the level assurance that the counselee has to have in order to be successful with overcoming anxiety. This might be viewed as an implicit conditional promise for success for clients with an anxiety difficulty. However, the more serious anxiety conditions may have a much more remote opportunity for successful remediation than the less serious type of anxiety problems, but they can improve their management of the more serious anxiety conditions. Also, anxiety sufferers are likely convinced that they are never going to be able to resolve their anxiety difficulty and that only terrifies them further. To have the counselor express that it is possible for the client to overcome this problem under these applied strategies in itself provides for an opportunity for profound relief. However, the promise of cure should be given with some reservation, especially in cases where the counselor recognizes that the client is unlikely or unwilling to apply the steps outlined in this chapter. Success through assurance

alone will have merely a placebo effect and will not be lasting. Assurance of success is related to the commitment of the client and the assurance is possible as the counselor effectively assesses the client's commitment.

7. The counselor should refer those serious cases of anxiety for medical treatment so that the emotional distress of the client might be reduced sufficiently to prepare the way for counseling the person more effectively. It is important to check the person's dietary regimen that may also contribute to anxiety, sleeplessness, and depression. Be aware that excessive caffeine intake may exacerbate anxiety conditions, especially panic disorder (Veleber & Templer, 1984).[9]

Background Information on Depression

Depression and anxiety have the same basic orientation in the context of the discussion of the spiritual formation perspectives. According to this thesis, both anxiety and depression ultimately proceed from the self-effacing, self-critical response that human beings utilize to modify the impact of the convincing work of the Spirit of God. While the model uses the term fear as the primary emotional response for the self-effacing strategy, depression can also be the result of that same reaction. As well, depression can be the result of the pleasure-seeking strategy as indicated by the word "despair" in figure 2.2.4. A distinction should be made between the terms used for the clinical diagnosis of depression and anxiety and the terms used in this model. The pleasure-seeking strategy may not necessarily lead to a formal diagnosis of depression and that is one of the reasons for the use of the term despair in this figure. Despair is a broader and more generic term that includes other lesser conditions resulting from pleasure-seeking, and fear is also generic to self-effacing strategies that also include various clinical diagnoses of depression and anxiety, as well as lesser forms not so formally diagnosed.

Figure 2.2.4

Style of Relief	Pleasure-seeking	Denial	Self-effacing	Blame-shifting
Self-concept	Helpless	Autonomous	Inferior	Justified
Social Interaction	Selfish	Shallow	Avoidant	Aggressive
Behaviors	Addictive	Rationalizing	Blaming	Controlling
Emotions	Despair	Worry	Fear	Anger

From this, two questions emerge. One question, that has already been answered in brief, is the question concerning the purpose of the Spirit in convicting someone whose source of depression is assumed to be from stressful circumstances beyond that individual's control. For what shortcoming, then, is this individual being convicted? This question could be answered in several ways. One way to answer the question is to recognize that the Spirit is not the source of the worsening state of affect in any given depressed person. Rather, it is the typical type of response human beings give in varied degrees to the Spirit's work that can worsen the suffering of the person to the point of depression. The intent of the Spirit, so named the Comforter, is to bring care to and for that person, and the Spirit's convicting work when responded to with repentance and faith provides opportunity to find relief. Another way to answer the aforementioned question is to understand that depression is a physiological state that is independently related to any particular spiritual response to the preconditioning work of the Spirit. Nonetheless, even in circumstances where the initial cause of depression could be purely assigned to physical dysfunctions, such as hormonal imbalances, chemical exposure, physical injury, terminal diseases, cardiac and respiratory disease, the comorbid depression could be ameliorated by how the person responds to these physical challenges by means of spiritual formation strategy.

The intent of the Spirit is to reveal himself to the suffering person through the very struggles that human beings face. The work of the Spirit is evident in any event of difficulty that human beings might encounter along the way whether the individual is a Christian or not. This was the case with Balaam who was considered to be an idolater but knew about the God of Israel in a very peculiar way and was later confronted by the voice of God speaking through the mouth of the animal that he was riding that warned him concerning the wrong he was about to commit against Israel for praying down curses upon them. The Spirit may use various avenues, even depression itself, as a means to reveal his life-giving truth to help those human beings yet to be unshackled from their past and changed from their former course in life.

Depression is not simply the result of the Spirit's work nor is the cause of depression essentially understood to proceed from the being expressed here. Job was a man in whom God himself found no person's commission of a particular sin. Job is a great example of what is being expressed here. Job was a man in whom God himself found no fault, yet he suffered tremendously. In the end, he was challenged to understand the true nature of the God and to stop his protest over what he perceived to be the injustice of his suffering. Job did not sin so that he suffered as much as he was being tempted to sin because of his suffering.

The relationship between sin and depression is an interesting topic, for certainly the idea of a relationship has passed through the mind of many depressed person. And it is true, the source of depression can be a particular sin, such as in the unending bitterness that one harbors over some perceived past injustice. There is also the more subtle relationship that sin has with depression because there are some benefits for staying depressed, such as others expecting less effort from the depressed individual by which the depressed person takes less personal responsibility. There are other factors that may contribute to this aforementioned phenomenon because very few depressed persons would consciously plan to remain depressed for the payoff of diminished expectations from others. Another explanation for this phenomenon is the physiological homeostasis of depression that finds a neurological balance around the state of being depressed. Expressed in scientific terms, neurons in a state of depression express genes that maintain this organic state of being depressed. Therefore, the body may actually resist any behavioral or cognitive measures that attempt to change the person's steady state of mood. This is why depression takes time to remediate, regardless of the therapeutic approach. Another factor that builds on the former perspective is that the long, seemingly unending experience of trying to overcome depression is very discouraging to the counselee to the point of making this person give up on any hope of relief.

Even though the person suffering from depression may be aware that recovery takes time, he tends to grow weary of trying his own methods to feel better prior to coming to counseling because of the elusiveness of these efforts' all too distant promise of relief. They may even stop applying the suggestions of the counselor and stop taking the antidepressant medication because they are not sensing any benefit in the short term for their effort. The relief for their depression is not immediate and serves to maintain the depressed person in an even more depressed state. This may be the major difference between anxiety conditions without comorbid depression and conditions of depression. Other than symptomatic differences, the course of depression has rendered the person to a state of resignation, whereas the person with anxiety conditions may be counter productively exercising fight and flight responses without this sense of resignation that depression carries. The challenge for the depressed person is continue to do what they would do or should do even when they still depressed. To stop would only double the hazard for depression.

Attributional theory similarly supports not only the notion that "self-blame" is considered a common source of both anxiety and other mood disorders such as depression. Attributional theorists also recognize that there is a precipitating event of either the physical or psychological stress event for various mood disorders (Anderson et. al., 1994; Mantler et. al, 2003 & Victorson et.al. 2004). The idea of precipitating events for mood disorders is compatible with the idea of this written work that indicates that a diminished self-concept and a perceived incapacity to overcome the magnitude of these events is responsible for these various affective conditions. Attributional theorists apply its principles to depression in much the same way they apply them to anxiety. These concepts also lie at the foundation of the thinking that is the basis of cognitive behaviorism (Vanderbeeken et. al. 2002). Aaron Beck (1979) wrote extensively about how to use cognitive approaches for affective conditions like anxiety and depression. Basically, cognitive behaviorists catalogued to various mood disorders. It may look like a simple means to help someone who has a profound affective problem, but the process is made more complicated than it may appear at first glance when practitioners try to successfully manage the method in a clinical context. Cognitive-behavioral concepts do give more than a two dimensional view of human beings with affective difficulty, but other than the absence of the work of the Spirit in cognitive behaviorism (as we would expect from a secular model that does not intend to infuse any religious point of view), it also does not account for other dimensions of human beings that are important for effective recovery from depression.

One such dimension is the circumstance of the depressed human being's complex motivational system where, in general, human beings passionately hold onto behaviors and cognitions that produce both unwanted and wanted consequences while legitimately desiring a much more pleasant result for themselves in their affective and social experiences. Cognitive behaviorism, as it is practiced, also lacks the feature of considering the potentially positive purpose for depression. The goal of spiritual formation concepts when helping the depressed is to learn how depression might serve to direct the depressed person to the profile of Christ to conform to his image that involves a human being finding a real hope and a clear sense of purpose, even when the person endures suffering. The newly proposed positive psychology similarly critiques cognitive behaviorism for not considering the endowed assets and talents of depressed people that they have and that they are able to use as a therapeutic means to overcome their depression (Karwoski et. al 2006).

Cognitive behaviorism is incomplete in at least three dimensions: primarily the lack of recognition of the preconditioning of the Spirit, a lack of a comprehensive view of human nature by not recognizing how human beings passionately maintain their pathology for other purposes while suffering unwanted consequences, and finally a lack of understanding of the ultimate purpose for suffering. All of the above matters are necessary for successful therapy so that any human being might fully overcome depression. Cognitive behaviorists would also assume that their clients would be thoroughly consistent in their motivation system without any conflicting cognitive patterns in order to be successful in their therapy. Cognitive behaviorism may work in the short term as it is applied to specific cognitions within a solitary schema of cognitive experience. But cognitive behaviorism lacks the desired comprehensive view of human personality that spans the complexities of human thought, motivation, and affect.

Formal Diagnoses of Depression

There are a number of formal diagnostic categories that are contained in clinical manuals, such as Adjustment Disorder with depressed mood and Depressive Disorder not otherwise specified, but for the purpose of this discussion the list below will describe depression subcategories of Major Depression, Manic Depression, and Persistent Depression Disorder (PDD) that formerly named Dysthymia to be considered more specifically:

1. Major Depression must first be understood in light of the criteria for an episode of depression. For the diagnosis of major depression, at least one episode of major depression is required in the client's history for the diagnosis and some subcategories of major depression have multiple episodes that are required by the type indicated as the "recurrent type." A major depressive episode must be distinguished from depression found in manic depression, schizophrenia, and other psychotic disorders and by not having its source in medical or

biological conditions. Five or more of the following symptoms must be present at the same time during a two-week period and must represent a change in previous functioning. Either depressed mood or a loss of interest or pleasure in the person's former activities must be present that are the first two items in the following list found in the Diagnostic Statistical Manual, Fourth Edition, Text Revision (DSM-IV-TR 2000, 168–169):

1. Depressed mood most of the day, nearly every day during the episode.
2. Loss of interest or pleasure in activities most of the day, almost every day.
3. Significant weight loss when not dieting or weight gain or de crease or increase or decrease in appetite.
4. Insomnia or hypersomnia nearly every day.
5. Psychomotor retardation or agitation most every day.
6. Fatigue or loss of energy nearly every day.
7. Feelings of unworthiness or excessive or inappropriate guilt.
8. Diminished ability to think or concentrate, or indecisiveness, nearly every day.
9. Recurrent thoughts of death, recurrent suicidal ideation, with or without a specific plan.

The specific diagnosis of major depression would also need to specify whether the depression is single episode or recurrent episodes. The diagnosis may be further identified with features of depression such as mild, moderate, severe, with psychotic features, with melancholic features, with atypical features, with postpartum onset, in partial remission, or in full remission. The residual effects of major depression may appear to be similar to persistent mood disorder formerly called dysthymia.

One man in his late forties who worked in a grocery store was placed on disability after a stack of milk cartons on wooden pilot had fallen on the backside of both of his legs. This injury required several knee surgeries that ended without his complete satisfaction that his injury was completely resolved. He swore that he still had pain even though doctors could not corroborate any basis for his experience with this level of pain. The gate theory for pain may be an explanation for this phenomenon. Pain signals are emitted from the body continually regardless of any reason for pain to exist that are then intercepted by endogenous anti-pain transmitters in the brain when there is no injury or physiological basis for the pain. In the brain, perception of pain relies not only the blockage of Substance P by endorphins but can be inhibited by depression when other neurotransmitters are depleted. Facilitating neurotransmitters for endorphins such as serotonin and as well norepinephrine are also depleted in depression.

His depression was determined to be unrelated to the injury itself, but his depression did grow out of the despair of his losses in life that were indirectly related to his injury. He wept during sessions frequently and wished that he could die. He had withdrawn from most of the activities that he had formerly enjoyed. One activity that he was still willing to continue was his cooking because he was at home all day while his wife went to work. This was one activity on which a therapeutic plan could initially build. As well, he had grown attached to a preschool neighbor boy and would act as his sitter enjoying this young boy as his only social outlet. He and his wife did not have children. He was resentful of his wife thinking that she did not respect him because he did not work. His contentions with her in this regard seemed very petty; however, they were needlessly offensive to her. As a result, they slept in separate rooms and he would lay awake all night angry at what his life had become. A friend of his had lived at their home but recently left the home prior to the counseling process because his friend's daughter thought that he had an unnatural relationship with him. He went to his estranged friend's apartment to reconcile their differences but this man refused to talk with him. Very slowly the counselor started to work from two therapeutic perspectives, reframing his cognitive concept that defined his relationships with others and reentering purposeful activity that formerly gave him a meaning for his life.

2. Manic Depression can be separated into basically two categories, namely bipolar I and II conditions. Both bipolar conditions must meet the criteria for at least one major depressive episode, and there must be at least one manic episode for bipolar I and for bipolar II at least one hypomanic episode. The difference between bipolar I and II condition is that depression is the primary feature for bipolar II, indicating a greater need for antidepressant action than with bipolar I (Berk & Dodd, 2005). However, antidepressant medications with mood stabilizing agents should not be used for bipolar patients, risking the consequence of producing an acute manic episode that involves psychosis. In bipolar I, manic episodes involve frequent bouts of mild to severe psychosis, indicating a greater need for the atypical antipsychotic action are needed with bipolar(McIntyre & Katzman, 2003).9 The bipolar I condition has a greater comorbidity with anxiety disorders such as OCD (Gaudiano & Miller, 2005), and bipolar II has a greater comorbidity with personality disorders (Joyce et.al, 2004). (Comorbid or comorbidity means the two or more conditions occur at the same time). As in the case of the criteria for major depression, there cannot be a diagnosis of comorbid schizophrenia or other psychotic disorders and the manic condition cannot be the result or medical difficulty, neurological disease, or from the use of drugs or alcohol. The difference between mania and hypomania is that the following symptoms must coexist for at least one week during an episode of mania and at least four days for hypomania. Both mania and hypomania must have either elevated, expansive, or irritable mood and at least three symptoms from the following list of symptoms and four symptoms if the person experiences only irritable mood (DSM IV-TR 2000, 169–170)

    1. Inflated self-esteem or grandiosity
    2. Decreased need for sleep (satisfied with 3 hours or less)

3. More talkative than usual or pressure to keep on talking
4. Flight of ideas or subjective experience that thoughts are racing
5. Distractibility
6. Increase in goal directed activity or psychomotor agitation
7. Excessive involvement in pleasurable activities that have a high potential for harmful consequences.

Bipolar I could be further specified with a single manic episode, most recent episode hypomanic, most recent episode manic, most recent episode depressed, most recent episode mixed.

Bipolar II can be specified with recurrent major depression or recurrent hypomanic episodes. Both can be further identified with features of mild, moderate, severe, with psychotic features, with melancholic features, with atypical features, with postpartum onset, in partial remission, or in full remission.

A middle-aged woman lived her life in constant conflict with others. She developed a long list of battery charges on her rap sheet until she was in her mid-twenties when she started to raise her family. Her troubled history started with her dad who was an alcoholic and when she went to elementary school, she felt ashamed of this family secret. He self-medicated his yet undiagnosed manic depression until much later in life. However, even though no one else dared to mention her father's alcoholism, she realized that her childhood peers were aware of her father's problem, and she felt so ashamed that they knew.

The second major crisis of her development happened in the sixth grade when her teacher openly expressed a dislike for her in front of the entire class, while her classmates laughed. She vowed that she would get even. Her mother did not believe that her teacher would do this, and therefore she was made to sit through this outrage until near the end of the school year when the whole ordeal was revealed and teacher was dismissed from the school for this and other unethical practices. In high school, she developed a relationship with the star on the football team. The relationship was not a public one and was extensively sexual in nature—meeting for secret rendezvous. The young man later professed to be naïve about what she was doing to protect herself against an unwanted pregnancy. Likewise, she would not explain what led her to not take precautions that led to the birth of her first child. She graduated from high school and her "boyfriend" went off to college, resisted any financial responsibility, and had little contact with the child until she was age nine. From this point, she was so bitter and angry that she began to pick fights with anyone, sometimes with perfect strangers in public that would as much as look cross-eyed at her.

She attempted working at a large building supply chain store stocking shelves and conducting inventory. While employed, she struggled with sleeping and then would spend days in bed on a sleep rebound. She would get into fights with customers in the store and with her fellow employees. By the time she had started treatment, she was no longer having physical fistfights but when she became angry with anyone, she would use words that would make a sailor blush. Her employer requested that she be placed on disability for her missed days at work and for her behavior of fighting with supervisors, fellow employees, and customers.

When counseling began, she had already started a number of medications, but the first several sessions of counseling were spent largely on sorting out what was fact or fiction regarding what she assumed to be the side-effects of a given medication. She discontinued a number of medications so that it was hard to find a physician that would continue to prescribe for her. Another element in those initial sessions was to help her recognize how she could take responsibility for her own care so that she might improve regardless of the medications that she used. She found this very difficult to believe, that she could make any difference on her own—thinking that the medication or the counselor would have the major responsibility for her improvement. Her greatest challenge was her hopeless despair, which also increased her guilt and her sense of culpability. Therefore, her responses to others were prickly and her patience with any annoyance was paper-thin. She would call her mother three or four times a day. However, if her mother would try to advise her against taking reprisals on others whom she thought had offended her in the slightest way, she would blast her mother with a retort that was so harsh and demeaning that it took all that mother could do to continue to answer the phone when she would call.

Obviously, her depression was through a sense of resignation from ever being successful, feeling no hope for forgiveness from those whom she had offended. She sensed little peace, thinking that her life would never have any merit. In moments of calmer reflection, she would admit that she had unnecessarily offended others but offered only, "That's just the way I am," as if still angry at the same individuals. Her vision for the future was indelibly marred by the past, but on her persona, she had a built-in response that was automatic and without fail: attack whoever was there to validate her sense of failure. The counselor's non-judgmental relationship went a long way to prevent her from reacting to the counselor's admonitions in the same manner that she would typically respond to others. Very slowly the counselor started to work from two therapeutic perspectives, a loosening of these old constructs that made her feel so very condemned and that found no redeeming quality to her life and a reframing of her cognitive concept that would define her relationships with others in a manner that gave the option to start over with a clean slate that was founded on the love of God.

3. Dysthymia must meet the criteria of being depressed most of the day almost every day for at least two years and one year for children and adolescents and during that period must have at least two of the following symptoms (DSM-IV-TR 2000, 176–177):

   1. Poor appetite or overeating
   2. Insomnia or hypersomnia
   3. Low energy or fatigue

4. Low self-esteem
5. Poor concentration or difficulty making decisions
6. Feelings of hopelessness

The symptoms for dysthymia cannot be due to or explained by other major diagnoses like major depression, mania, hypomania, schizophrenia, or any of the major psychotic disorders. Symptoms must not be due to the direct physiological effects of substance abuse or general medical condition.

One woman in her late fifties always lived a thrifty lifestyle. She had seven children that were all grown with families of their own. She grew up in a rural area without a father. She was always careful about taking any risks in life, even adventures that others might consider to be important to take. She found herself being repetitious in her life patterns, and these habitual patterns took on a life of their own. If she could not maintain these habitual patterns for living for some legitimate reason, she felt like a failure and became sad and sullen to the extent that it was difficult to get started in her routine again.

She would often question herself as to the reason that she had to do things a certain way day after day and year after year. She also wondered why she felt frustration with those who did things differently than she or why she felt a little angry if others would suggest another way. She began to realize after some counseling that her walls of protection had become her prison and that she was attempting to overcome her sense of culpability by her orderliness of life. She recognized that she completed her tasks according to an acquired narrowly defined protocol with little toleration for change. Through counseling, she was admonished that she should not conduct efforts to be justified before God or others, but her work out should be from a heart that had already been blessed. When she realized her new freedom to make her personal choices free of these encumbrances, she began to feel less depressed and sensed that she was truly free to make her own choices.

The biological correlates for depression involve major neurotransmitter systems known as the biogenic amines, also known as monoamines. The monoamines are a family of neurotransmitters in the brain such as serotonin (5HT), dopamine (DA), and norepinephrine (NE). Certainly, there are other biological systems that are involved in depression, but the site of action for depression is majorly thought to be on the cell level of the brain and explained by what has become known as the monoamine hypothesis (Stahl, 2000). Brain cells are called neurons and a neuron conducts electrical flow like the chemical charge of a battery from neuron to neuron that lie end to end in the brain. The site of action is, more specifically, the microscopic gap or cleft between the neurotransmitter-sending end of one neuron and the neurotransmitter-receiving end of the next neuron. It is important to recognize that the pathway for these various monoamine neurotransmitters are throughout the brain and pass through structures along these specific pathways that are indicative of the symptoms that are exhibited in depression. In major depression and PDD, neurotransmitters NE, DA, and 5HT are mostly depleted.

Major Mood Disorders and the Brain

In mania, the same neurotransmitters are unstable. Subsets of DA and subsets of 5HT when in excess are mostly responsible for psychotic symptoms. Both major depression and manic depression can present psychosis but may do so by a very different means. DA is on the same synthetic chain as NE, and when synthesis of NE is truncated during its synthesis, the over-production of DA is the result and vice versa. This is the basis for psychosis in depression. A subtype receptor for NE, the α-2 receptor, inhibits both 5HT and NE so that all these biogenic amines tend to regulate themselves by a delicate balance with each other (Stahl, 2000). When NE is not regulated very well, as in the case of manic depression, excess DA may be the result and may be the basis for psychosis during manic depression.

The pathways for the biogenic amines are very similar starting in the brain stem, flowing through the midbrain toward the frontal lobe, then proceeding toward the parietal lobe on top of the brain, and ending on the backside of the brain, known as the occipital lobe. NE emanates throughout the midbrain, passes through the frontal lobe, and emanates throughout the parietal lobe. 5HT emanates in every lobe that it passes. DA does this as well but in more highly concentrated areas of the frontal lobe (Ka-plan & Saddock, 1998). The brain stem is responsible for attention, sleep, and appetite; the mid brain is responsible for memory, concentration, and emotions; the frontal lobe is responsible for planning and executive function of activities; and the parietal lobe is responsible for body movement and orientation to space and time.

When considering the biological correlates to depression, one may ask what causes depression. Is the disorder of the brain causing depression or is depression causing brain malfunction? If one decides that depression causes brain malfunction, then medical interventions would be used then counseling and psychotherapy would be exclusively supportive for the depressed person with the major focus of therapy on the brain's activity and the resulting condition. Most scholarly articles recommend mostly for symptomatic relief. If brain malfunction causes depression, both psychotherapy and pharmacotherapy in the treatment of depression (Ebmeier, Donaghey & Steele 2006). However, there are skeptics on both sides (Miller 2006; Miller 2006). The best explanation might lie somewhere in between the two extremes at various points of view depending on the type of condition presented. This question involves the theoretical discussion of the body-mind construct for human personality. Welch (1998) has given his answer to the question by indicating that the two entities relate to each other in four different ways. He says that the body and mind relate to each other in the following manner: the body affects the mind, the mind affects the body, the body does not affect the mind and the mind does not affect the body. This may appear to be the case, but also it may be difficult to be certain if there are circumstances where the body does not affect the mind or where the mind does not affect the body because the effect from one to the other may be so subtle and immeasurable at the time that it may only appear that it did not at all have an effect. The basis of Welch's thesis is to avoid the tendency to "blame it on the brain" when attempting to explain emotional problems or of the counselee avoiding any personal responsibility for the difficulty at hand.

The relationship between the two is conceivably correlated as the term "biological correlates" suggests so that this term also implies that there is a cause that is neither solely physical nor solely metaphysical for any resulting condition. What happens in the mind is likely processed in the brain and what happens in the brain is likely processed in the mind but not necessarily one causing the other. This explanation does not abrogate personal responsibility nor does it blame the body or the mind for difficulties that the person develops. The person is influenced by forces within body and brain and in the social environment that impact the metaphysical mind to cause some reaction or malfunction. That reaction and/or malfunction of the mind will in turn impact the body and the brain, but that all depends on the character of the individual person, what that individual person believes. Personal responsibility does not reside solely in the mind nor solely in the brain. The mind is not housed in the physical brain but works alongside the mind, mind reflects what is happening with the neurochemicals in the brain and the neurochemicals reflects what is going on in the mind. And yet there can be such an inaction of neurotransmitters that produces depression without the person necessarily becoming as depressed and visa versa. An illustration that might explain the body-mind construct is like the two rails of the railroad track. They are perfectly parallel and yet distinctly separate from one another. For the train to run smoothly, both rails need to be perfectly correlated at a slope of +1.00 or -1.00. They must work together as though they were one or the train on the track will derail with accident and injury to its passengers. The physical brain and metaphysical mind are the means by which the person expresses the entirety of his living being.

Formation Interventions for Depression and Other Mood Disorders

The most important feature of an intervention strategy for the depressed person involves the two primary symptoms of depression. One of these two possible symptoms is essential for the diagnosis. One symptom that the person must present is the "depressed mood" and the other symptom is the person's "loss of interest or pleasure in activities" that the person used to enjoy. While for the purpose of diagnosis one of the two must be present, a logical analysis of the two indicates that these two characteristics are intertwined in a way that makes them difficult to distinguish one from the other. The net idea about how these two primary criteria combine to suggest that it is the person's life and activity outside the counseling relationship that is the center for the focus of the focus for the remediation of depression involves these life-change dynamics.

Thase & Callan (2006) indicate in their study that there are three aspects of "homework" that need to be considered to be effective in treating major depressive disorder. The threefold assessment of homework should focus on the relationship of homework to its adherence to a planned outcome, on the relationship of therapist behavior to homework completion, and on the relationship of patient variables to homework adherence. In other words, homework should be appropriate and congruent to the established goal of the counseling process. Also, as indicated, when the counselor carefully assesses, follows, and encourages progress in the depressed person's homework, the assignment of homework will be more effective. Thirdly, when the counselor takes into account the counselee's personality traits and characteristics assigning homework that the depressed person will more likely complete and benefit from the homework.

One of the two characteristics of depression that are essential for diagnosis—the loss of interest or pleasure in activities—impacts greatly and is greatly impacted by this person's relationships, especially in those relationships with significant others, family members, work-place associates, and in fellowship with friends. Others who depend on this person, such as employers and family members, become frustrated with the depressed person as he is often saddled with this person's responsibilities. Depression progresses until the depressed person is socially isolated and cannot foresee any means to personally recover those former social relationships or complete the tasks of past responsibilities. Recovery from the vantage point of the counselor should take incremental steps of restoring the person's relational functioning in whatever way that would bring greater harmony to those relationships without sacrificing the s too depressed person's personal integrity. In this process, the depressed person should be set free to do what is necessary to improve his affective state and to do what is important to improve his relationships. However, the depressed person mostly regards those steps a painful to attempt, but taking them is exactly what he should do to recover. The depressed person is reinforced to avoid these steps, especially ones that involve renewing or restoring relationships by this sense of despair, and so further isolate and become more depressed.

Four major categories of homework assignments might be considered for the depressed person. Communication projects are important assignments to consider for depressed people. The communication homework assignments involve the implementation of anything from informal exchanges with significant others to that of more formal family conferences. The manner of communication and the content of communication should be carefully rehearsed during counseling sessions. There is the great potential for the depressed person to make a bad situation in their relationships worse while attempting to make them better. The counselor should be sure that the depressed person is ready emotionally and spiritually to take the step of communicating with another with whom he had ceased communicating or with whom he had poor communication in the past. The counselor should have a grasp of issues to know of the hidden dangers in attempting to have a counselee reestablish communication.

Family conferences should have an established agenda and purpose so that the session does not deteriorate into arguments. However, in many cases the family situation may have already deteriorated to the point that such formal measures are not as likely to occur, let alone be successful. It is likely that the depressed person has already given up on communicating prior to counseling, assuming that it would not change the outcome or the opinion of others about anything relevant to his point of view. The depressed person may have withdrawn from the most significant relationships, convinced that nothing can be established so that he will quickly withdraw from communication attempts when others respond to them with any of the former resistance that he experienced in past attempts.

It is likely that depressed people have also neglected their responsibilities. This is not to say that the depressed person takes any comfort in this problem because his is the larger price to pay in terms of his loss of personal self-confidence, loss of income, the potential loss of life in suicide, and especially in the sense of guilt that he feels from neglecting these responsibilities. In other cases, depressed people have been too indulgent by taking on too much of others' responsibilities (such as the responsibilities of other family members), and they may have been obliged to do so by those very people. In many of these cases, the depressed person will complain about how this other person has taken advantage of his assistance and yet continues to help this person. Depressed people may also complain about the ingratitude or even rudeness of this other person who gives little credit for his assistance. Even though depressed people may realize that they should withdraw from this circumstance, they may continue to make significant contributions to the other's success and reputation, propping him up against his own eminent disastrous consequences. Depressed people, in this case, rely too heavily on what esteem they can create for this significant other or from this significant other as though it will directly impact their own self-concept as well. Perhaps they have given up on ever having a positive view of themselves without this type of bondage to another. Whatever the circumstance, the depressed person should carefully select what is their person's rightful responsibilities in order to schedule the appropriate activities and responsibilities to be completed that are commensurate with an appropriate self-concept that is based on his true identity as creature of God or an identity that is based on his relationship with the Son of God.

Frequently, depressed people can trace the beginning of their condition of depression to an event in life (if they are willing to reveal it) when they or close allies were seriously offended or even abused. The offended person may have become embittered by the circumstance where the offender seems to have gotten away with this act of treachery without facing the essential justice for his deed (Romans 12: 19–20, Galatians 6: 9–10, Psalms 37 and 73). In this case, the depressed person has lost faith with the human race that anyone in the present circumstance would care sufficiently enough to correct this grave injustice. Forgiveness projects may be an appropriate step for the counselor to consider in this case, but the counselor should carefully assess the circumstances and the state of mind of the depressed person. Where the depressed person was offended in a way that instigated a reaction that was intended to retaliate or seek vengeance for the aggression, depression might more closely represent a form of anger and vindictive bitterness. Depression in this case might also represent unsuccessful attempts to retaliate or blocked attempts to bring some justice to the situation. By the time depression sets in, the opportunity for any further correction is seemingly no longer possible. Not all offenses incur such vindictive feelings upon the victim, perhaps, because the circumstances involve a love-hate relationship or the depressed person was too young at the time of abuse to understand how offended he was by this abuse. While this text will reserve the greater comment about the abused counselee for chapter four, there are circumstances where offenses against the counselee do not require the counselor to instruct the counselee to formally forgive that person. Although forgiveness may be an important consideration, the counselor should focus rather on the steps for the restoration of the person's God-given identity of the depressed person that has been held hostage through the act of abuse or mistreatment, which identity now needs to be restored. Abused/ depressed people using a transformed communication strategy might begin to lay claim on this new identity by the declaring their freedom from the domination of their former identity perpetrated on them by the offender. Through such communication strategies, these people may now be free to express a new identity.

Formation interventions should use several formation principles throughout this restoration process. When using biblical/ spiritual concepts with depressed people from varied spiritual backgrounds, the information cited below might be more appropriately used as a benefit to the counselor's understanding of the counselee initially. Later, spiritual formation concepts may be used in the development of the counseling process to communicate more directly to depressed person. The decision to communicate these principles directly or indirectly would be based on the assessment of the spiritual background of the person, bearing in mind the preconditioning of Spirit in every person's life. The concern is for the impact of these principles, when communicated directly to the unprepared counselee, might create defensiveness in the counselee. Therefore, the intended impact might be lost. Counseling is a narrative dialogue between two people, but the distinctive part of Christian counseling is the element of instruction. Cognitive-behavioral therapy also considers early experiences, formation of dysfunctional assumptions, and more recent critical incidents for identifying the "logical errors" that bend the person toward depression (Power, 2004). But the instruction element of Christian counseling is distinctive in its more positive content, as well by its Socratic style of weaving short elements of instruction into the exchanges between the counselor and the depressed person. The content of instruction would mostly be the relevant application of formation principles rather than the these personal applications should not be a secret to the depressed formal exegesis of scripture. The source of counselor's ideas about person. For counselors to conceal their theoretical basis for counseling practice would be unethical. And more specifically by the following formation concepts, counselors may advance people who are in a depressed state to have the opportunity to approach (Power & Schmidt, 2004; Markowitz, 2004). The following spiritual formation concepts below include cognitive, relational, or emotional-based concepts that are dynamically integrated.

1. Guilt is invariably the underlying dynamic to depression. However, understanding the various nuances of guilt might make it a more complex issue to rectify. There may a good reason for the person to feel guilty due to known offenses that he has committed. In any case, with or without known offenses, to know the forgiveness and grace of God as well as the forgiveness from others would be centrally important for depressed people. But many who experience a subjective form of guilt seem to have as their source of guilt what others think about them, rather than what is accurately true of them—an objective point of view related to what God thinks is true of them. However, from a Christian Formation perspective, even subjective guilt cannot be thought of as false guilt because it truly represents objective guilt in a different form.

    The work of the Spirit in the world is to convict the world with respect to sin, righteousness, and judgment (John 16:7–11). Surprisingly, the passage explains that the Spirit convicts the world of sin for the purpose of pointing out their unbelief instead of pointing out their specific transgressions. Rather than this convicting work pointing out the most embarrassing characteristics in a person, it points out the ultimate source that produces all evil, namely unbelief. Faith is the focus for overcoming any form of guilt that the depressed person may exhibit. Where the person does already relate to the Person of Christ who is the ultimate object of faith, it may be observed in the life of the counselor. This is not to say that the counselor should hold herself out as a superior example but for an example of a person that depends on God. For the person that may not have this Christian background, there may be an opportunity to provide an example of a person that does. Preferably a person that would be an example of God's grace. Any human example that is used should provide a segway to the ultimate example. In chapter one of this text, the formation concept related to inner conflict used the passage of I Corinthians 4, concerning the life of Paul and his relationship with the Corinthian church, illustrates how faith may be used to avoid the typical personal interference of others' opinions with a client's conscience. This concept bears relevance to people who permit others to have the authority to negatively affect their sense of well-being, resulting in a greater sense of condemnation that has no remedy. When the Holy Spirit convicts, it is combined with the understanding for a constructive change and the conviction directs the person to find solutions for the wrongs that the person has committed. The Spirit's work ultimately leads to faith. The first step that needs to be taken in this case is to discern the source of the person's guilt. The more evident reason for guilt may be found by this person allowing others to have a more significant role than appropriate that consequently makes him feel guilty. At the rudimentary level of helping depressed people who may not have an evangelical background, faith can be first explained to this person. Observing that Jesus experienced suffering for a meaningful reason. By searching for the reason for their suffering, some relief may be afforded to the depressed person as well. This may prospectively contribute to the potential for faith by Christ's example. Faith and the Kingdom of God are like the mustard seed, as Jesus described, that has meager beginnings but eventually can produce great results.

2. *The sovereignty of God*, in concept, can further develop formation strategy. The depressed person has practiced avoidance of both physical contact and/or mental memory of the shattering echoes of past failed relationships, offensive acts of others, tragic loss, announcement of terminal disease, public knowledge of their most grievous sins, persecution, and rejection. The counselor's attempt to open the doors of memory of these events will not be met with open arms or open minds even when the person is seeking help. This may be the reason why he might prefer a chemical cure rather than to face the real issues. The important aspect of this formation concept is to assist depressed people to reframe their mental image of these pivotal experiences. Secular psychotherapy realizes this to some degree when utilizing positive imagery and methods of suggestibility, such as hypnosis or a form of self-hypnosis. However,

formation concepts give the Christian counselor a more realistic means to gain this positive perspective on their problems that have accrued from past, unresolved experiences.

The passage of I Corinthians 10:13 indicates two very interesting perspectives on this matter. The first perspective is that God, in his sovereign care, does not allow more tragedy to come into one's life than what that person can bear. This is God's perspective and not the perspective of the depressed person, and so if one does not believe what God says then this will be of little comfort. The second element of this instruction is that it is through this tragedy that one may find an escape from it. The last thing that depressed people want to do is remain depressed, but depression, according to this formation concept, is the means to the resolution of depression. The counselor cannot coerce the depressed person to take this step of cure, but the counselor can be straightforward about the failed expectations of the person related to avoidance of this step. The corrective procedure is to take steps to learn to live effectively with depression, and depression will most likely take care of itself over time.

3. *Effective handling of personal disappointments* builds on the previous concept because depressed people have grown to believe that their tragic experience is greater than they can endure. If anyone has experienced even a momentary bout of depression, he might tend to agree with this perception. But again, as it was stated in the opening comments of background information for depression, depression is a physiological state that is correlated but not necessarily caused from a person's personal struggles or shortcomings and likewise, corrective procedures that one may take will not directly impact the depression itself immediately. The grave disappointments to which the person now responds in depression require a response. Such a response should not be based on whether or not it will immediately relieve depression. However, the burden of unresolved disappointments may contribute to the overall burden of depression. The cause of these disappointments is probably much more personal

than the depressed person realizes. This was the case for the twelve tribes scattered abroad that James 1:1 made reference.

The people referred to in James 1 were obviously of Jewish descent, but they were also the first generation of believers in Jesus. At the time of the writing of this epistle, there were "scattered" by persecution, rejected by their family members who did not believe, experiencing famine, and imposing death threats upon those who believed. Nonetheless, James refused to allow these suffering people to blame God or their circumstances for their sense of despair, even though they lost their homes, their incomes, their families, and for some their very lives for the cause of Christ. He states, **"But each one is tempted by his own evil desire."**

What were these people being tempted to do? It is apparent from verse 6 that they were tempted to doubt. To amplify, these new Christians of Jewish descent might have been thinking or even saying, "Where is this abundant life that Jesus promised? We have never had such a hardship in life prior to believing in Jesus."

Second, what was their evil desire? The meaning of the term used for **"evil desire"** needs to be clarified. It is a term that is commonly used in the New Testament to mean **"lust"** or **"desire for something evil."** However, there is at least one place where it tends to have a slightly different nuance. The passage of Galatians 5:17 uses the term when it states, **"For the sinful nature desires what is contrary to the Spirit, and the Spirit what is contrary to the sinful nature."** The connotation for the term as desiring evil as determined by the term επιθυμια alone is not workable when it is used in reference to the Holy Spirit. Also, the context of James 1 does not support the typical meaning of **"evil desire"** because these people were likely desirous of nothing more than their homes, families, source of income, and their safety returning to them rather than wanting to acquire anything indecent. James elaborates on the various means to overcome these tragic disappointments by avoiding the human propensity to doubt and despair. It is when one wants what one thinks are basic needs that are at the time also denied when the related disappointments can be so overwhelming. By this, James indicates that the first step to bring comfort to these people is to *evaluate what is their true need when they do not have what they think they do need.* Disappointments such as these naturally lead people to judge God as being unfair, but a fair evaluation of the person compared to nature of God would cancel out any such thinking, even in the midst of great deprivation.

James outlines at least four more ways to overcome their serious disappointments. The second way that he recommends to these suffering people is to believe consistently in God's loving care despite circumstances that seem contrary to that perspective. As James indicates, *their error is in losing sight of how much they are loved by God.* The extent of his love is not measured by our circumstances but by his revealed truth to us. This is confirmed by the words found in verse 17 where James indicates that God is giving good and perfect gifts, even when suffering human beings observe the matter quite differently with no earthly evidence of these gifts at all. How could there be such disconnect between the perspective of God and the perspective of mortal beings? Jeremiah blasts the apostasy of Israel because they had turned from the Living God and had hewn out broken cisterns that can hold no water (2:13). The analogy of God raining down blessings to his people unchangingly, even when there is no earthly evidence of such blessing to human beings that blinded by their disappointments and their expectations are greater than their need. This type of disappointment exemplifies that he is doing so much what Jeremiah is indicating to the people of his day that were experiencing what they thought was unbearable difficulty. It is, rather, their leaking cisterns that need the repair that is referring their tendency to judge God by their circumstances rather to define their circumstances by what they knew about God (Proverbs 3:5–6). This is the true test of faith in God's love. He also continues to recommend that a person needs to be in a listening mode with God to be directed to do what he hears him say. James asks them to place themselves in submission to God's perspective.

In so doing, they are also recommended to put their faith to task, as he states, "He will be blessed in his deed." There is nothing more comforting in the time of tragic events than to know what one can do about them. Lastly, the recommendation of James is to make sure that they place a major part of this type of activity in helping those whose disappointments are greater than their own.

4. *As it was already mentioned faith can change the unchangeable.* Faith does not function well through the cognitive and affective resources of human beings as Proverbs 3:5–6 indicates. But faith transforms human vision and potential. As Hebrews 11:1 states, **"Now faith is being sure of what we hoped for and certain of what we do not see."** Depressed clients may see clearly the incontrovertible mess of their lives and may not see any relief or help out their despair, but that is just the circumstance in which God shines.

5. When faith is established, next in the order of virtues that despair, but that is just the circumstance in which God shines. Having hope complements the overall intervention for depressed people is hope. Knowing the true character of God does inspire human virtue even in circumstances and sometimes especially in circumstances of life that are not conducive to having any hope. The natural means that human beings try to develop hope is to find some earthly reason to have hope. Biblical hope is based on accepting God's perspective rather than having one's own finite abilities to have hope. The power of this hope is through believing in the Christ who was victorious over the ultimate disappointment and hopeless despair in death. The human race has largely become locked into a even more hopeless cycle of futility of thought, known as worry. Hope is not based on how much one desires or believes that they will procure relief, but on what basis that this hope is derived. II Peter 2:9 supports this perspective, **"The Lord knows how to rescue godly men from trials."**

6. *Patience* is not simply waiting for the deliverance that one desires to have from a given disturbance of mood or difficulty in life. Patience involves any activity that validates faith in the revealed truth about God's provision, even when deliverance has not yet become evident. Patience requires a person to transcend circumstances and defy his own sense to believe what God says is true about the most immediate circumstances. Depressed people need to maintain the application of what they have learned in counseling even when they have had little noticeable difference in their relief from depression. Romans 8:22–25 describes both the now and the not yet of the depressed person's hope for relief, indicating that the formation of faith sustains the person until the promise of complete relief is fulfilled. Depressed people do not need to hope for what they already have by their willingness to believe in the promise of relief. Relief can be experienced simply from having the assurance of knowing that relief from depression will come. Hope generates a solution to the question of persistent depression before there is any relief.

7. Prayer is the natural extension of the aforementioned interventions and has a significant role in making a difference on the prognosis of care for depressed people. Jesus taught a number of things about prayer, but to mention a few he taught that prayer should not involve meaningless repetition but rather it should petition God's will done on earth as it is in heaven. This manner of prayer continues more of the reframing process that is needed in the depressed person's life. Prayer also needs to be focused on the perspective on that need. Psalm 37 and 73 demonstrate how David candidly prayed from a human frame of reference lamenting about how evil men seem to go free from justice regarding their misdeeds, while righteous people seem to never get a break. On the other hand, he continued his prayer by reframing this former perspective when he entered the house of the Lord with a different understanding of the same situations that realizes the matter from God's perspective.

An older woman with Multiple Sclerosis (MS), a brain disease that involves localized but progressive destruction of its neurons, sought counsel. Symptoms for MS are consistent with the location in the brain where this destruction may occur. The disease preponderantly affects the brain stem that depletes the synthesis of neurochemicals that maintain the person's mood. Her mood would also impact her behavior. She was married to a man who had been a merchant marine and she was fixated on his past indiscretions of leaving her for long periods of time alone with their three sons. She was not as warmed by his presence when he returned from sea duty as she was hoping to be because he found odd jobs among his neighbors to occupy his time. Her approach early in the marriage before she was diagnosed with MS was not much different than it was currently, except that her despair seemed to be much more progressed. From her perspective, she lacked any viable means to respectably disagree and calmly communicate her frustration and sadness with her husband's lack of attention for her. He later retired from the merchant marines and worked for large business conglomerate.

He seemed to be more aware of her difficulty than she had recognized, but he did carry a certain air of indifference about her expressed need for his attention and affection accounting for that expressed need by citing her depression and by focusing citing her depression and by focusing behavior. When he made major decisions without regard to her wishes, she would become sullen and start to weep and then enact self-destructive behavior, such as banging her head on the wall. She literally gave him an excuse to be less attentive by her child-like protest The adult sons were divided on the topic, but they mostly supported their father when the argument reached the level of intensity that sides in this ongoing argument were formed concerning whose fault it was that she threw such a fit. On the last occasion, she was taken to the hospital after her husband called the police. She blamed the pain of MS and the abandonment of her husband for these episodes and was even more greatly depressed by her husband calling the police and sending her with them to the hospital.

It was not long after counseling had started that she modified her present form of communication of her feelings of abandonment to make some attempt at calmly presenting her case to her husband. While she was gratified to have a counselor listen to her lament, she did not gain the satisfaction of a listening ear at home. Although a professing Christian, her mood was not elevated by this change in her outlook as the counselor had hoped. Her husband, even as a retiree, would tend to offer more reasons why she was depressed that did not focus on ways that he could be a part of the remedy. She stopped the self-destructive behavior, but she could not find any peace of mind with her marriage relationship and would offer more discouraging evidence of his lack of appropriate care in following sessions of counseling.

At several cycles of the counseling process, the counselor would bring her to the objective reality of her dependence on her husband for her emotional needs that were not being met by the marriage. She would stubbornly resist the suggestions and the counselor would show her compassion by not pressing the matter until it came up again. She seemed to take the counsel and apply it to a degree after her initial resistance. In the end, the counselor would visit the home that made both husband and wife less resistant to the path that they were learning to take. The progress was ever so slight until her health had so declined that she was having difficulty driving, but this gave rise to a new controversy. Her husband was unable to gently help her to understand his fear of her driving with her MS, instead he had utilized her physician's help to remove her license without her approval. She was unwilling to surrender her license, and therefore she refused to continue counseling as well.

While there are differences among the various mood disorders, whether manic or major depression, these categories mostly present a depressed mood. The more specific differences between them do not change the formation concepts that may apply to a counseling strategy for them as much it may change the intensity of their presentation of symptoms. One study indicated that the differences between various mood disorders are not so much a diagnostic difference as it is a difference in personal background and experience (Clayton, 1977). Both manic depression and major depression may present with the symptom of psychosis. For that reason, this discussion will continue with a short discussion of background information and formation strategies for psychotic conditions.

Schizophrenia and Other Psychotic Disorders

When any of the psychotic disorders are considered, the organicity of the symptoms is greater than it is with other diagnostic conditions. The origin of the symptoms may be partly biogenic or partly psychogenic, but psychosis itself is considered to be a mostly biogenic condition that creates profound psychological effects, whereas depression and anxiety are mostly psychogenic. The severity of psychosis may also be determined by the client history and the severity may be somewhat predicted by the nature of onset when the onset is more greatly organic. Greater organicity indicates that medical care professionals would have the greater responsibility for the client's care. Delusions and sometimes hallucinations provide some helpful information about the person's innermost emotionally charged perceptions and deep images that the person carries about self and others. The psychotic person bears some responsibility to reduce his delusions and hallucinations. No-psychosis contracts have been utilized to reduce psychotic symptoms by helping the patient to observe the early warning signs related to the onset of psychotic episodes, enabling the patient to make prescribed decisions to opt for a different direction. In this case, psychotic patients will then decisively use the instruction received during the counseling process to avert the ordinary course of psychosis that would follow those early signs of onset in order to avoid the inevitable result.

Formation strategies are focused on the issue of anxiety that is a triggering mechanism for the onset of psychotic episodes. The psychotic person often experiences bouts of anxiety when control over the person's mind is being dramatically challenged (Naeem et. al, 2006). Therefore, this strategy would utilize a modified version of the same strategy for anxiety reduction that is recorded in the beginning of this chapter. Further, the counselor should find a window for the psychotic person to develop some self-reflection. The counselor should probe the individual's unusual defenses for a more open line of communication. When an open line of communication is established, the counselor can assign an appropriate level of responsibility. With one Amish Mennonite farmer who had been diagnosed with schizophrenia, the only means to prevent him from regressing further into his world of paranoia was his children, especially his four-year-old daughter who would treat her father like nothing was wrong with him and would readily ask him to play checkers with her each day. The counselor can assist the psychotic person by encouraging a reframing of these sometimes-bizarre cognitions that can be accomplished at a time when the psychotic person is more lucid. For this Determining the prognosis for a given person with psychosis is found in the saying. "When the onset is gradual, the prognosis is usually poor! When the onset is fast, the prognosis is usually better. When the distortions of reality are specific, the cognitions that occur during psychosis at a time when the person is more lucid." The delusions and hallucinations do serve a purpose for psychotic patients are working out some of their distorted innermost emotions based on their warped perceptions of their relationships with others. For this reason, the schizophrenic naturally will offer resistance to the reframing of these feelings and cognitions. The counselor must reduce the anxiety that magnifies the threat that the schizophrenic person perceives in relationships. Philippians 4: 7 adds, **"The peace of God ... will guard your hearts and minds in Christ Jesus."** Compassion and gentleness will go a long way to prevent further deterioration of the person into psychosis. The counselor should make progress reports readily available to the other professionals on the treatment team and request feedback of the same professionals regularly.

CHAPTER THREE

THE BLAME-SHIFTING RESPONSE

Blame shifters use their controlling behaviors t o preempt others from posing any credible threat to control them even when others pose no real threat to control. Their highly reactive character is one that others most often with the greatest a mount of disdain or fear, but the controlling person's view of self typically does not reflect this same regard for self that others may observe. While angry and aggressive on the outside, these controlling individuals are actually fearful of others, but they cover their fear by an aggressive agenda to control their circumstances of life. They perceive others as trying to take advantage of them, even when others are not attempting to do so. Without strongly sensing goodwill from others or accurately viewing the grace of God emanating through the behavior of others, blame-shifting people tend to keep all threats at bay by working to maintain absolute control over all of their circumstances in life. Significant others in relationship with blame-shifting people are likely to feel oppressed by their overbearing control. However, the blame shifter's fear of being controlled is almost as great as their aggressive manipulation of those that deem as their greatest threat. Their focus on those that threaten their dominance may blind them to how oppressing and manipulative their behavior might be to others.

Background Information for the Controlling Counselee

Paramount to any other topics mentioned in this chapter, the controlling type of person is its major focus. *Anger* and *unwillingness* are also featured in this category of controlling behaviors, but anger and unwillingness are distinctly described in this chapter due to their profound impact that they have on their relationships. The tendency to seek control is a common characteristic for any human being. Manipulation is a generic way of expressing the more extreme form of personality disorder, and to a lesser extent the way of expressing the most basic propensity that is generally observed in all of human behavior. When this characteristic is extreme enough, it impacts marriages in a destructive way that obscures many of the virtues and assets that might have been found in the marriage relationship. The controlling characteristic in a person's life is most visible when conflict is expressed in relationships, but the source of conflict may be disguised as from a source other than from the controller's behavior. Conflict in marriage or in any other type of relationship may also be caused by a given partner's personal inner conflict that will be discussed later in section three, but for the purpose of this section, conflict will be understood as a function of the controller's passive-aggressive manipulation. Most people, including the controller, know the ugliness of what an over-bearing controller looks like and for that reason the controller is also clever enough to sustain a manner of controlling behavior that is mostly obscure and unobvious.

They will often seek for relationships with those who are readily manipulated, making this controlling behavior even more difficult to detect as the source of any conflict. Whether or not controllers are fully conscious of their motive to control, much by design they find that the best means to gain control is to cause others to lose control to remove any suspicion from them. It has always been a remarkable phenomenon that a married couple may find compatibility not in so much the way that they have a mutually satisfying relationship with each other, but often in what they believe that they are getting from the other partner and what the other gives back may not be what the controlling person wants. Controllers are deceived by the presumption that their partners in marriage will be the fulfillment of their long-held desire for marriage believing that partners want to give them the control that they want. For a while, this circumstance seems to provide a mutually satisfying goal for each partner until the reality of this exchange is discovered. How is it possible for two people who have been together for a number of years to not really know much about the other person with whom they live? Often, a person so passionately desires a certain result from his/his relationship with another so much so that one partner or the other is blinded to the reality of the other person's true nature. One person intending to build a relationship with another may believe that he can mold the other person into what he wants without pondering long enough to find out what the other person wants. In one way or another, one person usually seeks to be the more dominant of the two in a relationship, and the opposite partner in this relationship may be willing to be more submissive, finding security by maintaining the relationship by this means. While this may be somewhat typical for all marriages, the suffering and hardship that is found in some relationships where controllers are overreacting to the fear of the other partner's control by using manipulative behaviors creates a tragedy of destructiveness for their spouses and other family members.

This *controlling behavior is reinforced by the success* it has in its ability to reach, with regularity, its desired goal of having the primary control in the relationship. Techniques used for controlling behavior are interesting as well. One method is the *wounded bird technique* where the controller feigns or exaggerates injury at the hands or words of the significant other. In this approach, controllers may reduce the significant other's resistance to be controlled by inflicting that person with unfair guilt and with accusations that are not at all true or not entirely true. A second approach is t*he invisible trigger finger* that injures the significant other while hiding any intention and/ or means to bring that harm to another. In this case, the controller can baffle others by making them responsible for the injury that the controller has inflicted. A third method for controlling is the multiple choices where the controller poses as the mediator and the contender, the victim and the perpetrator, or the actor and the reactor all at the same time. This approach keeps the significant other confused about the controller's actions or statements that are neither clear nor distinct in meaning, hoping to mystify the significant other in such a way that makes the controller's purpose and intention difficult to comprehend. Often, this type of controlling behavior attempts to remove all accountability so that this controlling person may be free to continue more passive-aggressive activity. A fourth method is the truth vs. desired version of the truth that involves the worst form of manipulation. In this case, the controller attempts to convince others of what he wishes the truth would be rather than letting the truth be the truth. This approach becomes so habitual and does not require much deliberation by the controller so that the controller will also have greater and greater difficulty recognizing the real truth. Through the passage of time, the controller, as well as his victims, will gradually gain the better discernment to know what the truth really is. The smoking gun technique uses the other partner's existing fear to maintain control over that other person. The controller will exploit this fear by pretending that harm to the other person happened accidentally without any intent on the part the controller to harm this person—like a smoking gun in the hand of one who exclaims, "It went off by itself!"

The thesis of this written work has already described the somewhat paradoxical motivation behind controlling behavior:

Figure 2.3.1

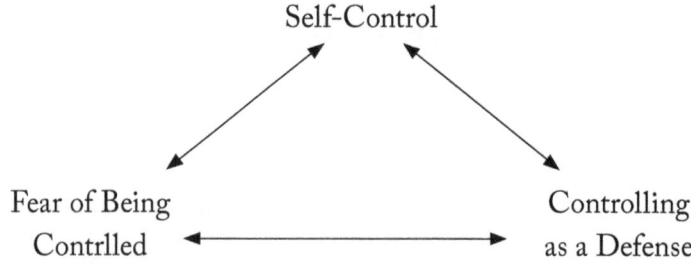

Controlling behavior is the result of the fear of losing control and controlling others is motivated by the controller's fear of losing control to others. Controllers may not appear to be so threatening! Their motivation for manipulative behavior may seem fairly innocuous when it is unmasked in this way (i.e. that they are motivated by fear). The counselor may use this information wisely to gain an inside advantage when attempting to remediate the controller's behavior. Also, the partners that are married to an overly controlling person might benefit from this insight if they will not use the same information in a manipulative way as well.

In some of the more obscure personality disorder diagnoses, it may not be so evident that the entire class of personality disorders are overtly controlling in behavior. However, while all personality disorders may seem to exhibit passive-aggressive behavior, there are basically two paradigms for this type of controlling behavior (Alicke, 2000). One paradigm indicates an aggressive behavior that passively disguises the motive for aggression, and the other paradigm indicates a more passive behavior that is inadvertently aggressive by means of being more withdrawn than the other paradigm of controlling behavior. Research has often suggested that the etiology for the clinically diagnosed personality disorders is found to be multifactored, including the factor of the disordered childhood family (Garmezy, 2005). The etiology of personality disorders is understood to be related to a developmental framework of persistent, long-standing, and inflexible patterns of behavior that belong to the Axis II category of diagnoses (Davison et. al. 2004) Also, there has also been evidence to suggest that the diagnoses have a biological and, therefore, genetic linkage (Coolidge et. al. 2004; Rettew et. al. 2005). The best explanation for the onset of any of the Axis I or Axis II conditions would be the diathesis stress model (Davison et. al. 2004). This diathesis stress model explains that most diagnostic conditions do have some genetic predisposition, but that stress acts upon genetics to push the prospective diagnosis toward the threshold of onset. The diathesis stress model best explains all available data related to the development of any given diagnostic condition, including personality disorders. It is also is an explanation that is most compatible with a spiritual formation perspective on personality development in general.

Formal Diagnoses of Personality Disorders

Personality disorders were thought to belong to a subcategory of schizophrenia at one time in the history and development of the Diagnostic Statistical Manual (DSM). It was the DSM-II (second edition) that finally moved these personality prototypes to Axis II. The only other Axis II diagnoses are the four levels of mental retardation. They are so categorized with mental retardation and sequestered from the Axis I diagnoses because of their developmental etiology and because they represent a very steady state of condition. There are three so-called clusters of personality disorders: wild, weird, and withdrawn. The wild personality disorders are the antisocial personality disorder (APD), the borderline personality disorder (BPD), the histrionic personality disorder (HPD), and the narcissistic personality disorder (NPD). The weird personality disorders are the schizoid personality disorder (SPD), the paranoid personality disorder (PPD), and the schizotypal personality disorder (STPD). The withdrawn personality disorders are the dependent personality disorder (DPD), the avoidant personality disorder (AVPD), and the obsessive-compulsive personality disorder (OCPD).

1. The Personality Disorder–Not Otherwise Specified (PD-NOS) is an admixture of various traits that do not distinguish the person of this diagnosis into one of the other former types. Are reactionary to authority figures. In the DSM-V, personality disorders are not separated from the former Axis I as this distinction does not exist any longer.[1]

2. Antisocial Personality represents the adult version of the childhood Axis I diagnosis, Oppositional Defiant Disorder (ODD). The personality type is not to be confused with sociopathic behavior that

exhibits little conscience for misdeeds done to harm others. However, persons with APD have been known to have minor skirmishes with the law, often do not finish school but personality disorders were ultimately separated from the schizophrenia diagnosis because the positive symptoms of hallucinations and delusions were either not present or not in sufficient magnitude to merit that diagnosis. It is thought that the only means to modify their behavior effectively is to remove financial reinforcement. Physical punishment is thought to motivate rather than to discourage their misbehavior. APD is the most researched personality disorder in the class.[2]

One man had been arrested for drunk and disorderly conduct a number of times and was placed on probation. His childhood was riddled with truancy from school and he and his three brothers could always be found drinking and fighting with each other from early adolescence. Before his last arrest, he became interested in a young woman who left the area to return to home, a rural community over 200 hundred miles away from his home. He followed to her home area ignoring the fact that he was in violation of his probation. He found a job as a farmhand just minutes away from where she lived, but she did not know that he was in the area. The judge who presided over his case found out that he was in violation but ruled that he would allow him to stay where he was instead of rearresting him. He thought that the rural life would be a better influence on this man than the urban scene. In time, he made his presence known to the young woman. She barely knew him prior to leaving the city but was surprised that he had followed her there. She expressed that she did not want him to stay as she too was leaving behind her past in the city. He was furious and he assumed that her request had an ulterior motive. He went back to his job and watched her movements and later found out that she was engaged to a young man from the local area. What he did not know was that she had run away from her home because she was running from this engagement prior to leaving for the city.

When he found out to whom she was engaged, he walked on foot in the direction of this other man's home so that he might confront the man to show him who was the better man for her. As he went on his way, he passed a church and for a moment he thought that he might ask a pastor inside to convince him that he should not go and do what he planned, fearing that he might end up with much greater legal problems. The pastor offered this man the plan of salvation and the man made a commitment to Christ. He attended that same church for many years and married one of the women in the congregation. He obtained a job driving a truck for a feed mill. They had two children and seemed to have a wonderful story of redemption to tell. Later, he appeared in a counselor's office one Saturday afternoon making an urgent request for some emergency help. His wife had reported an incident to the elders of the church. She often found that he was not in bed when she awoke in the middle of the night. He always had some curious explanation the next morning to tell when she would ask him where he was. On this occasion, she went to look for him. She found him in her oldest daughter's room with his hands up under the blanket. The elders of the church removed him from the home and they hoped that the counselor could assist them further without informing any outside authorities. The counselor realized that he would be in an ethical violation if he would concur with this plan. He informed the counselee that he must report the matter to the legal authorities after which he was promptly arrested. For the Children and Youth Agency, he was an easy case to prosecute with his admission of guilt. For the counselor, there was more work to be done.

The counselor found that there were many secrets that he had been keeping, such as a bottle of whiskey in his truck, but there were more pernicious secrets in his life than this one. He always had problems with authority figures. He would feign humbleness over his failures in life without true remorse and typically go through the motions of trying to look like a Christian and a good citizen, at least while others were watching. He would rely on some sensational relief such as alcohol to compensate for his boredom with trying to act respectable. He had no friends because he was mostly disinterested in any positive personal development. He mostly sought for shortcuts in life and thought those who were rich and more fortunate have it easy in life. Three sessions into the process, he was asking the counselor how these prospective changes could become more automatic—always looking for easy solutions.

With his confession, he was sentenced to eighteen months in jail.

The counselor went to the prison to counsel him. The prison was actually very useful to the intervention. Fearing reprisal from other inmates in prison for his offenses, he attempted to hide the reason for his incarceration. Even when he was confronted by other inmates, he tried to deny that he had molested his daughter. Inmates have their means to find everything that there is to know about their fellow prisoners. He was beaten on several occasions and the guards looked the other way. To help him further the counselor implemented the biblical story of David when Absalom rebelled and stormed the palace. On that fateful day, David barely escaped with only his elite guard and a few of his family by his side. On a nearby hill stood a descendant of Saul, as they were leaving the back door of the palace, cursing and working his revenge against David. One of David's guards requested to climb the hill and violently silence this man's rage. David resisted this request by saying to his guard that they should let the man alone because what he said was true.

The imprisoned man understood the application of the story well enough to implement, and on the next incident within prison walls, he told his fellow prisoners that there was nothing that they could do to him that he would not deserve and offered them no resistance. Later, he commented that this was the first time in his life that he sensed the meaning of true repentance for the wrongs he had committed during his lifetime.

3. *Borderline Personality* the most well-known of all personality disorders and it has three clusters of symptoms: affective, impulsive, and identity clusters. The affective cluster is responsible for the set of symptoms that bear the profile of the love-hate relationship. They cannot seem to believe that significant others could or would really love them. They will often make it nearly impossible for others to love them. Nonetheless BPD people strongly desire to be loved as if their whole identity depended on it. In order to find out if the significant other does love them, they might place many obstacles in the other's path to test the other's resolve to see if they are able to break through all barriers to prove their love after all suspicion to the contrary. Combined BPD and drug abuse disorders are the best predictors of suicide attempts among all other diagnostic conditions where there is also a worsening course of major mood disorder and drug abuse in the months preceding the suicide attempt (Yen et. al., 2003). This identity cluster of the borderline personality best defines the condition as one in which the person cannot be intimate due to an inadequately developed personal identity. They do not seem to have a focal point of identity that they can reliably use to bring order to their personal self-concept. The identity cluster tends to overlap with the affective cluster at this point of explanation. This identity cluster of border-line symptoms is thought to represent people who live in their mask who are dependent on what esteem others give them in order for them to know who they are. The impulse cluster of symptoms is most responsible for the high incidence of successful suicide because they have a deficit regarding the internal mechanism of self-control. This is probably the most well-known personality disorder.[3]

One woman had already attempted suicide several times when she came for counseling. She was mistreated and physically abused by a stepfather according to the "account" of that she gave childhood story. Her current struggle with her husband was her major concern during these counseling sessions. She was open about her role in their battles, but she was also very stubborn and manipulative toward him and toward the counselor. She was never convinced that her husband loved her, and she would test his resolve to commit himself to the relationship in a manner quite opposite from what would encourage him to make such a commitment. Rather than to request some charity from him, she would challenge him with accusation of his un-kindness doubting that he could ever initiate any action of benevolence toward her. Further, she would often wait behind the door when he arrived from work and physically attack him because their arguments were never resolved to her satisfaction and she did not want him to forget that they were still at odds over the matter. He was not so discerning of her underlying motivation and would repel her attacks with one grand swat of his bear-like-arms. He was a large man that found her convoluted way of requesting affection as annoying and responded to it in the same way it was received. She was hospitalized after another unsuccessful attempt to buy a weapon to commit suicide, but she concluded in the hospital that her relationship with her husband was the source of her pathology, or so she thought.

She was finally released from the hospital with the condition that she would live with a family who had volunteered to take her in. All seemed well for two weeks until she decided to drop off her two small children at the home where she was staying. She commented to her oldest child as she was leaving that she wanted to return to her house to pick up a few things. More than curiously, she planned to return to her home at the very time that she knew her husband would be returning from his workplace. An argument began shortly after her arrival and she left the home stating that this was enough for her. Her body was found in her car the next day with a rifle propped through the steering wheel and aimed in the direction of her head.

4. *Histrionic Personality* diagnosis by its very terms describes a person who is very dramatic. The histrionic person is often flirtatious but does not necessarily want by this behavior to develop into a

relationship with the person with whom he is being flirtatious. He seeks a disproportionate amount of attention that would greatly exaggerate his personal appeal or abilities. However, if the flirtations are unsuccessful, histrionic people becomes more sullen, morose, and angry regarding their lack of success by seeing this reaction from others as an unfair rejection rather than looking at their attempt to gain affection by this means as egregious itself. Histrionic people are also bankrupt for a reliable means to establish a personal identity and use what is most familiar to them so that histrionic people most often rely on their alleged physical attraction to construct a personal identity regardless of how insignificant and/or physically unattractive they might be to others.[4]

One female client had insisted on receiving help but had little to say about any specific problems. She tossed her hair and laughed as if to flirt with the counselor while speaking with him. After much ado about nothing, the counselor expressed that he was reluctant to proceed with further appointments because no goals for counseling were established. She seemed insulted at the suggestion and rose from her seat and turned to go out of the door, but she stalled her movement to the door until the counselor approached behind her. She proceeded further until reaching the threshold of the door and then had a fainting spell. The counselor tried to check her fall, but he was rather knocked down by her force backward because she was a very large woman. His feet pinned under the weight of her body, and he could not roll her over because she was wedged in the doorway. A call for help and a glass of water seemed to bring her to consciousness. In fact, one woman said that she would throw the cup of water on her, but before she could act, this woman suddenly opened her eyes and rose to her feet.

5. Narcissistic Personality is portrayed by Greek mythology and in particular by the Greek god named Narcissus who could not stop admiring his reflection in the pond because of his penchant for self-admiration, This tale epitomizes the diagnostic category.

The narcissistic person may feel slighted if he is not given better treatment than all others. After all, they are the premier type of selfish person who seems to have no conscience about their self-centeredness. They develop poor attitudes and behaviors, will want a greater advantage over others and may jump ahead in long lines that are waiting for services, thinking that it is their right to be first in line. In a similar fashion to the HPD, the narcissistic types build their identity on how much attention they can receive, but narcissists use more of their ability to gain special privileges than to have the greater physical appeal when carrying out their manipulation. They can be vicious in their attacks upon others who are unwilling to allow them to have these special privileges.[5]

The example of one woman illustrates these first three points of intervention: She had cost her husband a small fortune in household items that she destroyed to say nothing of the emotional anguish. She would do this by her tirades when she threw household items at her husband at the time when he would arrive at home from work. Her husband was stunned by her denial of these upheavals shortly after they had happened and so was drawn to contact a counselor. The counselor asked if she would come if she were invited by her husband to participate in marital counseling and her husband thought she would agree as long as she would not be the major focus of the counseling process. The counselor reluctantly agreed, indicating that eventually the more obvious difficulties would need to be addressed, but also concluded that trust-building should be the first priority. As the counseling relationship progressed, trust was slowly acquired by talking to each person separately and conjointly and asking some hard questions of each person. Drug and alcohol problems were considered as a part of the inventory process to rule out other possible explanations for these bouts of rage and anger. Both denied that there were substance issues sufficient to claim of a substance abuse problem.

Both were asked to take the Minnesota Multi-Phasic Inventory Second Edition (MMPI-II), a highly regarded test for personality analysis. After the results of the MMPI were analyzed, she asked the counselor what her results indicated. While the counselor found evidence of a borderline personality condition, he did not think that she was prepared to accept these results. He answered her by telling her that the results were majorly a tool for the counselor's understanding her and that in due time he would explain her results to her more completely. Meanwhile, her husband would call the counselor and ask for help by indicating that the tirades were continuing. When the counselor had achieved sufficient level of trust, the counselor instructed the husband that on the next occasion of a tirade that he should wait until she had calmed down, call the counselor, and then talk to his wife about what he had described to the counselor. The counselor did receive a phone call one late afternoon, the husband described an event of his wife having another tirade that had just happened in their home, and continued by saying that she is now in the bedroom banging her head on the wall. He held out the receiver and the counselor could hear the thumping of her head on the wall. The counselor asked the husband to walk into the bedroom and quietly announce that he had just called the counselor and that the counselor would like to speak to her alone that very evening. Long after these events, her husband described her response after he followed the counselor's instructions, "She stopped banging her head when I finished talking to her and without a word she went to the closet to get her coat, picked up her car keys and purse, and went out the door."

When she arrived at the counselor's office, she was quiet and somewhat different than she was in previous sessions. The counselor was a little nervous about how she might respond during this impromptu session. He started by reminding her of her earlier question when she asked about her MMPI results. He indicated that he would like to explain these results to her now in light of her recent actions to clarify her difficulty in a meaningful way. It is best to avoid showing the graphs and interpretative reports of an MMPI result because of the clinical language and the cold impersonal tone that it uses. The skilled assessment interview will couch these test results in an interpretation with language that will benefit the counselee with achievable solutions rather than with the indictments of diagnostic terms. As the counselor interpreted the results, the words were penetrating to her in a very personal and meaningful way, describing how she had forced her husband to bear the brunt of her guilt and rage because she did not have any means to deal with it herself. Even though she had attended an evangelical church, she had not made the connection between redemptive truth and the dilemma of her past or present life. She began to weep, and the counselor did not assume that the tears were relevant to a genuine desire to change at first because tears had been expressed in sessions prior in order to manipulate. This time, however, her tears were expressed in a different context and by a comment that was different than comments before, "Have you ever met anyone like me before? Is there anything that can help me?" The counselor responded that this would take a long time and that she might likely revert to her old, familiar ways before she can fully accept the feedback that the counselor, her husband, or others might give. She decided to commit herself to a residential facility where they specifically dealt with personality disorders in an intensive treatment protocol until she could return to outpatient counseling. After the residential treatment, the process continued with the following steps of personality reorientation.

6. *Schizoid Personality* is a very unusual type of personality disorder and perhaps one that is more difficult to detect. Two words that be st describe this condition are anhedonia and amotivation. The two terms are tied together by implication in the SPD condition. Despite their lack of motivation, many SPD people continue to work successfully in positions of responsibility, but a closer look at the person will reveal that he has problems with taking appropriate responsibility. Many other SPDs do have difficulty maintaining adequate vocational interest. Behaviorally, they appear to be timid

and to feel inadequate, but they do not apparently seem to be so emotionally affected. Anhedonia means that they have little pleasure in life and therefore, they are not motivated in a manner that is commonly observed in people in general.[5]

One man who was the top administrator of a high-rise retirement community had recently become a Christian, and even though most of the residents and those on the board of corporation were Jewish, he held Bible studies in defiance to their misgivings. The greater problem was what they did not know about his lack of leadership that he was displaying in his executive position. Many of his responsibilities fell to mid-level managers from whom he was detached, and he was mostly unaware of how they continued the day-to-day operations in the absence of his direction. Even his administrative assistant was more aware of what it took to manage this retirement community than he. She would ask him about what to do about various personnel decisions to which questions he would defer by telling her to make the decision herself about what should be done. Some of his mid-level managers enjoyed his hands-off approach, but when there was a conflict between these mid-level managers, they became frustrated with his lack of decisive action. His administrative assistant was very angry with him for asking her to draft all necessary correspondence and reports without giving her much of any direction to their content to which he would then assign his name. She was also disturbed by how he would tell her as soon he arrived in the morning to hold all his calls and then would close his door and asked not to be interrupted. When the counselor asked what he was doing in his office all day, he replied by informing him that he was opening his junk mail and answering e-mail.

One might think that he was just irresponsible and lazy until he was asked about how he felt about his role in an executive position in this retirement community, to which he would respond that he liked the income and prestige associated with his role and nothing more. When he indicated that he did not immediately see anything wrong with how he handled his position, it was apparent that he was not the stereotypically indigent man. In response to this, he was brought to the knowledge of how he had wronged his administrative assistant, his staff, and his employers. He was asked to consider apologizing to her, asking her to make him accountable not to defer all of his responsibilities on to her for reports and correspondence. He was also instructed to spend a half hour with her each morning to go over the daily business. Although he was very intelligent and had a graduate level degree in business management and knew the standards for conducting his responsibility, he had not initiated these matters himself. He was encouraged to recognize that he should establish a multi-level mentoring and managing of his staff that was consistent with his training. Thirdly, he was also advised to visit three residents each week on a rotating basis to ask them how services might improve in the retirement community. Lastly, he was asked to speak to his board about what they would want him to do in regard to having a more acceptable plan for Bible studies in the facilities. After he had made these changes, he found greater satisfaction with the responsibilities of his position than he had prior to these changes, but unless others were willing to continue to make him accountable to follow through with these plans he would likely regress into his room and continue to open his junk mail.

7. *Paranoid Personality* is to be distinguish from paranoid schizophrenia of which this personality disorder is the lesser of the two. As an Axis II diagnosis of the DSM-IV-TR, the (PPD) condition is not to be mutually exclusive with schizophrenia and may represent the contingency diagnosis of paranoid schizophrenia when the schizophrenia is in remission. Paranoia is a common condition when consideering how often people have assumed that others were plotting aginst them. The condition represents a quantitative rather than a qualitative difference from the average person. This condition personifies the third part of the threefold response that people give to the perception of the world as a threatening environment as

described in Psalm 1:1. The average paranoid person responds to the imposition of the worldly philiosophy in the world by **"sitting in the seat of scornful."** Rather than by as the first part of the verse suggests, to embrace this philosohy of the world in a wholesale fashion **"walking in counsel of the ungodly"** or the alternative to be reluctantanly coopted by the forces in the world **"to stand in the way of sinners."** The world as John describes, **"For all that is in the world—the desires of the flesh and desires if the eyes and pride of life—is not from the Father but is from the world."** (I John 2:16) The paranoid person has reasin to be afraid of the world but without and security against its threat, they cannot discern nor overcome that fear to act in a more positive manner with other centeredness in any of their relationships. The characteristic of paranoia has as its source the personal attributes of the person and a certain level of reinforcement from within family and community. This personality disorder has been often linked to Axis I anxiety conditions.[6]

One man was considered to be a very demanding employer who had angry confrontations with some of his employees. Those who managed to win his trust had an unusually familiar relationship between employer and employee. His confrontation with others seemed to be related to him thinking that the employee did not respect his judgment and did not follow appropriate communication and protocol with him. Many of these employees would leave their jobs to find another and would report back to other employees that they were having a much better experience in their new job. One of the employer's trusted employees had the courage to let him know what was happening to these other former employees whom he had predicted would fail at any other job. At first, he explained to himself that their success in their new employment was due to his teaching them appropriate behavior while in his employ. However, there were many of these employees who left his employ, and too many of these who left were finding success elsewhere. He began to doubt his judgment. The counselor focused on the mission of his workplace and how his role had become too focused on his success and competence and not so focused on his leadership to make others successful. Further, he spent too much time preserving his power and fighting off what he perceived to be dissidents rather than seeking how his place of employment could serve others better and the higher ordered purpose of the kingdom of God.[7]

8. *Schizotypal Personality* people are very odd and eccentric. Their sense of auspicious, magical thinking is borderline delusional and borderline psychotic. This condition is thought to represent the genetic predisposition to schizophrenia. However, some of the class never develop full-blown schizophrenia and most schizophrenics are not previously diagnosed with STPD. STPD may, at times, simply represent the residual state of schizophrenia when it is in remission.[8]

9. *Dependent Personality* is thought to be the central character type for all other personality disorders (Millon, 2000). Dependency may be the first stage of the development of BPD, AVPD, and more remotely related to other personality disorders, but Millon's idea is not to establish that all personality disorders find their onset by starting out with pathological dependency. He is merely indicating that the progression of each disorder is a variant response to a sense of dependency. It is only a slightly different perspective to say that each person with this diagnosis uses some form of control as a defense against the fear of being controlled, as indicated by the thesis of this text. Passive-aggressiveness is a characteristic of DPD; passive aggressiveness was also a distinct personality disorder listed in control because of feeling of this text. Passive aggressiveness is a characteristic of DPD; passive-aggressiveness was also a distinct personality disorder listed in the DSM until it was later removed. The DPD person is one who does not have an identity apart from what the presence of others. It is thought to represent the personality that did progress much beyond the symbiosis (attachment) between child and parent of early childhood.[9]

10. Avoidant Personality involves a distancing of self from others because of feeling inadequate. Avoidance is a very common response when one does not want to appear to be controlling by the stigmas attached to that behavior. On the other hand, the avoidant person may be in a position of having been so manipulated so that he withdraws, attempting to be totally independent of what others are doing, or he may be futilely attempting to be unaffected by what he perceives as others' controlling behavior. There is a certain pretense on the part of AVPD condition that presumes that they can remove themselves from the impact of others' control by placing physical distance between themselves and others. This is lifestyle approach that is somewhat delusional about how isolating themselves has already impacted their life. Their walls of protection become their own prison. AVPD is one personality disorder that seems to be an unlikely fit for the profile of a controlling person, but this type of behavior is one that most likely shows itself as being inadvertently or truly passive about their controlling.[10]

11. OCPD should be distinguished from OCD as the lesser of the two categories, but they also possess some qualitative differences as well. OCPD is a residual state of focus on things to divert attention and the tension that might be felt from relationships with others. The category does not require a total withdrawal from people, but it does advocate a focus on tasks and things that inappropriately substitute for failed relationships with people. Controlling objects substitutes for controlling people; much in the same way, people are attracted to pets when having them provides a favorable alternative to loss of relationships with people. Objects cannot fight back and are easier for the controlling person to manipulate than people. OCPD people are list makers who make lists at times to inventory what is on other lists. List making is not a bad habit to have except when it becomes a substitute for establishing appropriate order and a commitment to responsibilities for others without regret.[11]

12. Personality Not Otherwise Specified is a category for those individuals who exhibit certain odd or controlling behaviors that are not able to be placed into any of the above categories. At

one time, there was a category of passive aggressiveness in the DSM that is no longer a separate personality disorder. Currently, passive aggressiveness is thought to be a prototype characteristic of almost all of these disorders. Passive aggressiveness also could be understood to be the major criteria for PDNOS. Also, if related symptoms were insufficient to meet the criteria of one of the above categories, the symptoms might be sufficient enough to meet the criteria for PDNOS.[11]

Formation Interventions for Controllers

It is important for the diagnostician to recognize that those diagnosed with personality disorders are not completely depleted of appropriate motivations nor are their behaviors always extreme and socially inappropriate (Beck, 1990). Thus, there remains sufficient character in this person's life on which the counselor can build. However, these more inappropriate personal characteristics are quantitatively greater and may be modified only as the person's fear of control is reduced. The following methods are stated for the purpose of improving the helping relationship through Christian Formation concepts:

1. The primary task when helping the person that is a manipulative, aggressive, and controlling person is to win this person's trust. This may be as difficult to do with the dependent client as much as it is with the paranoid client. The first method in developing the appropriate relationship of trust would be to avoid being manipulated and to not minimize their controlling behavior. The person helping the controlling person is readily susceptible to being manipulated by the controlling person to whom he is trying to show warmth. By this, the helping person should be cautioned instead to identify these manipulations that are regularly used by the controlling person. Also, the helping person may be overly cautious about accepting the controller's portrayal of events, increasing this type of client's already profound level of distrust. Whether accurate

or not, the helper should at least accept the counselee's point of view, as it is his point of view. It is, at minimum, information about how controllers would like to portray themselves, regardless of the accuracy of these explanations. The standard policy for any practitioner is to give every counselee hope. The reason for giving hope to the counselee who may have a greater tendency to distort his circumstances is that by giving hope, real change for that behavior is made possible. As Romans 2:4 suggests, even the most incorrigible person has the potential for change when he gains an appropriate perspective on the grace of God, "... **realizing that God's kindness leads you toward repentance.**" By showing kindness and trust to the controlling person, a helping person might arrest their fear of being controlled, thus changing their response with a much different behavior.

2. As well, the timing for when the helping person gives his insight or interpretation of the dynamics of this person's controlling behavior is extremely important. The counselor should recognize the sovereign care of God in leading the helping person the appropriate timing for such a confrontational insight. However, there are specific identifiable circumstances for revealing these insights to the client. When trust has been established, the controlling person might react negatively to these perceptions that might be shared by a helping person. In the event that the controlling person cannot accept the helping person's evaluation when it is given, a contingency plan would involve the use of understanding the controller's development of these personality characteristics. The use of clinical language would only serve to further confuse and distort reality for this person, regardless of how accurate the language might be. The counselor should express the interpretation of the problem in terms that the controller would understand. Like, "You were already thinking that everyone would laugh at you for this so you unfairly criticized their work ahead of your presentation!" Explain their manipulative behavior in a way that the controlling person could effectively

change the outcome of his behavior. The helper should avoid the cliffhanger that occurs when this person rather than accepting the interpretation channels to resistance and then presumes that the helping relationship will end immediately. The helping person should anticipate gradual improvement with persistence in a way that convinces the controlling person to be willing to accept a viable plan for success. With the permission of the controlling person, family members and friends of the controller should also be utilized for several reasons:

- Friends and family members have likely sustained some hardship, if not profound manipulation, and so they may need to obtain some debriefing themselves in order to remove these stigmas from their self-concept and from their relationship with the controlling person.
- The best intervention for the controller is one where friends and associates are not so readily manipulated, but rather actively identify and avoid this person's manipulation in order to have a greater positive effect on the controller as well. Each participant should be interviewed for their ability to both be resilient against manipulation and not to overreact with anger to create additional problems.
- Without the input of close associates of the controller, the helping person may never ascertain the truth about this person's controlling behavior.

3. The helping person may need to use self-concept measures or clinical personality inventories. To do so may require a referral to a person familiar and qualified to use such measures. The counselor should have the essential training necessary to use these evaluative tools according to the ethical trilogy for using personality and related inventories of both the American Psychological Association (APA) and the American Counseling Association (ACA) guidelines for competence is education, training, and supervision (Herlihy &

Corey, 1996; Pope & Vasquez, 2001). Contained in the introduction to section three, there is further discussion about the appropriate use of these self-concept inventories. The inventory results may be regarded as information that is direct and firsthand from the controlling person. These inventories also serve a secondary purpose of corroboration of the classification and diagnosis of the controller that is gained by the helping person previously and informally conducted in the initial interview.

4. Continuing the counseling process after the client has acknowledged his controlling behavior involves a reorientation process for the client. When any person is highly charged with the sensitivity and fear of others' controlling behavior, such as in the case of the personality disorders, life becomes a series of dramatic episodes in which the actor tends to wear certain masks to compensate for that fear. It is important after some unmasking has been accomplished, as defined in the previous steps, that the clients begin to peel back these layers of personality by considering the following avenues of personality development:

   a. The counselor should consider what roles the client has played in various social relationships, how he differed across these various social conventions, what the client perceived about these intimate social interactions that served to create these roles, and how he might be more open and honest in these relationships presently. The Controlling person will need to learn how to meet their personal needs through direct requests of significant others rather than through attempts to manipulate others to give them what they desire. As well, they will need to learn to be more other centered in their perspective on life rather than be so focused on meeting their self needs that has been fostered by the underlying and exaggerated fear of others' controlling. They will learn that in trusting others gives to them the opportunity to see themselves reflected especially as they make it a priority to meet others concerns and needs before their own needs (Philippians 2:1-10).

b. The helping person needs to identify the common practice of controlling behavior by observing how controllers tell the truth according to how he wants the truth to be believed and told rather than telling it as it really is. Once the real and relevant truth has been identified, the best approach that avoids driving the person back into his defenses is to ask questions such as, "Is this really the case or is it better described another way such as?" or, "It may seem to be that way to you but if you believe this to be true, what will be the likely outcome?" The benefit of this approach is that it poses an alternative basis for the action or reaction that the counselee may take rather than to be left to defend past habitual response patterns. This approach may give this person the opportunity to make a decision rather than to react habitually in a way that leads him to an inevitable destination.

c. This controlling behavior has a strong spiritual dynamic that compounds the problem that could be viewed as similar to personal idolatries that the person has developed over time. Idolatries such as these are not of the nature that involves the worship of icons that the person superstitiously reveres as representing the powerful forces of a god. As well, this kind of idolatry does not involve the stereotypical love for material things that people want and worship by giving those things more importance than they should be given. In this case, idolatry is related to anything that exercises greater power and influence over the person than any person or circumstance should. Similarly, the ancient idolatries were seldom about gods whom they loved and adored, but often they were about gods whom they feared, to whom they were enslaved, and to whom they offered their children in sacrifice to preempt the gods of these idols' uncharitable deeds toward them. The fear of control and the consequent controlling response to that fear represent the same type of spiritual stronghold that is found in these ancient idolatries. As Jesus reminded his disciples, these demons cannot be cast out except through much fasting and prayer. This biblical concept of prayer and fasting is not being applied to this circumstance of controlling behavior to make the presumption that controlling behavior involves demon possession, but rather to indicate that the approach of patience, undivided focus (fasting), and prayerfulness (submission vs. controlling) is necessary to help the person overcome this tendency. Consistent controlling behavior infects the person's identity and enslaves his soul. As persistent as this person's behavioral patterns are to create this behavior so is the person's persistence necessary to correct these pathological patterns. The controlling person who can separate his identity from this habitual propensity to control is the person who can develop a more positive personality change.

One man was obligated to seek counsel because he had been found to use the services of an escort service at a hotel where he had stayed on a business trip. This was not the first time that his wife had discovered inexplicable charges on his credit card, but in the past after he explained these charges as having to do with perfectly legitimate and respectable activity. She was amazed at herself for saying, "Well, okay then!"

This last occasion had awakened her to his comorbid condition of manipulative behavior with his sexual addiction. When he arrived at the counseling center, he was astute and well dressed. He wasted no time to explain his resume of being of person of means who worked for a mega-corporation as a training officer who traveled from plant to plant. He only briefly gave way to the questions of the counselor about himself and his reasons for his behavior while away from home on business. He explained, when directed to describe his family of origin, that his parents were of a lower socioeconomic class and that his parents had frequently partied with another man in the neighborhood, but he quickly changed the subject to be critical of his wife whom he had observed as being ashamed to express her sexuality openly to him in a way that made her sufficiently attractive to him.

The counselor indicated that he was not going to be able to counsel him without the focus of their attention being appropriately placed on him and his motivation to do what he did. This man seemed oblivious to the comment of the counselor because he adjusted by saying, "Well, that's what I thought that I was doing."

It was not as obvious to the counselee that he was focused more on blaming his wife than was necessary. The denial and blame-shift was so incredible that as the counselor looked at this astute-looking man, the counselor was somewhat neutralized by his appearance to redirect him before regaining his composure. The counselor finally responded with the assertion that he may not recognize the difference between looking at his wife as the reason for his behavior and his own lack of means to control his own behavior. In addition to that, he did not fully recognize how exceedingly wrong his offenses were that had so injured his wife for many years. And further, his focus was on his needs so he did not even realize the nature of his offense.

True to form, this man decided to put on a face of disgust and anguish at the thought of the topic of conversation in a direction that enabled him to look more like the victim to maintain control, resisting every assertion of the counselor to dodge the issue. Though he attended an evangelical church where the former pastor had learned of the problem, he did not have a strong grasp of the grace of God or how he could absorb the guilt for his transgressions. It was important for a successful outcome that his wife become involved in the process. At a minimum, she might be better equipped to deal with her husband of his manipulation. This would also have the optimum effect on her husband to bring her some solace to her own confusion that he had inspired.

The next meeting was with her alone in order to bring her back to some level of trust with her own judgment that had been so very manipulated by her husband. It was true what her husband had said about her timidity to speak openly in regard to sexual matters, but she was after all made to feel this way by his constant badgering her over the way he wanted her to dress and act when he was around the home. She felt used and abused by this unseemly attention. She was able to handle his anger without a great amount of expressed fear, but she adjusted to his rants by appearing to be naïve, contrived as a subconscious defense that would tend to disarm his suspicion of her resistance to him. She was reluctant to be more discerning in her conversation with him because of the possible consequences for speaking with him more frankly.

The next session scheduled gained a commitment from him to attend training and support groups for sexual addictions, and he subsequently attended a retreat for the national organization, American Family Association (AFA). A little more of his family background was discussed and contrasted with God's plan for family life and the work of redemption that the Spirit was prompting in his life, but at the AFA retreat he got into an argument with the person who led the training group. He was interested in the comments of this leader, but when he went up to the leader after several sessions, and attempted to place his own spin on the application of the information, but the leader quickly identified his maneuver.

Several sessions later, he was not happy that he had not reached the completion of his probationary status and turned to his original plea that his wife did not complement his therapy. The counselor asked her to accompany him at the next session. After this final session, it became apparent to the counselor what this man had instigated. They came to the session, and before a word was spoken the counselee was noticeably disturbed. Nothing that was said or done in earlier sessions was different in this session, but he wanted to convince his wife of how intolerant he was of the counselor and fifteen minutes into the session, he growled, stood up, and walked out the door. She was shaking and the counselor knew then that this man had orchestrated a manipulative attempt to blame the counselor for the reason that he could not return. He wanted to blame the counselor so that he could justify his commitment to not return to counseling by indicating that he would never trust another counselor ever again

Years later, she returned to counseling, recognizing the futility of reinforcing his manipulations by allowing herself to accept his arguments at face value. She was unaware of any further acting out on sexual encounters, perhaps because he was too cunning to make the same mistakes that led to his discovery in the past. The most remarkable outcome was how she had matured and gained the wisdom that she needed to endure in this relationship. She expressed that he was more than curious about her returning to the same counselor of years prior, but she was convinced that counseling had helped her to realize many things and indicated that returning was a subtle statement to him that she had not been at last manipulated by his behavior that had ended the counseling years ago.

The Angry Person

The angry person is an example of how an individual fearing external control often commits the ultimate error of futilely attempting to control these external forces by responding to this fear by an equally profound affective state. On one hand, anxiety, depression, and anger have a similar orientation as suggested by the given model of control and by the experiential partnership that anger has with both anxiety and depression. On the other hand, the consequent emotional response to these futile attempts to control others' issues naturally toward frustration and anger that controlling people experience is when they attempt to control that which they know they cannot control.

Background Information to the Angry Person

Additional dynamics for anger are found in the components of *cognition, behavior, and the person's neuroanatomy*. The issue of cognition, as it is related to anger, conforms similarly to ideas of attribution theory that were explained in the previous chapter (Barclay, et. al., 2005). The angry person's expectations and perception of circumstances in regard to his relationship with others are dynamically related to the development of anger. The factor of cognition alone can prepare the person for the onset of anger. As it is also indicated from scripture, anger should be understood as a learned behavior. This perspective on anger mixes both cognitive and behavioral factors in the same experience. The neuroanatomy of anger has been implicated from the way in which Prozac has been blamed for acts of violence for which it has also been prescribed (New, et. al. 2004). It is understood that the asymmetrical stimulation of the frontal lobe activity in the brain can also create greater agitation of purposive behavior (Harmon-Jones, et. al. 2002). Also, alcohol and substance abuse have been known to create the phenomenon known as angry blackouts followed by amnesia subsequent to these violently rage-filled activities that had preceded the onset of amnesia of their preceding behavior (Miller, et. al. 1994; Aharonovich, et. al. 2001). There are some angry people who externalize their anger and others who are more self-conscious who tend to internalize anger in the form of bitterness. The variety of forms through which anger is expressed is indicated by the various terms used for anger in scripture (Ephesians 4: 31). Also, as one may observe from the context (Ephesians 4:15–32), the two topics of anger and communication are intertwined. For that reason, anger may also be understood as the failure to successfully communicate. To handle anger is to develop constructive communication that constructively builds stronger relationships with other people. To become angry is to eliminate those constructive efforts. Similarly, the passage of Proverbs 22: 24 cautions its readers not to spend time with angry people to avoid learning to be angry as well.

Formation Intervention for the Angry Counselee

Various passages of scripture, such as James 1:20 and Ephesians 4:15-32, are helpful in forming a good counseling methodology for angry people:

1. James 1: 20 states, "For man's anger does not bring about the righteous life that God desires." It is apparent that the intentions of those who are angry are mostly to achieve a good result and

not all anger is intent upon destructiveness. *Anger may be defined as the intense will of man to do that which God has not yet permitted.* Anger may have the lofty goal of making things right or correcting some perceived injustice, but it does not yield to the timing and/ or to the sovereign choice of God's method. Angry people exhibit behavior characterized by great impatience, if not with slanderous abusiveness, to those who disagree with them or with those who do not cooperate with their ultimate goal. Anger is entirely focused on the perspective that is human and does not have the godly characteristic of submission to God's plan. The solution for anger that focuses on an understanding of God's sovereign care involves the far reaching benefits for mediating angry impulses. A commitment to the truth that believes that God does have benevolent control over all circumstances is necessary to overcome the angry impulse:

> Benevolence is a basic dimension of God's love. By this we mean God's concern for the welfare of those whom he loves. He unselfishly seeks our ultimate welfare. God's love is an unselfish interest in us for our sake as seen the life Joseph, Genesis 50:20 (Erickson 1998, 318–319).

2. A contingency plan would provide an alternate plan for the person being frustrated by unmet expectations. A contingency plan would involve an alternate plan from the one that is incurring the person's anger with a different cognitive and behavioral process that is consistent with conflict resolution. A literal paradigm shift should be made from the context of the person's immediate ideals, goals, and behaviors to that of easing of those current constructs that had produced so much anger. After this is accomplished, the formerly angry person may consider what God would want this person to do when God did not permit the previous plan to come into fruition.

Another question emerges over the issue over whether or not the person actually knows what his plan or strategy might be that had produced so much angst in the first place. Many angry people continue on a certain directional pattern in life without a clear understanding of the ultimate destination where it will end and/or why they are going in that direction. The helping person should counsel this person to commit to no activity without having a good reason and coherent purpose for his behavior, not just for the purpose of mediating anger but to enhance cognitive development in general. This is where the study of abnormal psychology and the psychology of normal personality development regarding the formation of cognition and decision converge.

3. Impulse control reduction mechanisms involve anything that helps slow down the tempo of angry impulses. The passage of Proverbs 7:15 indicates that anger and contentiousness is a continual **"dripping of water."** Many of the older generation remember the fairy tale story of the little Dutch boy who sent his friends for help as he held back the North Sea with his finger. The story had a purpose to help all Dutch people, young and old, to use vigilance in guarding the status of their dikes that kept them safe and dry as they lived under sea level. For one little leak would soon become a torrent flooding and eroding the whole wall of the dike. Certain therapeutic models for anger involve the pressure cooker concept rather than the erosion analogy as a means of explaining anger and to develop an intervention strategy. The pressure cooker idea proposes that interventions should give vent to anger so that it will not build up and be expressed in an extreme and malicious way. This has been long discounted as a viable method (Mayne & Ambrose, 1999). The practice of controlled venting may not reduce anger as much as it may erode the person's control over impulses. Rather than controlled venting, it would be better to use the early detection and hold method as the Dutch boy did with the hole in the dike. Without early detection, the flood of anger will be impossible to contain when it is unleashed. Without holding it back when it is possible to do so, anger will likely become habitual.

For early detection to work, the person must readily confess his anger problem. Early confession of anger by itself provides some immediate relief for the one struggling with an anger problem.

There may be *medical and physical problems* associated with anger. One physical cause for anger may be substance abuse, presenting in a range from constant irritation to that of the violent acts (Graham, et. al. 2004). There is also the residual state of manic depression that posts irritability as a major symptom (Harmon-Jones et. al. 2002). Anger may also be the effect of hormonal dysregulation and depression (VanGoozen et. al. 1994; Harmon-Jones, 2003). The therapeutic approach for anger that has an implicit physiological basis should first focus on the possible underlying physical problems that may exist. However, counseling interventions may continue as these underlying physical problems are dealt with through medical means.

4. Cognitive mechanisms that are involved in anger need to be examined for clues that could also be used to remediate angry responses. Cognitive mechanisms and past experiences are connected and mounted on present frustrations. As in the case of a car mechanic who had the reputation for his constant anger, many people were afraid to bring their vehicles to him because he would complain that they should take their car to the junkyard rather than waste their money on repairs, referring to their vehicles as "that pile of junk." If he would not also have a reputation for being a good and honest mechanic, no one would bother to try to bring vehicles for repair. At times, he was observed in a fit of rage with wrenches being thrown from underneath vehicles when he engaged some obstacle upon repair. Oil cans were kicked over when scheduled repairs would have unexpected delays. He was a deacon in his church and aspired to live a better life, but he focused more on his failures, and his anger was so entertaining to some of his customers. His wife would complain that their teenage daughters were not respectful to her and when he came to his home he would hit the roof at the news of their

misbehavior. He would brood all day about his daughters' behavior and add more negative, hopeless thinking about how overwhelming his responsibility in car repair had become. His cognitive set needed a paradigm shift from this state of worry, fretting, and brooding that led him to regularly explode with anger.

5. Anger and communication are interrelated as the passage of Ephesians 4: 15–32 indicate. The passage begins with the words "speaking the truth in love" and later in verse 26, "in your anger do not sin" (NIV). *Anger is the antithesis of communication and good communication is the antithesis of anger.* Effective counsel for the person with an anger problem would be to increase the effectiveness of his communication. Later in verse 29, Paul instructs them to not let any unwholesome words come out of their mouths but that they should speak in a manner to edify the other person. Good communication that reverses the tendency toward anger involves speaking in a way that builds up the other person to whom communication is being directed. In verse 31, several terms are used to describe the various forms of anger. The list of terms depicts explosive anger, bitterness, irritation, and loud expletives and then ends with a term that is best translated with the word blasphemy. This may indicate that all anger ultimately leads to blasphemy, rather than simply representing another more egregious form of anger. It is the blasphemy of refusing to accept what God wants! In verse 32, the passage deals with the relational aspect of anger where Paul instructs the Ephesians to forgive as Christ forgave them. To forgive others is the antithesis of controlling others, and to control others is the antithesis of forgiving others. Forgiveness with an attitude of submission to God's sovereign will is essential to remedy impulse control problems that will ultimately check anger that has been reinforced by unsuccessful attempts to control others inappropriately. Anger can also be a problem related to the counseling relationship because angry people may want to ventilate their anger on those who are urging them toward change. The scriptures indicate that

anger in itself is not wrong when it is redirected toward constructive activities and attitudes. When it is expressed during the session, it is an opportunity to turn that intense emotion into a virtue for the counselee. Furthermore, anger expressed in the counseling session is also an opportunity for the counselor to demonstrate the balance between compassion and confidence. In the face of the intimidation of the anger that is being expressed, it is an uncommon reaction that angry people receive from others outside counseling sessions so that the counselor may help the angry person by the way he responds. Often, the angry person is not willing to come for counseling nor willing to speak with a helping friend, but the significant other in a relationship with the angry person often is willing. In the next chapter, the abused and intimidated counselee will be discussed. It is probable that the person in a relationship with an angry person is also abused that angry person. The principle of Proverbs 15:1 gives the basic parameters for counseling this person. It is a proverb and not a promise and represents the best policy for responding to anger. Expressly, **"A gentle answer turns away wrath."** First, a person should answer an angry person in a gentle rather than an emotionally-charged manner. The common scenario is that the angry person instigates another to respond in a way to escalate the expression of anger back and forth between the two people. Second, a gentle answer is a confident answer, demonstrating that the angry person cannot successfully intimidate the other person. Third, it is an answer possibly indicating a solution or redirection of the other's anger that may initiate some constructive redirection of activity.

The Person Unwilling to Change

It is always a struggle for the counselor to understand what the specific cause is for a client discontinuing the counseling process. Not knowing the specific reason for this breakdown may frequently contribute to the burnout of counselors and psychologists. In one study with a sample of 1000 surveys where 425 were returned (Gilroy, Carroll, & Murray

2002). Even if it were assumed that those surveys that did not returned were sent to those who did not identify themselves as depressed, the sample would indicate a rate of 62% of returned surveys were depressed psychologists or 26% of mailed surveys. The cause of such a high rate of depression may be multi-factored, but the authors of this study rightly recommend some kind of self-care. Specifically, interventions may take the form of mentoring and supervision that involves a debriefing of the counselor over incidents that are related to clients that have withdrawn from counseling or with whom the counselor has not been effective. Therefore, it is important for counselors to understand the possible factors and characteristics of the person that is unwilling to change.

The counselor may assume some personal failure to be the cause of the unsuccessful contact with clients without any basis for knowing this to be the case. The counselor, no matter how experienced, should debrief through supervision or by consulting another professional. This may produce the self-care needed after a client discontinues counseling, postpones appointments, regularly forgets appointment time, or is reluctant to reschedule. This could be happening because the counselor may not be making a personal connection with the client or it could be because the client is simply unwilling to really place himself in a position to receive effective counseling. The following characteristics of the unwilling client may help the counselor to discern the characteristics of client resistance.

1. The client's observed lack of motivation or initiative to establish a change of direction for his life.
2. The client's lifestyle of avoidance of confrontation or disagreement with significant others in regard to the client's self-concept.
3. The client's tendency to procrastinate on important initiatives.
4. The client's contradiction in the person's cognitive process, known as cognitive dissonance that is defined as holding two opposing streams of thought simultaneously by the same person.
5. The client's persona of being withdrawn and mysterious.

6. The client's obvious lack of insight and disinterest in gaining significant personal insight.
7. The predominant tendency to be reactionary rather to take the initiative
8. Ephesians 4: 18–19 also indicates that resistance to godly counsel is the typical human response.

It is important to understand that the unwilling person will likely want to discharge early from the counseling process early, rather than risk any detection that he is unwilling to change. This leaves many questions unanswered and especially the question about their reasons for wanting to leave the helping relationship early. Most conscientious counselors want to know if they did anything wrong when the client leaves early in the process. For that reason, it is important for the helping person or advocate (I like the word "advocate" over "helper" because the latter suggests a kind of superiority on the part of the helper) to gain a commitment from the one that is perceived to be unwilling early in the process. Second, this must be done with a great amount of compassion and gentleness by openly thanking this person for allowing this advocate to partner with this person in their privileged communication. Third, the advocate could ask what topics of information would this person be unwilling to tell the advocate about himself. Most are unwilling because they already feel overly blamed by others, feeling guilty or giving information that would further implicate them. The information that they are expected to share may be perceived as disqualification of their last remaining attempt at dignifying themselves to serve in roles that wish not to risk. Mask wearing is not uncommon and may be the only barrier that unwilling feel that remains for them as their last defense. It would be appreciated as a act of mercy to spare them complete exposure of everything that is wrong with them. They believe that most people do not use that exposed information compassionately. The first rule for this work is "don't rip off the unwilling person's mask indiscriminately." There must a really good reason for any exposure and it is important the exposure would give a greater benefit when the person involved is treated with respect and compassion. The advocate must win the unwilling person's trust. Boundaries between the advocate and the unwilling person must be established whereby the unwilling is not manipulated, coerced or shamed into revealing personal information a well as any other type of client. Worse than ripping off masks of is putting words in their mouths of the these who are unwilling. The unwilling do not change by telling them what to do! Trust from their client to their advocate must not be presumed, but rather it be should be won. This author is regularly surprised by clients for whom I did nothing to help, but listen to their sordid story, and I did not flinch when they used every kind of vulgar expression to tell their stories, and they just open up with more and more. They seem to feel tremendous relief with depositing this crud on my floor and I accepted it!

SECTION THREE

THE EXCUSING FACTORS

The coping strategies of denial and pleasure seeking are identified as excusing factors in this text. Conflict gives impetus to the use of these same two strategies that are utilized as attempts to reduce a sense of inner conflict but may also result with a reduced impact of the Spirit's work upon the person as well. An inner conflict can also become an interpersonal conflict that may, in turn, also return again to an inner conflict. Denial creates conflict with others by avoiding responsibility and producing difficulties both personal and interpersonal that are characterized by attempts to rationalize these difficulties away. Denial results in the habitual pattern of unwillingness to recognize how unresolved personal difficulties are impacting others. On the other hand, pleasure seeking creates conflict with others by substituting a short-term relief with an impersonal, feel-good stimulus rather than develop real solutions to life's problems that create difficulties in relationships. For pleasure seekers, these missed opportunities to strengthen themselves spiritually through the use of the chemical cop-out also decreases the level of intimacy in their relationships that ultimately leads them down the road of increasingly making substance and other pleasurable stimuli more significant in life than their relationships with others. The destructive aspects of the pleasure-seeking approach are readily demonstrated with the problems that are associated with the impact that addictions have on marriages and families.

Consequently, people seeking pleasure override the message of their conscience to be accountable for their own responsibilities, resulting in a reputation of helplessness. This, in turn, forces the greater responsibility upon other people who have relationships with these addicted people.

Figure 3.0.1

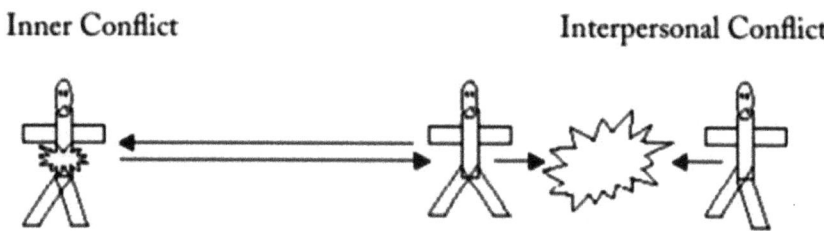

Inner Conflict   **Interpersonal Conflict**

The Person Lacking Insight

Not all people who are lacking insight in what others clearly observe to be their most obvious liabilities are in denial. It is possible that a person could be blind to his most relevant personality features that others may be very aware. This phenomenon may also be accounted for by the differences in personal values among various people that make one person more aware of certain personal features in another that another may not consider to be important to assess. Thus, self-awareness may be considered in a four-dimensional analysis:

Figure 3.0.1

	Others Aware	Others Not Aware
Self Aware	Arena Self	Private Self
Self Not Aware	Blind Self	Unconscious Self

The following comments in regard to this figure will be focused on the blind self that may represent a denial of one's most salient and personal characteristics. However, such a person may be only insufficiently self-aware of these characteristics rather than be in denial. The typical human evaluation of self or others narrowly utilizes factual information that appears on the surface to judge that person's true character. From some perspectives, one person may impose incomparable high expectations upon a person's character, while another person may expect much less so that the imbalance produces great disparity in judgment from one person to the next. The truth about a human being, as human beings understand the truth, is, after all, in the eyes of the beholder.

A common experience for counselors is one where the counselee describes the circumstance of acquiring feedback from others that are from different social settings and the feedback from these varied sources have a common theme and commentary on their personal character. Often, people in denial or in addictions seem bewildered by the frequently similar feed-back that they receive. They had not, to that point, considered what they had gathered that was to the denier and pleasure seeker to be indicative of truthfully who they are! God may be using other people that have become like angels from whom the individual lacking personal insight receives light from God. When people are in denial or involved in an addictions and experience this type of conflict between their own view of self and the feedback that they receive from others, there is usually some difficulty in these relationships as well. The outcome may be an inner conflict that is based on a lack of insight or self-awareness that is reflected by conflict in those relationships. On the surface, people in denial appear to have some incongruency in their relationships with others involving prolific misunderstandings on one side and dependency on substance to create unreality on the other extreme. However, the problem may be more personal than interpersonal. This shows how much healthy relationships depend on being accurately self-aware partners and how good communication with others is also based on an accurate self awareness. Also, anxiety may not be always apparent for the person who possesses an inaccurate self-awareness, but often through conversation with someone who openly and unconditionally accepts them, the presence of that anxiety may be observed.

The greater problem is how to help a person who does not possess an accurate self-concept or who does not understand the nature of their difficulty. Denial and addiction have the common characteristic of cognitive distortion to the point of delusion that is not necessarily from the use of any particular drug. Those in addiction seem to use denial of their addiction to their drug(s) of choice by replacing the unpleasantness in residual guilt with a pleasurable sensation from their drug of choice. Those in denial have failed to remove the impact of the conviction of the Spirit that produces guilt by attempting to pretend that it does not exist. Both of these choices are the natural and creative responses of human beings to minimize the work of the Spirit to reduce guilt and conviction and to overturn the natural course of problem-solving drawing them closer to rocks for an imminent shipwreck on the shores of Sirens[1] to destroy themselves with almost complete loss of their cognitive abilities. Also, prolonged denial and addiction may be due to suppressed anger and/or guilt when the person cannot accept the truth. To assist in the unraveling of the client, the counselor may use formal self-concept measures, but there some restrictions in their use. Most formal measures require training in statistics, formal training in tests and measurements. After that, they must have supervision while using the measure to gain the privilege to use the inventory. One may arrive at an inference with or without formal personality inventories and without as much cost that these more formal measures create. Suppressed anger is the fuel for the suppression of the truth by those that are attempting to erase that truth and create their own version of the truth. The counselor may look instead for strategic behaviors, ideas and people that enable the person to improve his or her life situation when they were feeling like a failure, and by discovering those that enable them in their failures. Search for explanations that challenge them to consider seriously making essential changes or those ideas that empower this person deal successfully with their problems. Once a probable inference is found by this means, the people in denial and deceive themselves by substituting an addiction for the solution to their guilt should use this inference in logical progression to see if this inference has given them some measurable success. Person analysis has some real benefits for those in denial and addictions because before they deceive others, they first must deceive themselves. While they have already engaged in openly or consciously internalizing within themselves those mot regretful experiences in their pasts, they often build imaginary identities to confront or avoid their past life by pretending that these past experiences ever had happened. In other cases, they may use substance to bury their conscience remembrance or find alter states mind generated by denial into a pathology. If none of things work, they will seem to automatically choose a life of a slow death or more deliberately seek suicide. Alcoholics also do not present their struggles to others openly but hide it within themselves. During times of intoxication and even when they are sober, they try to convince themselves that they have their substance abuse under control. The think that are in control by successfully hiding their problem from their conscious mind as if that will hide it from others.

Once personal analysis is complete the question about the arrangement of factors remains. The more primitive idea would be the simple linear arrangement of factors or variables that is described as "A" leads to "B." This idea may be a naïve misunderstanding of the person because, as the Psalmist indicates, we are fearfully and wonderfully made, indicating the significance of a more dynamic analysis of the complex human being than a simple one (Psalm 139:14). Nor is the unity of the person honored by assessing the person from a list of mostly unrelated factors to explain the sum total of a human being to consider. There are the empirical and behavioral features of a human being that make our analysis even more complicated than we could ever understand, but the Spirit assists us in the areas that are almost impossible to comprehend. The person's dynamic relationship of factors that seem to be more cyclical than linear in nature.

There are also philosophical perspectives to personal analysis to human personality that is seen by how Jesus challenged the Jews,

"**If anyone chooses to do God's will, he will find out whether my teaching comes from God or whether I speak on my own**" (John 717, NIV). If you wish to be sure of who Christ is, try to follow his teachings, or so John suggests. Jesus is the key to understanding human beings as John 1:4ndicates, "**In him was life and {this} life was the light of men.**" I would suggest that the term, "**life**" is the life-giving force of the Spirit. Jesus is a better measurement of what a human being really looks like in his original form as he is the perfect human specimen. However, there is the exception of the human beings fallen condition of total depravity. Fallen man is the example of abnormal psychology but Jesus in the example of normal psychology. Philippians 2: 5-6, "**Have this mind among yourselves which is yours in Christ Jesus: who, though he was in the form of God, did not count equality with God a thing to be grasped. (ESV).** Rather than telling the Philippians what they should do in every instance, he just provides them with a construct so that can build their own discernment from that construct. The construct is that he put there interests before his own as the cross of Christ aptly and dynamically represents. He even gives the general principle that is derived from that construct to get them started: "**Let each of you, look not only to his own interests, but also to the interests of others**" (ESV). There is also an analytical element to the features of human personality that has to do with changing behavior and changing life's direction after gaining insight about one's self. It is not within the realm of human possibility to know exactly or completely if such insights are really true. As Jeremiah indicates, "**The heart is deceitful and beyond cure. Who can understand it?**" (NIV) But we still have hope for validation through the Spirit, he adds to the human beings innermost thoughts a greater dimension of personal problem solving. "**We have not received the spirit of the world but the Spirit who is from God, that we may understand what God has freely given to us**" (I Corinthians 2: 11–12). He does simply give the human mind a divine data dump, the Spirit lives within us to provides us with access to the mind of God. Just as Jesus did not have to grasp for his own deity, the believer Spirit of God is freely given to us! What is freely given to us?

No! It is "Who is freely given to us?" This gift is not self-contained, but is other-centered in the person of God.

The gift of God is not independent of our relationship with God: The believer does do anything for this gift, and we still have our propensity for reducing the impact of the Spirit and often lose the opportunity for the personal application of the truth through the indwelling Spirit. The believer does not become a spiritual powerhouse to be credited for our success or to be punished for failures. The Spirit cares for us even when we are straying from him. We are compelled to acknowledge all praise and honor is due to Son that has defeated every foe, and to the Father that has had everlasting love, and to his Spirit that has pursued us through every experience to develop a stronger fellowship for us with God.

CHAPTER FOUR

DENIAL, THE PRETENDED NO NEED FOR A RESPONSE

enial is probably the mostly widely used strategy in the human race to reduce the impact of the Spirit's work. This text observes the concept of denial in the passage of Ephesians 4:19 where it says that human beings have **"lost all sensitivity."** Denial is a self-reinforcing response that dulls the senses to feel little or no compunction-neither for guilt of transgressions committed against others nor through compassion for those that would be benefited by our better understanding or showing compassion for those that presume to have a relationship with us. Instead of being motivated by selfish ambition, they live to be free of accusation. The ongoing conviction of the Spirit will give us opportunities for a different course in life to preempt additional threads of denial from adhering to the conscience. However, the person in denial often channels Spirit conviction along with other sources of negative assessment of themselves to create anxiety that receives superficial relief from sacrificing themselves as a trade-off for identifying their obvious threat or their obvious guilt.

The Defensive Person

Defensive people typically have grown up in an environment where family members were concerned more about results than they were with quality relationships. Likewise, the defensive person's background would likely be a home where parents see children as a means to gain stature from them and avoid the ignominy of their children's failures. They are more likely concerned about raising their children as prove their own competence rather than to help sustain their child's hope or rather than for the purpose of helping them to know how to live through their failures. They would be more disparaging of the struggling family member rather than show them uncommon encouragement. A genetically informed study conducted on twin parents and their offspring showed that harsh treatment by the parents was more greatly associated with long-term behavioral and emotional disturbance in their offspring than it was associated with genetic factors for the same result (Lynch, et. al. 2006). Defensive people that have grown up in an environment such as the family dynamics described above. At the minimum, defensive people have perceived that a constant harsh treatment from others has existed in their formative years of life, whether or not harsh treatment can be factually verified.

For this reason, defensiveness may be understood as a learned behavior, but it also represents much more than that. It is an example of a person who feels that he has not been free to function as an independent person. The normal development of a child involves a caring environment that fosters not only independence but also one that gradually increases the child's ability to assume personal responsibility and competence for managing one's life. One study corroborates this view by showing that as children get older, they are less likely to feel like any praise or blame that an adult gives as feedback accurately validates their effort and ability for academic tasks (Barker & Graham, 1987). For a defensive person, a large shadow has been cast over everything that this defensive person does.

While this person may blame others for his not having a chance to realize his dreams of success and happiness, he will never have a true opportunity to take full responsibility for himself while feeling so profusely blamed and criticized in that way. Another element to the defensive person is the apparent cross-purposes that exist as evidenced by this person's behavior and thought process. Cross purposes exist basically because of the environment of the home where the child's rebellion was reinforced by the constant din of a caregiver whose sharp, critical comments of impatience and disapproval that were regularly communicated to the child. On one hand, children grow up protesting the unfairness of their parents' judgment of them and yet wanting to gain the certainty of their acceptance and wanting their parents to believe in their competence by receiving the validation from these same critical caregivers.

To untangle the web of opposing aspects to the person's childhood story, one needs to view the larger picture. This is the circumstance of where the devil is in the details. The details serve to confuse the person in denial, but also to confuse those in a relationship with the person in denial. The advocate should identify the irrational beliefs that contribute to the distress of the person in denial. The advocate can further illustrate to this person how irrational some of these beliefs may be by carrying the same beliefs to their logical and active conclusion to help the person in denial understand the ultimate result of each competing idea. The person in denial is highly reactive to change that ordinarily occurs in life by thinking that the worst result will come from any considered change and that any change may cause the tragic outcome, losing the desired result even if past outcomes from the status quo were not what the person really wanted. The person in denial often appears to be secure in the uncertainty of the situation presumably feeling more comfortable with chaos than with the correction of these problems. They may seem to prefer problems that have no solutions than to be active in making things better. They have often felt a greater burden of blame and guilt than they have had opportunity to find forgiveness and grace necessary to admit or to confess their true needs, shortcomings, and misdeeds. The sense of being trapped by the decisions and perspectives of others results in denial—the only means of relief that they may know. Defensive people often see themselves through the critical eyes of others who may not have been as critical of them as they might have assumed. They also may feel that their identities are frozen in the past—from circumstances when their behavior or experiences with others was judged to be at its worst. They fear the shame related to the alleged negative characteristics that others will always see in them indicative of these past memories. They tend to depend on others too much to know who they are even though they are very uncomfortable with the conclusions that others would make about them. Formation strategies for the dynamics of change used to assist the defensive person are fourfold: First, the defensive should identify the past patterns for how this defensive person in denial gained approval and disapproval from within his childhood family setting. From this information, it will be easier to understand the purpose of the twists and turns in the person's story. As the defensive people recognize the significance benefit of seeing how their childhood experiences have prepared them for a life of defensiveness real life changes can begin. The advocate should adopt strategies that counter the past failed strategies of the defensive person that was used to gain approval to develop a perspective on spiritual formation solutions. By this, the advocate may be helping the defensive person to recognize viable and relevant alternative explanations for their struggles that reflect true difficulty in regard to their thoughts and feelings. From this, the procedure related to correcting this person's defensiveness might be better understood and established. The defensive person should simultaneously *structure patterns for thinking and behaving* that reflect the integrity, worth and justification of the person that is based on God's love for that person and that is not based on defensive persons' feeble attempts to justify themselves through the failed strategies of the past. Typically, the defensive person attempts to conduct what resembles a works-righteousness strategy to construct a viable pattern of behavior.

The defensive person that purposes to use activities with only inherent reason for engaging in them is to be engaged in efforts that are seeking that elusive approval from others. The governing principle is to do the good and right thing because it is the good and right thing to do. This should be the ultimate goal for the counselee to be truly independently motivated rather than disturbingly defensive. The apostle John in his first epistle recognized this above motivational principle. He said, **"let no one deceive you,"** as he presents to the path to identifying righteousness, **whoever practices righteousness is righteous, as he is righteous."** By comparison of this verse in 3:7 with the following verse in 3:8, it is apparent that he is saying that if you practice righteousness, you have Christ-likeness because verse 8 reads that with the practice of sinning you have devil likeness. This passage of scripture infers that as we anticipate doing the good and right thing, our motivation should not to become a good person by doing that task. We are often deceived to chase the proverbial dangling carrot seeking for the appearance of righteousness without the reality of being righteous in Christ Jesus. We ruin our opportunities to do good by importing our self-centered needs into that good deed to become a good person when the two are antithetical. We should be free from the need of approval from other human beings when we anticipate doing good. It would be so emancipating to be able to do a good deed just because it is a good thing to do! One such ten-year old boy's mother brought him to a counselor after she had caught him with a knife in hand chasing his younger brother around their kitchen table. She was so startled by the vision of her younger son being murdered by his older brother that she was frantic to know what had brought on this murderous intent. After telling the counselor everything that she knew about the situation that did not seem to be a great amount of information, the counselor asked if the young alleged perpetrator would like to come into the session himself. The counselor found him to be a precocious child who was angry but thoughtful regarding his actions, explaining that the knife was used more to scare his brother than it was used to harm him. The child was more than willing to talk about the circumstances than the counselor had anticipated. He described how his younger brother managed to ruin every pick-up baseball game with his neighborhood friends by insisting that he would be allowed to play. If the older brother would not permit him to be on the team, he would go to Mom and Mom would come to the field and tell him that he must let his brother play as well. His younger brother would not only lack the same level of skills as his same-aged friends, he would also pull stunts to cover up his lack of skill that further irritated his older brother's friends. With this, one by one, his friends would begin to quit the game and go home until it was just him and his brother left on the field of play. At home, his brother continued his antics by coming up behind him and popping him on the shoulder with his fist. The younger brother would do this when his mother was nearby and would scream for his mother's rescue when his older brother would try to retaliate. The older brother would be the one who would always get caught in his retaliatory attempts, and the scolding that he would receive from his mother would further elate his younger brother.

The counselor asked the young counselee what he thought his younger brother was trying to do, and he rightly answered, "He was trying to get me into trouble!" The counselor replied with another question, "And are you going to help him?" This younger brother wanted from him. At first, he answered by shrugging his shoulders, but the counselor admonished him by indicating that he was intelligent enough to give a better answer and finally replied, "I guess he just wants attention!"

The counselor connected the two perceptive answers that he gave and worked out a strategy. First, the response to his brother's attempts to instigate getting him into trouble with his mother needed a better response from him that also did not give his brother what he wanted. Rather than giving the retaliatory type of response, he would attempt to be brave, applying the "turning of the other cheek" doctrine of scripture with the emphasis of the doctrine that it does not represent a response of weakness but a response of strength. This type of response is one that would not allow his brother to control him and would place the control of matters in regard to his brother in God's hands. He would instead respond with comments like, "Are you satisfied with yourself?!" The young client anticipated that his younger brother1w60ould not know how to respond to this type of response and that he would hit him harder the next time, but he also surmised that he would also eventually lose the purpose for trying it. Second, he was also to be proactive in his brother's attempts to seek attention. Rather than waiting until his brother sought some type of inappropriate attention, he would initiate spending time with his brother involving activities chosen by his brother and use this to curtail his brother's interference with activities that he would have with his peer group.

Not everything worked out so ideally, but this young client was soon convinced that he now had a better means to achieve peace of mind and a better influence over his younger brother. Th e counselor waited until his young counselee had some measurable success with this before informing his mother of the adopted strategy for a number of reasons. The greatest of these reasons was to convince Mom and Dad of the need for a more personal involvement with their offspring that gets results like the ones that they were already observing in their oldest son.

Background Information for the Abused Person

By discussing the topic of abuse under the heading of denial, the reader of this text might already assume what perspective the author is taking on this topic. An assessment of abuse history is secondary to the level of denial that the abuse person his use to live with their abuse unresolved. The relationship between the abuse experience the subsequent pathology is not that of a cause and feel between the two. However, the prospect of an intervening variable that is involved in one's abuse history provides some interesting explanation of how variables constellate provides a more viable understanding of the abused person. This also indicates that there is hope for abused people as the effect of abuse is indirect on outcomes because abused people do not have a singular outcome of profound pathology and may not have a pathological outcome at all. Also, the abuse victim may be able to greatly reduce the effects of abuse when the intervening variable for determining such outcomes involves greater support for the development of autonomy and personal responsibility. However, there are a majority of abuse victims who do present with dramatic difficulties that are not readily overcome and that they seem to endure for their entire lifetime. There is a strong tendency for abuse victims to use denial as their most reliable means for relief that some others have called repression. In other case, denial may be as extreme as to create amnesia for past events of abuse that many victims experience (Rob, 2004; Middleton, 2005). It is likely what begins in childhood as denial or suppression of these abuse memories, later in life becomes repression. (Repression refers to an unconscious act of a loss of memory, whereas suppression is more intentional loss of memory.) And it is important to realize that abused children may have little else at their disposal other than denial to reduce the devastation of their abuse. The larger difficulty for the victim is that this pattern of response continues long after the original abuse has been discontinued (Middleton, 2005). Abuse outcomes may not have a simple cause and effect relationship between incidents of abuse and future outcomes, but the greater determining factor may be the way that the abused person responds to that abuse over time. The number of diagnostic categories and other problems that have a high percentage of people reporting an abuse history illustrate this perspective. There is the more obvious category of post-traumatic stress disorder (PTSD) where traumatic stress, like abuse, is inherent to the diagnosis of PTSD (Van Den Bosch, et. al., 2003). There is a high incidence of abuse history reported for the various personality disorders, especially antisocial and borderline personality disorders (Bergen, et. al., 2004; Stovall-McClough & Cloitre, 2006; Van Den Bosch, et. al., 2003). Further, there is high incidence of abuse reported among categories of dissociative identity disorder (Steele, 2003), eating disorders (Hund et. al., 2005), substance abuse (Markof, et. al., 2005), and depression (Meston et. al., 2006). Childhood sexual abuse has been closely associated with sexual dysfunction in women and often represents the major outcome for women who were profoundly sexually abused though between the past abuse experience and the resultant pathology, it may be untenable to believe in a cause effect relationship there may be at least a catalytic relationship between the two (Pugh,1993):

Figure 3.4.1

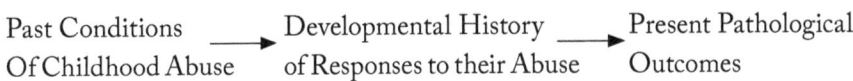

Past Conditions ⟶ Developmental History ⟶ Present Pathological
Of Childhood Abuse   of Responses to their Abuse   Outcomes

The abuse victim's response to the abuse provides the intervening variable that preponderantly influences the course and eventually the outcome. This also provides an explanation for the phenomenon (though rare) of those abused as children who present seemingly without any pathological outcomes. The pattern of suppression to repression becomes a way of life for most abused people, affecting their identity construction over time (Steele, 2003). This pattern is not strangely different from how others who have not been abused formulate their identity and memory of personal experiences of the past. There is interplay between the components of the person's personality, the objective appraisal of the person by others, identity formation, and the inward aspiration about self within the person (Luyckx et. al. 2006). Human personality maintains a plastic state similar to what was first conceived and modified throughout time but does not lose many of the features of its initial state (Luyckx et. al. 2006).

I had a rich childhood in a rural community living on a farm. It was rich with experiences of learning to grow into adulthood by taking personal responsibility. The operation of the farm and taking the responsibilities inherent to it were assigned early in life. Although I may not have appreciated the discipline of rigorous work much at the time, I was better equipped for my future because of this experience. When I speak with my younger brother about my memory of events, he has a somewhat different version of the same events. It is not that either one of us has exaggerated or was in a fugue state during some of these common childhood experiences, but it is rather that memory has the function of identity not so much in relation to the facts of the memory, but in relation to what those memories mean to each person or how these memories made them feel about themselves.

Several seminal authors in the field of secular theory and research have provided some very helpful information in the last several decades that is useful to clarify the impact of abuse upon the person of the victim. Such are the studies done by Browne, Finkelhor, Carmen & Reiker and Peskin. Finkelhor has written extensively about abuse especially through the 80s and 90s when abuse was the number one social crisis in the minds of people in the western culture. This was the period of time in recent history when there were also some highly speculative ideas that were forwarded about how abuse would be discovered that also created some hysteria by which there were many cases of alleged perpetrators that were falsely accused. But during this same period of time, some issues related to this national tragedy were also helpful in understanding the problem.

Finkelhor rightly identified the basic effect on the victim of sexual abuse by indicating that the identity of the victim becomes obscured and dominated by abuse so that the person does not have a distinct personal identity Browne & Finkelhor, 1986.

This circumstance reflects the sentiments of Jesus when he said that a person that abused a child would be better off to have a millstone hung around his neck and to be cast into the deep (Mark 9:42, ASV). The Greek term for "offend" from "σκανδαλίζω" carries both an active and a reflexive action and such is case with the victim of abuse (Bauer, 1957). Conceivably, Jesus understood that to abuse a child robs the child of the means to freely choose his own path in life, but more importantly the abused child is prohibited from expressing a childlike faith in order to receive the spiritual endowment of faith and trust. By that means, that child is prohibited by the abuse experience to find a new identity that is based in a relationship with Christ. This perspective is so basic to the development of Christian spiritual formation in general and for personality development in particular.

Carmen & Reiker (1986) clarified what abuse means in its role and relationship within the family system. Many questions arise concerning the development of pathology and psychological effects when the person experiences abuse early in life. A more important question that is somewhat answered by Carmen & Reiker is how psychological abuse might exist apart from physical or sexual abuse. Their study indicates that abuse is effectively a role reversal between the caregiver and the care receiver. The alleged caregiver subtly removes the child from the position of receiving parental care and manipulatively obligates the child to meet the needs of the alleged caregiver instead. It has been observed that the outcome of abuse is far more pathological where the element of psychological abuse is more severe (Stalker et. al. 2005). From this concept, the devastating effects of psychological abuse are better understood. In fact, physical trauma alone cannot explain the outcome that is observed in most cases of physical and sexual abuse. As Jesus indicated, we should fear him who can harm us spiritually more than we do the one who can harm us physically (Luke 12: 4–5). Psychological abuse might be expressed as the rock inside the snowball. While it may be difficult to separate physical effects from the psychological effects, it is possible to observe that in some circumstances psychological abuse may occur apart from any physical trauma with more devastating effects than thought possible. Recent trends in diagnosis has forwarded the idea that dysfunction is not always within the individual but us found in the relationship, touted as relational disorders between two otherwise normal people (Wakefield, 2006). The trauma that occurs in relationships by far has the greater impact upon the person's self-concept and self-appraisal (Pugh, 1993).

Peskin (1992) considered two distinct outcomes for victims of abuse related to the developmental stage of the child when the abuse had occurred. He said that until age four or five, children do not understand the mental representations of the other's actions toward them so that the child does not comprehend in what way the other person's actions are dependent upon that person's "epistemic state."

Accordingly, if the child cannot represent the beliefs of another person, it is impossible for the child to use those representational states to predict the behavior of that person. Primarily for this reason, very young children cannot effectively resist an abuser's manipulation and without appropriate feedback may continue to have difficulty in reading other's motives [for abusing] throughout prepubescence and adolescence (Pugh 2003, 30).

Heyman, et. al. (1992) further reason that children who are abused approximately before age five think that abusive acts against them generally infer that they are "bad," and when they are abused after age five, they think that they are "dumb." When abused, the victim's integrity as a person is threatened and the victim is in constant fear. More significantly, the child's personal identity has been stolen and recovery will take a long and arduous path because of the victim's undermined identity development. Young children depend on their relationship with their parents and immediate caregivers to know who they are. And in relation to this topic, it is important to understand that the younger the child the greater the dependence! When parents sense some unresolved conflict within themselves, they often turn to their child to resolve their own personal conflict in an unhealthy way.

This idea is the basic hypothesis of this chapter that when inner conflict for adults rages unabated and unresolved, it will eventually result with tactics that use and abuse children and others inappropriately for the purpose resolving them. This process of deferring inner conflict on to others will inevitably pass on from parent to child—generation after generation. In ordinary circumstances, a child will formulate identity in those formative years by relying on the immediate caregiver. Children need constructive feedback from a significant caregiver in order to thrive and mature successfully into their next developmental stage. When that caregiver is in the mode of receiving rather than giving reassuring feedback, the whole developmental process for the child is in jeopardy. Further, when the caregiver has been so frustrated for not receiving constructive feedback throughout life, he will often seek for feedback in any form that is consistent with his own identification process that inevitably becomes abusive to the child, rather than developing into something that is constructive for that child's development.

The role of the perpetrator of abuse is important to consider. In light of the need that the child has for identity construction, it is apparent that it is not so much what this alleged caregiver does, but what the caregiver is that makes the circumstance of abuse so very devastating to the child. Inter-generational transmission of abuse is so prevalent because each successive generation continues to use their offspring to meet their own personal needs. Their needs cannot be met by this means and this only leads to greater dissatisfaction and more abnormal requests made of their children. The nature of the perpetrator's alleged needs are evil and gruesome distorted from what was the original conviction of the Spirit and the basic spiritual needs that God had created within that person. Now, the person of the perpetrator is reduced to live for procuring some sort of tantalizing sensation or validation from that sense of failure instead of finding personal peace and reassurance by wholesome relationships as content and sincere people. Their current attempts to resolve inner conflict gives only temporal relief, creating successive steps to procure more. From this, one may observe the affinity be tween the approaches to minimize the work of Spirit of denial and that of pleasure seeking that leads to addiction as they are both attempting to enact inner conflict resolution by these inappropriate interpersonal methods. The implication is that the basic spiritual need for children is to grow into adulthood with the encouragement of being able to attain the essential security, integrity and confidence to be successful and content with adult responsibility. All of this short circuits when abusiveness functions to destroy the positive aspirations of the child that is also exacerbated by the loss of support for the child's future endeavors with something even more gruesome in its place. Elizabeth Gershoff (2002) researched spanking among various religious groups and found that conservative Protestants were more likely to use spanking as a means of discipline and to believe that spanking is instrumental in successful parenting than mainline Protestant, Catholic, and Non Affiliated parents. Although she distinguished serious physical abuse from spanking by both its intent and its effects on children, she attempted to establish that there is some deleterious effect for spanking a child. In answer to Gershoff, Baumrind et. al. (2002) indicated that her meta-analytic study was flawed because those previous studies that were included in her study did not consistently distinguish spanking from violent acts of parents inflicted upon their children.

Should the Christian counselor support those client who decide to use spanking in the discipline of their children? While the "sparing of the rod" is not recommended in scripture, the rod should be used sparingly. Spanking seems to be best applied in cases when there is an expressed disrespect for the parent and when the child is very young. A "rod" is a "switch" as in the case of Aaron's rod that budded after it was broken from the bush with no possible basis for causing the child permanent physical harm. It has been the experience of many parents that the child's knowledge of the possible use of spanking was enough to maintain discipline, seldom needing to use it. Some children do not respond well to spanking and there are many other means to effectively discipline children (Tripp, 1995). In many cases, it is the lack of positive activity and training for children and the lack of positive relationship with parents that puts them in a position to react negatively to their parents in the first place. For this circumstance as well, it is understood that inner conflict is the source of interpersonal conflict both for the parent and for the child.

Some general distinctions between types of abuse and their effects will provide further implications for the victim's treatment. Martsolf & Drauker (2005) detail five different types of abuse: sexual abuse, physical abuse, emotional abuse, emotional neglect, and physical neglect. For the purposes of writing this text, the term "psychological abuse" will substitute for the terms "emotional abuse" and "emotional neglect," and "neglect" will substitute for the term "physical neglect." Victims of psychological abuse typically experience an inability to differentiate themselves from others and to confidently establish relationships with others with their own specific identities intact. More generally, it is true that insensitive and unreliable parenting results in the child feeling unworthy and distrustful of others (Bowlby, 1982), and further, that it is not so much the quantity but the quality of contact between parent and child that makes the difference (Kenny & Sirin, 2006). With physical abuse, the nature of the abuse is one where the perpetrator lacks impulse control involving anger. Physical abuse carries with it the effects of psychological abuse and female victims often experience an inward rage and males often have rage and impatience with others as a result (Pugh, 1993). Physical abuse is observed in spousal abuse, elder abuse, and in child abuse. Sexual abuse usually victimizes children and women by those who are seeking sexual mastery, as a lack of mastery is highly suspect in the mind of these perpetrators. However, the ultra-feminist view of male toxicity do not adhere to the idea that there are any male victims at the hands of women that has created an under-served populations of male victims of female perpetrators. Female victims tend to withdraw and have serious identity and body image issues to overcome. Also, sexual identity as it is taught in some public schools having been counseled to do so without parents' knowledge. These programs have encouraged, and some say would have manipulated children as young as 10 years old to take hormonal replacement and have surgeries on genitalia to change their gender. This is a new class of victims. The young people that were put through this ordeal are now adults and the reports of these atrocities are now being published. Males are typically invalidated sexually by sexual abuse and seek to compensate for sexual identity deficits and some in a sexually flagrant manner (Pugh, 1993). With neglect, there is a serious developmental lag and anger (Pugh, 1993). In all forms of abuse, it is the prospect of a tragedy of an unlived life!

Formation Intervention for the Abused Person

The central concern for all forms of abuse is the psychological effects of abuse. Without the psychological effects, the overall effects of abuse would be less difficult to overcome and would be comparable to recovery from some accidental trauma. Abuse impacts to the person of the victim so extremely that the perpetrators of abuse continue to exact a toll on their victims long after the occurrence of the abuse and it is more than just memories that invade the victims of abuse, it is their relationships their emotions, and their cognitive process that is now tainted and disoriented. Caregivers often overlook the potential abuse are disguise by its source through the presentation of various major diagnostic conditions that have high incident of cases independent of abuse, but also his great number of moderately high incidence of an abuse history. Treating any diagnostic condition is made more difficult when an abuse history is present (Rodriguez et. al. 2005). There are also more specific issues for intervention for each specific category of abuse. However, there are some basic foundational interventions that the counselor should use to alleviate the psychological effects of abuse, as these psychological effects are present in any specific category of abuse:

1. The common theme found in the story is the abuse victim's quandary over how responsible the victim is for the abuse. This quandary intensifies into a pathological self-doubt, as perpetrators are more effective in their manipulation of the victim. The effectiveness of manipulation by the perpetrator depends on how long the abuse continued after its inception, the age of the victim when abuse began, the type of relationship between the victim and perpetrator, the strategy that the perpetrator used to induce victims, and the type of abuse that was perpetrated on the victim (Pugh,1993). The manipulation of the perpetrator has the profound effects on the victim, especially in the effect of creating within the victim a serious identity crisis. While victims may vigorously defend themselves against any charge of responsibility for their abuse, they may at the same time harbor some sense of responsibility for what happened. A major task for the abused victims is to differentiate between what is their responsibility and what is not! Out of this, two matters arise. One is the stigma that victims carry with them for having been abused. Usually, they do not literally think that they have

caused their abuse, but they may at the same time feel like they are unworthy of better treatment because this is what the perpetrator had manipulated the victim to think. This is the circumstance of the clinical dejevu where the victim is frozen in the developmental past. The victim often regresses to these past circumstances of abuse as a means to deal with more current challenges because the development of identity development is truncated at a level when the abuse began. Another matter that arises is that the victims have been led to believe that there is no alternative action to take in regard to how to respond to their past treatment by their perpetrators than to blame themselves. In most cases, it was the circumstance where the child depended on the same adult who had abused that had been the basis of forming the victim's identity. Therefore, it is an incomplete intervention to tell the abuse victim that the abuse is not the victim's fault and if there is no further help given to define what or how the victim should develop any alternatives for identity, interventions will fail. To derive such an identity that is not so strongly related to the victim's past or present abuse is major task of the abuse victim to accomplish, and the dynamics that change should involve a reevaluation of the past events from a different perspective—one that involves a redemptive look at the past. For mation strategies involve recognizing the care of God for them that is in direct contrast to the unchecked maltreatment the perpetrator was inflicting. A full range of discussion is found in the literature regarding religion and abuse. From one end of the discussion, it is thought that women in abusive relationships are kept in those abusive relationships by their faith and is meant as a disparaging perspective on their faith (Hage, 2006). At the other end of the discussion, it is thought that victims typically blame God for not intervening and make negative statements about the character of God because of His lack of intervention to stop the abuse. While some victims may dramatically change their tone over time, research does not indicate that there is a significant greater number of abuse victims who stop blaming God and find support in their faith in comparison to the number who continue to blame God (Murray-Swank & Pargament, 2005). However, the Christian counselor should not waiver at the prospect of the victim's protest. Instead, the counselor should give an answer that could *distinguish the role of God and the role of the perpetrator* that would also welcome such honest reflection.

One middle-aged woman struggled to understand how her abuse history was connected with some of the current health issues that she believed were psychosomatically induced. She told of her most recent battles and came back to the question of how these stress-related illnesses were related to her abuse so that she would know how to find a means to resolve these current health and emotional problems. In the meantime, she had heard on the radio that a pastor promised sure relief for abused people if they could only manage to forgive their abusers. She struggled to realize that resulting relief, but somehow it did not work for her. As she continued on her quest for answers, the counselor mentioned to her that she seemed to be doing to herself what she had hated her father for having done to her.

Although the counselor was focused more on the psychosomatic effects of medical conditions that were located in the trunk of her body, she was thinking about her mental and emotional state of remembering abuse. For her, the counselor's comment was like a light that was turned on in a dark room. She understood for the first time that she was exacerbating her condition by her constant internalization of the act of abuse. The counselor followed her consternation with another question that asked how many times approximately her father had sexually abused her. She surmised that if she were responsible for some continued mental activity of driving the abuse memory to greater destructiveness of her person, then she could also be responsible for marginalizing this practice as well. This somewhat paradoxically was already providing her with some hope!

During the course of the counseling, adult brothers and sisters asked her to attend a meeting where it would be decided what to do about their aging father to save their inheritance of the family estate as he was quite wealthy. They thought that his large number of sons and daughters could inherit more of their father's inheritance if they took turns in caring for him against the expense of placing him in a nursing home. She anticipated the worst and prepared to explain why she could not take her turn in caring for their aging father. She arrived at the home of one of her brothers and each adult sibling in his turn spoke about the benefits of the plan. She knew that one sister was also abused by their father and thought that she could rely on her for support, but that sister sat away from the family circle and looked nervously out the window. She spoke in her turn and revealed that she could not take her turn for caring for their father because he had sexually abused her as a child. She barely started to give her response when the remaining brothers and sisters became enraged at what they were hearing. Her husband came to her rescue and asked her if she wanted to leave and they did.

As counseling progressed, she changed her mind on her own about taking a turn caring for her aging father and thought she should demonstrate to him that he was not going to continue to dominate her mind in the present or future. Even though there were moments of regret, she found that she was able to overcome her fear and disdain for him because she no longer identified herself as one who was powerless in her father's presence nor did she regard him as the all-powerful one controlling her life.

2. Certain emotional stigmas continue long after the abusive relationship has ended and the attitude of dependency prevails and cripples what could be potentially the development of more wholesome relationships. Similarly, it is not sufficient to ask the client to stop being dependent, fearful and or distraught by the perpetrator. The deprogramming of dependency attitudes is twofold: One is to make the victim aware of the inherent dependency involved in abuse. Again, this type of dependency follows the trend of the ancient idolatries that did not regard the god of the idol with respect,

adoration, and appreciation but with fear and crippling terror. The other deprogramming aspect is *to introduce and to help the victim understand how the care of Lordship of Christ that was abused for us on a cross and by his resurrection can dissolved all of our dependencies.*

Victims of abuse need to be aware of their dependency attitudes and understand how controlling the past abuse is in the victim's present life, i.e., upon the type of decisions that they make and the thoughts that they think. On the other hand, there is the competing call for the surrender of one's life to God to find true relief. The battle for the victim's decision regarding to whom the person will yield control is the main concern for the counselor. Abuse and neglect creates a negative environment for the victim to react to any level of power and influence from others in the present in a most unpleasantly destructive way. Or they may openly express their depreciation of self in a way that makes them even more greatly dependent on others to know who they are! On the other hand, there is the competing call for the surrender of one's life to God to find true relief. The battle for the counselee's decision regarding to whom the person will yield control is the main concern for the counselor. Abuse and neglect create a negative environment for the victim to react to any level of power and influence from others and outside influences. Victims may construe any relationship as too controlling as a result of the internalizing of dependency attitudes. Or they may openly express their depreciation of self in a way that makes them even more greatly dependent on others.

When dealing with the topic of sexual identity, developmental psychological research considers various theories of sexual self-concept that also may be applied to abuse victims (Hammack, 2005). One is Life Course Theory that seems to follow the Hegelian trilogy of thesis, antithesis, and synthesis in regard to internal motivations and environmental obstacles that may block or reinforce those internal motivations. Another theory that is forwarded follows the philosophies of sexual sciences that posit the ideas of Construction ism and Essentialism. Constructionism indicates the course of development is a social product sustained by social processes. Essentialism defines identity development as a deep category of human nature. With sexual orientation, essentialism is thought to fit more with research on male development, and constructionism is thought to best fit more with research on female development. However, developmental theories of sexual self-cocept are thought to various degrees. Such thinking in the context of the abuse situation instigates some similar ideas on the effect of abuse on the person, but the involvement of spiritual formation has not been completely weighed into this equation of the person's development regarding the sexual self-concept as much the victim's self-concept in general from these theories.

The Lordship of Christ and the dismantling of the power construct of abuse works in totally opposite directions in the abuse victim's life. Romans 6:15–23 contrasts the liabilities of being under the control of the evil one as opposed to the benefits of being in the care of Christ or in army of Christ as opposed to the army of the Prince of this World. Christ gives us the choice to join whereas the evil one conscripts his soldiers. He leaves us to fight the battle and Jesus fights it for us. The summary of the contrast is when one has submitted or resigned to concede to Satan's control, the devil allows the person to suffer the consequences of his actions and when the consequences for his rebellion are experienced by human beings, he is of no support to his followers but leaves them to suffer on their own. In contrast, Jesus fights all of the battles for his army of followers; he pays for the consequences that were due to their transgressions and then rewards them for obedience as though they had been successfully fighting the battle themselves when they were not. The most telling detail of this contrast is that the conscription of the devil's followers is mostly without their conscious commitment to him being allured to do so by this world and their own carnality, whereas the Lord Jesus will not enlist anyone in his army without their open and conscious commitment to do so. The application of this passage to the abuse victim's self-concept is directly analogous.

The abuse victim is transported beyond just being a victim when in a relationship with Christ. In fact, the person with a victim identity is transformed when the victim assumes an identity of one who is dead unto sin but alive unto God according the impact of the gospel upon the human being.

3. Many abuse victims challenge the idea of God's care, asking where was the loving care of God when they were being abused. The believer in Christ should not overreact to such comments as these. This interaction may serve as a natural forum to examine the truth about God and the truth about their abuse not yet realized the believer's baptism. The debriefing process being imprisoned by enemy forces. The effect of the brain-washing of harsh treatment and imprisonment is that many soldiers would blame their country of origin for putting them into this circumstance rather than hold those who had mistreated them responsible. In debriefing, the reorientation of the soldiers involves a reintroduction to the care by their own country of origin at home away from the front of battle and in the comfort and care that the debriefing process affords to them in contrast to living in the context of their treatment in prison.

The most convincing way to debrief the abuse victim is to help that person understand the love of God in contrast to the abusive treatment of the perpetrator. The love of God is best represented to the victim by the examination of sufferings of Christ. For the abused person, there is an apparent role reversal between God and the abuser. To the victim, the abuser becomes God-like and God becomes abuser-like. When debriefing, the counselor should profile the abuser as weak and driven by forces not inherent to the abuser's person because the victim has been convinced that the abuser is omnipotent, omniscient, and immutable. In light of the sacrifice of Christ, God's love and patience as understood by the sacrifice of Christ, should give the victim reason to pause and consider an alternate path for thought and decision to follow. Debriefing continues as the victim's identity begins to be re-established on a different basis. The passage of Romans 6:1–4 indicates just such a reorientation. The key term in this passage is a term translated by the word baptism. From a human standpoint, the person's identity develops along the lines of environmental obstacles placed there by significant adults and peers during the person's childhood as they affect this person's internal character. The term baptism indicates that one who is baptized is placed n or under something, and in this context to be baptized, means to be placed in or under something, and in this context the believer is the one who is placed into Christ's body—in his death and resurrection. Presumably, this would serve potentially as a source for the victim's new identity. In other the way in which abuse victims understand themselves based on how words, victims are no longer to accept any other imputed identity but the identity that they have in Christ that he has given to them. He carries their identity to the depths of sin that is the believer is buried by his death and their future estate is to the height of his resurrection glory. Specifically, the abused person's mistakes, transgressions, and experiences of abuse that serve to establish that person's identity are now joined to Christ and to his death. Their future hope is now joined to the resurrection of Christ potentially transforming that person's identity from the past abuse as a victim to give the person the opportunity for a future that will create a new and confident identity. Those who are in a relationship of any kind with the abuse victim should also create provide a haven for this person that would be possibly the person's first introduction to the true character of God. The counseling relationship should also create the potential for a loosening of these old identity constructs so that the abuse victim may be encouraged by the example of the Christian counselor to have hope for a new life through the integrity of Christ.

4. Communication projects may commence before the goals of the previous strategies are completed. The identity for a victim of abuse is over-shadowed by the abuse incident and is reinforced by

almost every relationship the victim has developed in the present. It is that burden of an unwanted identity that victims bear most reluctantly—the reason for the victim's need for communication projects. This phenomenon of relationships reinforcing the abuse identity is due in part to victim's own depressed view of self that is also projected onto the victim's current relationships. Another part of this phenomenon is how others respond to the victim's projected identity as an abuse victim. This communication problem can happen even if others do not know about the victim's history of abuse, because the persona of the abuse victim often creates impressions on others that are consistent with the way in which abuse victims understand themselves based on how they were treated in the past that is inconsistent with the potential new identity that the victims would aspire to achieve. Abuse victims are more than just victims and should be challenged about how they perceive others so wrongly. They may be perceiving others in manner that ties others to a perpetratator-like personality even when others may be trying to encourage them. With this failed perception of receptive communication, this person in turn communicates to others accordingly. By this, they will unintentionally reinforce their past trauma. Victims usually do not say much when they encounter the past victim identity through their communication in relationship with others in the present. The victim identity has already overtaken the person's communication so that re-identification is essential to restore their life back to their own control.

The counselor may implement some atypical stress relief strategies that may act as projective techniques that help victims of abuse reframe their communication strategy with the goal to regain control over their self-image and communication with others. Painting, sculpting, music, gardening, and carpentry may serve as a constructive means to reframe the content of the abuse victim's self-concept and communication. But for the most part, counselors should simply listen to them. This may be at last the best therapeutic tool for the counselor for abuse victims to begin reframing his victim's identity. Any of the projective approaches should be implemented under the careful observation of the counselor to maintain the goals of the reidentification process. When communication is refined to the point of preparing the client to make a bona fide attempt to communicate with significant others, the counselor should be available to the client for honest feedback before any possible serious errors that are made in client's thought process. The communication project has as its ultimate goal of helping client declare to significant others in an appropriate way that they are building a new identity that is based in a newly found relationship with the truth.

5. Confidence projects are important to bolster the victims' attempts to establish a new identity. Many of the skills that others use without question may challenge the confidence of the victim of abuse. One woman was the oldest of three sisters who had two younger sisters that were profoundly sexually abused. When her father started to abuse her younger sisters, he also attempted to prepare her for abuse by his infamous sex talks, but her age and his perception of her potential resistance apparently dissuaded him from attempting to abuse her. He tried a more subtle approach to abuse her by telling her that she was not physically attractive enough to abuse and unfavorably compared her with his centerfold pornographic pictures. Even though he never touched her sexually, the effects of this treatment were devastating enough as it was. As the literature attests when a child is abused after age five, the victim thinks that she is dumb (Heyman et. a1.1992). These attempts by her father happened when she was approximately nine years old that, indeed, made her feel dumb.

    The counselor used an inexpensive and short IQ test to validate this woman's intelligence, as she was convinced that she was below normal intelligence. The results confirmed that she was actually above average intelligence as the counselor had anticipated. But she had tried to find a job after graduation from high school, and on the first day at a department store there was sidewalk sale. She was placed on the cash register to be trained by an older woman who was so very snippy about anything that she could not readily learn enough so that she quit the very next day. She was so embarrassed by her treatment that she never tried to find another job again. Later on, she married a man that she thought was giving her the benefit of the doubt, as she thought that he was doing her a favor to even consider marrying her. She had three children who were in their adolescent years at the time she came for counseling.

She never drove her car for more than two blocks and never pumped her gas at a self-service station. She was a pretty young woman despite her father's manipulative comments about her appearance. Conversely, she thought that she had created a great amount of pain for her husband because of her alleged lack of physical attractiveness. Simple practical assignments to complete tasks that she thought were impossible for her to accomplish helped her eventually to grow more confident of her ability that, in turn, improved her self-concept.

Special Conditions

The counselor should be aware of the special abuse conditions that may also require a specialized course of action because of them. The following special conditions of abuse mentioned in this section are the circumstances of active physical abuse of an adult female partner of a perpetrating spouse, the circumstance of current or recent physical and/ or sexual abuse of a child or adolescent, and the adult victim of past childhood neglect, physical, or sexual abuse. The circumstance of spousal abuse or abuse of a female partner is a very common example of the abuse culture in which we live. Commonly, spousal abuse occurs in conjunction with the male partner's involvement in substance abuse (Ritter et. al. 2002), but family violence of this type does not require the presence substance abuse. One woman with three children would have been thought to be happy in the circumstance of being married to a seminary student who was in an army reserve unit to be deployed as a chaplain after his graduation. However, what happened behind closed doors was truly detestable, as she was often threatened with an army issue, automatic rifle loaded and pointed at her head to warn her if she would breathe a word of the physical abuse that he had inflicted, he would use his weapon. She finally escaped one day when she gained an opportunity by his distraction to other matters, and because it was a spontaneous act she did not plan, so she brought precious little of her personal possessions with her. She arrived at her brother's home that already had five family members living within its confines. She did not acquire a job because every job opening required what she lacked as the necessary experience. Due to the fact that she had married right after high school graduation she could not afford a home of her own, and he kept all of their financial record locked away with all accounts in his name only. She was now living destitute in these crowded conditions of her brother's home for a few days when her husband started to call her at her brother's home. He would start out by telling her that he loved her and then he would beg her to come home. If she would hesitate to agree with him to return, he would begin to intermingle certain veiled threats of destruction of her personal property in conjunction with these expressions of affection. She came to counseling soon after she had arrived at her brother's home, appearing intimidated and worried. With the distance between her and her husband, she began to regain some clarity of thought. However, when he would call, fear and personal loss of confidence would appear once again at the same level that she had experienced when she lived at home. The culmination of these events occurred when he traveled the distance to visit her at her brother's home just prior to one of her scheduled counseling appointments, and so he accompanied her to the counseling office.

The counselor was surprised to learn of his presence in the waiting room. He was dressed in army camouflage with high strung black army boots. She entered the door of the counselor and nervously asked if her husband could accompany her to the session. While the request had no real purpose other than to comply with his wishes, it would be an opportunity for the counselor to demonstrate how the client should react to her husband's manipulations that the counselor had instructed her to react. She was visibly shaken by his presence, and the counselor asked him what his purpose might be for coming. His answer was less dominant than his demeanor, stating that he just wanted to know what the counselor was saying to his wife. There are times when the counselor needs to have the character to speak boldly and this was the occasion for just such a response. Abiding by his stated purpose that he did not have any other agenda other than to listen, the counselor would oblige him by giving him an earful as he would if her husband were not present. She experienced the ability to speak openly without his interruption or contradiction prior to his visit, but now all of that was lost for her on this occasion. The counselor directed all of his conversation to her, reciting all of the unseemly incidents and manipulations that she had described in earlier sessions. She confessed sheepishly that she was intending to return home anyhow, a comment that the counselor never heard her say prior to this session. She said that she believed that he had sufficiently apologized and would do better. The counselor's earlier assessment of the matter was reiterated—how her husband would no doubt disappoint her with these promises and that she would likely end up in a worse circumstance if she would return with him now.

The counselor never saw her again after that last session, but he did hear from the sister-in-law, wife to the brother where she had stayed. This battered wife had apparently applied the instruction of the counselor shortly after arriving at home. The counselor had discussed with her to prepare for a strategy of an escape plan that involved the elders of her church helping her move. Another part of protocol that was discussed was that the elders should then act as the buffer for the communication between her and her husband. She started to communicate with them shortly after arriving at her home, and the elders enacted the very strategy that was discussed in counseling when he began to break the promise of ceasing all violence and hostilities before they arrived at their home over 200 miles away.

There are several points of intervention involved here that need to be enlisted. First, there must be the presence of a viable position of strength. The victim's communication with the perpetrator of abuse needs to have a carefully devised escape plan. Second, there is the need for a practical means for the victim to sustain independent living free of contact from the perpetrator. This would place the victim in a identify free zone to correct the manipulations of the perpetrator in her own mind. In some circumstances, there needs to be adequate barriers in place to protect the person against the further manipulation of the perpetrator until the victim has sufficient confidence to face the perpetrator. If communication with the perpetrator cannot be avoided altogether, the perpetator's impulse control for his tendency for physical abuse could be verbally encouraged, such as saying something like, "You are better person than one that thinks he must threaten his wife to resolve this matter." If this is not possible or if the perpetrator is not inclined to acknowledge the behavior openly, he should be informed of the consequences of both compliance and noncompliance to the requested restrictions to his abusive behavior. In the case of the current physical abuse of a child, the counselor should seek to rescue the child by reporting the abuse and seeking for the involvement of other adult family members who may be secondary victims or may be complicit with the abuse of the victim (Pugh, 1993). Family counseling should be encouraged even when members are not permitted to be counseled separately by a counseling team with one lead counselor because the victim and perpetrator need to be directed through the same intervention that other family members are being debriefed. In counseling, the inner dynamics of the family system needs to be unveiled. Each person, including the victim, should be examined in regard to each person's contribution to the family violence, anger and impulse control issues that take place. When considering the collective forces within the family system, deal with the victim-to-abuser and the abuser-to-victim escalation of physical violence involving several family members.

In childhood sexual abuse, the counselor should attempt to rescue the child from abuse by reporting the abuse preserve as much of the family as possible. In one such case, a counselor was assigned to counsel the older brother who was about to graduate from high school and join the armed forces. He sexually abused his younger sisters while parents were working. The Children and Youth Authority was providing care for his sisters of eleven and twelve years of age. While the older brother did not respond well to any call for a change in his attitude and behavior for what he had done to his younger sisters, the counselor inquired of family services at the Children and Youth Authority regarding the welfare of his sisters. The caseworker commented by saying that she could not make much progress either and the sisters persistently requested that their brother be permitted to return home. She asked, "Should we devastate these girls by convincing them of how abused they are so that in the end we might bring comfort to them?"

With small children who have been sexually abused, the counselor might use the strategy of telling the child to not allow anyone to touch the area that is covered by the swimsuit to prevent future abuse. This strategy might work with younger children but younger children are also often unable to defend themselves, even if they would attempt to resist an adult. There are a number of steps that a counselor could take with children that have been abused. Building a relationship with the child and assisting the child or other family members to know how to identify and sufficiently commit to a commitment to the family's well-being may also provide for the protection of younger family members in the future when the child becomes an adolescent or adult to make a more viable intervention for the victim and the whole family. Such was the case of child who was an eight-year-old female who was brought to counseling by her parents. The counselor suspected something was amiss, but the little girl was not willing to communicate anything that related to the abuse that was taking place. The counselor did not have reason to take his suspicions any further than to talk to alone and ask her questions about her reasons for mixing gasoline in the milk and killing a kitten by running her bike wheel over its neck. The counselor asked the question in a fashion that it would be easier for a child to answer: "I don't think that you would have done that to an innocent kitten unless you were really afraid or really, What are you afraid of or upset by?" There was no pressure for her to answer the question, but only that if she told the counselor what was making her afraid, he would make sure that she was safe before he revealed to anyone. He, then, gave the little girl his business card and asked her to call when she was ready to talk about what was troubling her. She entered into counseling with the same counselor when she was twenty-one with the counselor's business card in hand. Thirteen years later, the only item on the card that was still valid was the counselor's name. Everything else had changed over those intervening years. She revealed that her stepfather had been abusing her physically by handcuffing her to her bed at night for alleged offenses that were not true. With neglect, there may be a delay of important developmental milestones in the child. Talking with the counselee may be initially unfruitful because of the absence of the person's ability to communicate any insightful information that is due to the victim's suppressed emotions, such as anger, sadness and grief, that often occur with neglected individuals. There may be some benefit in using creative art projects, observing this person as the victim works so that the counselor might be able to build a trusting relationship with the individual. When the emotional barriers lessen, more direct interventions for abuse may be applied.

Related to the topic of abuse is the phenomenon of recently recovered "traumatic memories" that were allegedly memories of events of abuse that the person was not conscious after they happened and later in life these traumatic memories were recovered. Several explanations could be given for this phenomenon. The first explanation is that the recovered memory could be of an actual event of abuse that was initially suppressed and then further repressed by the victim when the potential for remembering abuse would occur later through an onset of some difficulty that served as a cue for the person to recall the actual repressed material years later in life.

Sigmund Freud had an affinity to this point of view; in fact, it is the centerpiece of his theory that was built on the concept of repression. His theory, as described above, is defined as unconscious material of which the person cannot become aware except through an onset of anxiety that it may be revealed through dreams and slips of the tongue (Rychlak, 1981). Repression by this definition is in itself nearly synonymous with the phenomenon of recently recovered traumatic memories. His theory has found revival in recent decades in its application to traumatic abuse memories that are allegedly lost in childhood and then come back to life again in adulthood (McNally et. al. 2005). However, McNally and associates found a significantly lower incidence in the percentage of abuse memories reported by the continuous memory group as compared to the recalled memory group. This may indicate that abuse memories are as much suppressed as they are repressed because abuse itself does not necessitate the action of repression according to this study. Other therapeutic models struggle with the notion that the brain could sequester certain information without the person willingly and knowingly suppressing this information and without willingly forgetting it as well. However, one study concluded that there was greater evidence for the existence of incorrectly recalled memories than there was for the existence of false memories (Middleton et. al. 2005). The phenomenon of false memories indicates that a person's abuse memory is completely faulty; that is perhaps true! If an abuse memory is recalled after not having it for a number of years, how could it be a memory at all? Or is an incorrect recall of memory, simply a miscategorization of detail? Sometimes, the details of memory could make a huge difference if that memory involves a false accusation of an innocent person for alleged offenses.

One reason why recalled memories may not be always based on fact is that these memories may ironically provide a relief from guilt that is of greater interest to the distressed person than providing an accurate recall of past events. Memory researchers found that the best means to observe the phenomenon of repression was to pose a threat before rather than after the material to be remembered (Geisler, 1986). Therefore, the threat of exposure and/or guilt prior to the event to be remembered may preempt the person from accurately remembering these events rather than a threat posed after the fact. A second reason for false memories is that they may give sensational attention to the counselee in the therapeutic setting. Such was the case of the college-aged female who was the only child in a family whose parents had brought her to be counseled after she had convinced her cousins that her parents were the witch and warlock in a local coven. This undue attention may also serve to distract the counselor from other more pertinent matters because the same young adult female had long suffered from feeling very insignificant until she started telling these stories. Third, the counselee may honestly believe in the recently recalled memory because the person has a selective memory that the person uses to maintain a positive sense of personal self-esteem. Fourth, a much more intriguing idea is that the information is more of a cognitive device for the person to explain how the person feels more than it is a factually recalled account (Geisler, 1986). The fifth idea that may. He explains that the typical view is that there is a determining traumatic event that leads to memory fragments that are not so explicit because of trauma. Later on in life there is the onset of some difficulty that leads to some surfacing memory.

Figure 3.4.2

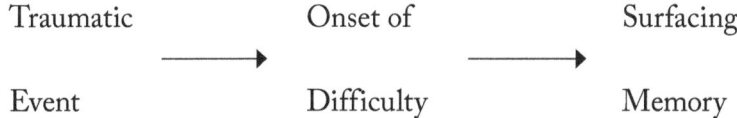

The alternative explanation that is espoused by Minuchin indicates that there is a current residual sense of unhappiness that creates the onset of difficulty, from the onset of difficulty memory is formed around the central affective state, and then from this affective state some relief is found through an abuse explanation:

Figure 3.4.3

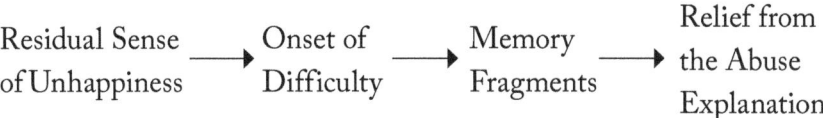

Are the two models incompatible or could both models have a valid application to the various scenarios of recovered memory? As far as spiritual formation concepts might be applied to this topic, both models may have some validity. However, both models are posed as mutually exclusive constructs for recovered memory. The first model recognizes the typical human reaction when the person is dependent on the one who offends by initially suppressing any knowledge of the event to be recalled and later forgetting it altogether. It is recorded of Elijah that Jezebel threatened him after he had stood alone against the prophets of Baal. While he was dauntless before all the prophets of Baal, he could not maintain his courage when one notorious Queen Jezebel threatened him (I Kings 19:1–5). He remembered the day's experiences quite differently at the end of the day than he did during the day when he routed and challenged the prophets of Baal. Then second issue is the resourcefulness of human beings' attempts to escape culpability either by a conscious or unconscious means of fabrication of truth (Romans 1:18).

The greater question is how should a Christian counselor respond to a counselee who years later recalls traumatic memories. First, memories do reveal something about the person's self-concept that would give the counselor an objective appraisal of the person, whether or not the counselee's account of memory is factually true. However, counseling should strive to bring a new mind and mood about the individual's role and identity that has been so impacted by the memory of abuse whether valid or not. Rather than the alleged memory of past abuse dominating the person's life becoming the focus of therapy, a future aspiration for and a redemptive view of self should prevail, even in the way the counselee might view the victim's personal past. Victims are not excused from all responsibility by virtue of being a victim and will, in fact, be benefited by understanding what their responsibility is. As they are empowered by a new identity to impact their perception of self and their view of these past events, they may find greater autonomy to feel, to behave, and to make decisions consistent with this new identity. The Spirit will invariably convey the message of Christ that will transform their self-perception of powerlessness from the identity that had been controlled by the memory of past abuse.

Multiple Personality Disorder

Multiple Personality Disorder (MPD) has a more technical and diagnostic name, Dissociative Identity Disorder (DID). As MPD, it would be the only personality disorder that is an Axis I rather than an Axis II disorder. MPD aligns with the criteria of the DID diagnosis prior to the DSM-V. MPD is a connotation that the condition impacts all aspects of the life resulting in a dissociative condition in the person's being, whereas DID indicates that dissociation is the central activity that produces that resulting condition. Delusional disorders provide a strong comparison for MPD called DID. Delusional disorders are similar to psychotic disorders with the exception that the psychotic disorders are often nearly global in their effect on the person, whereas delusional disorders are specific delusions affecting the person's cognitive function in isolated aspects of the person's life while other aspects to the person's cognitive processes seem relatively normal. Dissociations are very common in other diagnostic categories such as alcohol abuse and dependence where the alcoholic person pledges to stop drinking in one mode of existence that eventually gives the same person greater confidence that leads that person to act out with binging on alcohol in the next mode (Carnes, 1991). Dissociation is the activity of repression applied to one's personal identity and conscious awareness of self. DID may be understood as a very rare and dramatic form of repression. Dissociations impact not only the identity of the person, but also the person's ability to accurately recall memories (Bob, 2004). Dissociative memories may not be necessarily accurate, but they are probably an accurate recalling of past emotional states found through these dissociations. Dissociations may also represent the human being's fallen capacity to exercise faith due to a loss of object or inadequate object for faith. The similarity between faith and dissociations is striking. Faith looks away from the circumstance of an identity of sinfulness and assumes a new identity that is based on the death and resurrection of Christ. The precedence of the Spirit enacting spiritual formation is found by the way the abused child resorts to dissociation that avoids looking back to an unwanted event of abuse. To define one's identity by looking to various identities in order to feel safe from the abuse is the victim's only hope from their perspective. The abuse victim would bereft of the means to exercise faith in God. Switching to various coping identities is in essence exercising faith without an object of faith that is then the basis precluding the person from true faith in God to become the dependent of the abuser. The abuser has an omnipotent appearance to the victim as he or she is the only figure represents a God-like figure to the abused person. The stages of development for the person with DID involve a failed coping strategy of denial for the abuse victim. The repetition of dissociations throughout the early stages is reinforced by the same way phobic reactions of fight and flight are reinforced. As the person finds fewer identity-safe experiences, the person may splinter into isolated personalities with each having a different affective state from the other. Amnesia occurs in relation to the transitioning from of one personality to another, including the separation of thoughts, motives, and decisions of one personality from another. The person can enact splitting or dissociating at will, even though there appears to be a lack of conscious deliberation to do so—following the order of suppression to repression of these cognitive and affective states (Middleton, 2005).[1]

Counseling strategy should recognize that the person is not passive but active in the victim's symptomatology. When circumstances in the person's present life challenge the DID person's identity (Shaw, 2004), the individual cannot have a different emotional response without changing into another personality to experience that distinct emotion (Brenner, 1996). First, the counselor must consider a specifically defined profile for the counselor if the counselor is to intervene appropriately— that is characterized by genuineness, honest communication, and infinite patience. The counselor should be permissive with the client enough to allow for the expression of various affect-based personalities, but at the same time disclosing data to the client about the splits observed in the counselee's personality. Tactics that may enable data gathering to proceed in this unusual circumstance is to question who or what emotion is being expressed, even though this may be readily observed.

Orienting the person to mood or mode of the victim's identity falls into two categories. There is one type of persona that is relating to the traumatic past or there is the other type that is reacting to the current stressful situation. Another type of persona searches for a safe identity, such as the angry personality that is used to defend the person from abuse. The various personalities found in DID may simply represent the members of the family or community in the person's past childhood. The macrocosm of the childhood family is placed into the microcosm of the DID's various personalities of one person. However, the angry personality rather than protecting the person may be turned against itself in the form of suicide attempts and/or self-mutilation. The DID counselee may assume that another personality is doing this. One counselor looked at the four tracks of scars on the back of both hands from the knuckles to the wrist of one female counselee and asked, "Was it not this hand that has continually raked its fingernails across the back of the other hand?" *Confession* is a vital part for the integration of the person with DID. The counselor needs to process the events that occur by understanding that switching is the counselee's means to deal with current stresses upon the victim's identity and emotions. The counselor's instruction should inform the DID counselee that the victim can face these challenges and the clinical de je vu without splitting into different entities. The counselor should *confront* the person at a time when the victim is more lucid and can handle stresses without switching into another personality. Martsolf & Drauker (2005) find from an accumulation of research on therapies used for adult victims of childhood sexual abuse that group approaches are superior to other therapies, even though various individual therapies are beneficial as well. This validates the potential benefit that the healing community of the church can produce for dissociative counselees in the counseling process. Outcomes for therapy for those who have experienced childhood abuse were diminished when there was also an insecure attachment with parents in childhood (Stalker et. al. 2005). The most serious cases of dissociative conditions are where the person did not have early attachment and likely continued to live in virtual isolation. Again, counselors are not the entire solution to the person's problem, and the wise counselor will foster greater benefit for clients by using the family, community, and the church in the best possible way. One rare case of fictitious seizure disorder that is better understood as dissociative seizure disorder illustrates the above information.

A married man in his mid-thirties with two children exhibited pervasive and frequent seizures unlike typical seizure activity. He could not prevent himself from having these seizures, even during counseling sessions. Even though the symptoms were atypical, he experienced an aura prior to seizures of feeling nauseous. Often mid-way into the sessions, he would begin to stare as if he were about to lose consciousness, and then bow his head slightly forward with his eyes partially closed. Only the whites of his eyes were visible through the narrow slits still open. Soon he would begin to breathe heavily and growl like a mad bull with his nostrils flaring wide by means of his heavy breathing. The seizure, lasting only five to ten minutes, would abruptly end with a possibility of two events. Most of the time, he would hit himself on the forehead several times with his right-hand fist so hard that he would literally knock himself out of the chair. On other occasions, he would take both hands and placing them around his neck, as he would choke himself so violently that he would lift himself out of his chair. At the end of the seizure, he would either slump forward in his chair, as if sleeping, or fall on the floor, passed out in a semi-comatose state. The interesting information derived for this case that he was somewhat reluctant to reveal at first was the utter neglect and the physical and emotional abuse that he had endured in his childhood home. His seizures reflected obviously a great amount of self-punishment that he had used to preempt his mother from abusing him in the past. He was very insecure, mainly due the fact that she had prevented him from going to school because she had asserted that he was too dumb for school and should stay home to take care of her instead. He consequently never learned to read very well and parroted comments that he heard from his parents about others that made little common sense, and these repetitive comments greatly disturbed his wife. He would talk to himself this way frequently while in solitude, while walking down the street, or while engaged in a solitary task. He had witnessed sexual events of his mother with other men of the neighborhood so that he was very stigmatized sexually as an adult man with a short, stalky build. He was able at one point in counseling to seriously restrict his seizures when he had so determined that he would aspire to do better with his life than his parents had predicted for him. The seizures were reduced when he started to have greater confidence that he could live without seizures. When other disturbing events took place in his life, he would gradually lose this control over these seizures. He ordinarily resisted spiritual formation concepts to assist him in making a more comprehensive attempt to bring peace to his torturous path in life. However, he continues to seek help from the same counselor. More recently, he has stopped having seizures altogether of the type mentioned above. His current seizures may not be technically classified as seizures at all and are now characterized by muscle spasms in an arm or leg without losing consciousness during the episode.

CHAPTER FIVE

THE FEEL-GOOD STIMULUS SEEKER

People ordinarily seek pleasurable experiences for the purpose of giving themselves a sense of temporary relief from the ordinary stresses of life, but they also frequently overuse this response when faced with very painful personal experiences of perceived threats to their personal well-being. Pleasure seeking is used for this purpose, contrary to expectations; make this person personally more culpable and places further strain on their relationships with other people. In scripture, pleasure seeking is perceived to be one of the major means of resistance to the work of the Spirit, as Ephesians 4:18–19 indicates that "sensuality" is the character of one who is hardened to the truth of the gospel. The method of using pleasure to overcome the displeasure of guilt produced from conviction of the Spirit's work does not really relieve guilt or resolve the problems in relationships at all, but instead this method eventually makes guilt and difficulties in relationships worse than better. The Spirit intends to utilize both inner conflict and conflict in relationships to develop the person for further spiritual renewal and growth. Conversely, conflict in relationships typically instigates the opposite response that places the person in greater jeopardy to fail in overcoming those personal difficulties and difficulties in their relationships. Such painful experiences with conviction and guilt should be perceived as a positive means that would serve ultimately a good purpose i.e. to motivate the person to change and to make needed adjustments to what one understands to be the truth about oneself and about life in general. Seeking pleasure as a failed substitute for personal spiritual growth creates a temporary shortcut to relief that bypasses the opportunities for a person to experience positive adjustment in life and replaces these potentials with the greater personal degradation and decline of the person's character. Personal conflict could provide an impetus in the direction of helping the person to really learn how to solve problems and gain the spiritual benefit of knowing what God is revealing to that person through these difficulties. Conflict may find its source from within the person or from the conflict that one might have with other people. It is often uncertain which of the two comes first, as it seems to cycle back and forth between both of these difficulties. For the pleasure seeker, the amplitude of pleasure seeking must be increased from time to time to a level that compensates for the residual guilt that they carry, but it could lead this person to greater personal spiritual maturity that would also bring greater harmony to that person's relationships. Thus, it may be said that addictions perpetuate immaturity while hampering this same individual's steps toward spiritual maturity.

Inner Conflict   **Interpersonal Conflict**

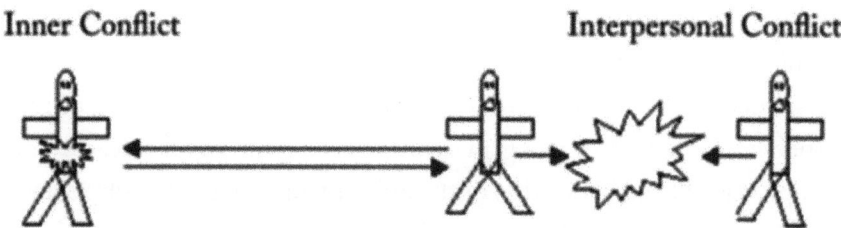

Addictions may be understood in the broadest sense as any activity involved in using a substance or pleasurable stimulus that is innate or foreign to the person's body that causes that people to behave in a manner that is detrimental for their integrity, spiritual growth and is destructive to their relationships. This is significant in light of study of the family transmission of addictions because research has more succinctly recognized that it is not the activity of abusing a substance itself that is transmitted intergenerationally. In the transmission, there are the associated behaviors and attitudes that are of greater influence to everything that is passed on from one generation to another (Burstein et. al. 2005). These behaviors and attitudes also affect the underlying dynamics for addictive behavior for each successive generation.

The issue of attachment has also been studied in relation to addiction and one study found that attachment difficulties were not associated with the severity of addiction but with the presence of comorbid psychiatric conditions (Schindler et. al. 2005). And according to this study, the loss of attachment may be more related to an addicted person who does not obtain or maintain a therapeutic alliance for either the addiction or the comorbid condition. As it was already stated, unresolved difficulties tend to find a short-term solution through the pleasure seeking of addiction that also subverts the person's opportunity for spiritual growth and maturity. Also, addiction develops relationships in an artificial way that may temporarily maintain the sense of having a relationship without correcting any of the behavioral problems that threaten these relationships. Building relationships with the false assurance of addiction only temporarily delays the person's brush with reality that is ultimately inevitable as internal conflict and inter-personal conflict worsens through the addiction. More specifically, many of the factors that lead to addiction demonstrate this theme and validate the concept that inner conflict may not only be the source of interpersonal conflict but also that conflict both from within and without may be the source of addictive behavior. This is understood by the factors that may lead to addictive behavior. Therefore, addiction is a cultured condition:

1. The disordered family
2. Lack of self-esteem
3. Peer pressure
4. Experimentation
5. Cultural influences
6. Parental drug use
7. Diverse personal values

In concert with the theme that addiction is associated with both inner conflict and conflict in relationships, the developmental background of the pleasure-seeking person may provide additional insights into the addiction process. In contrast, interpersonal conflict throughout child to adult development, as understood by scripture, is also the path to acquire virtue and maturity (James 1:1–2). Addiction and even lesser forms of pleasurable distraction effectively afford an escape for the pleasure seeker from the hardships of life and from difficulties in relationships inherent to these hardships. Rather, these hardships could serve to train the person to learn a more constructive behavior from them. Instead of learning how to behave more appropriately and to mature into adulthood, the pleasure seeker learns how substance and other addictive behaviors produce sufficient euphoria to avoid the pressure of the moment that could serve to produce a more positive goal of character development. They do this by using substance to impose more pleasurable stimuli of substance and/or pleasurable experiences, and by this, somewhat block the natural consequences of uncorrected behavior and unresolved conflict. Once introduced to this shortcut benefit, the person who is being addicted to substance seeks this euphoria more regularly. Soon all attempts at constructive resolution of conflict will be abandoned for the harmful dependence in the regular use of the substance. When addiction assumes this level of dependence, the person would feel compelled to use the substance in order to feel normal. Even when pleasure-seeking behaviors are not to the level of addiction, pleasurable stimuli may be used to avoid the opportunities for a more positive means to character development.

The interactions between the human body and any substance and/or pleasurable stimuli involve the cycle of tolerance and withdrawal. Both concepts are related to the body's chemistry and the balances that the body seeks to maintain. This balance in the body is known as homeostasis. Homeostasis may be as much affected by the psychological effects of the drug as they are by the chemistry of the substance. There are homeostatic reactions of the body to the drug known as pharmacokinetics. There are also homeostatic actions of the drug upon the body known as pharmacodynamics. Pharmacodynamic action of the drug on the body involves tolerance and withdrawal. There is also the socio-spiritual motivations in using the substance that are understood as running parallel to physiological homeostasis that is understood from the above explanations. Tolerance and withdrawal are so closely connected that it is nearly impossible to explain one without explaining the other.

Figure 3.5.2

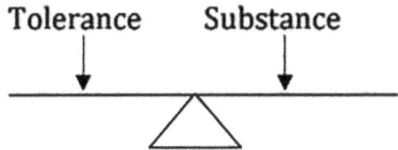

A plane and fulcrum may be the best means to illustrate both concepts. When a substance is introduced into (exogenous substance) or increased in the body (endogenous substance), the body also changes its chemistry to correspond with those changes introduced by the chemistry of the drug to maintain homeostasis or balance.

Tolerance is the body's chemical adjustment to the presence of substance in the body so that the body gradually achieves homeostasis or balance with the presence of this substance. The body will do so through a number of means. One means is to increase the rate of metabolism of the substance to eliminate it more rapidly from the body. However, because metabolism increases over repeated administrations of the substance, the person senses a decrease in the level of pleasurable stimulus from the substance, and this creates a greater motivation within the person to take more of the substance, even though it may also produce some undesirable effects. The person so motivated may want to change course and eliminate the substance or reduce the amount of substance previously taken. When this happens, the body may begin to withdraw. Withdrawal symptoms are unique to each substance and may have greater or lesser degree of severity.

Figure 3.5.3

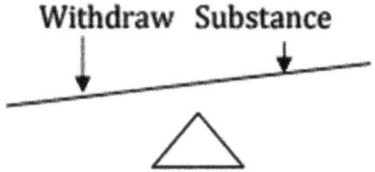

The chemistry of the body is imbalanced by the decrease of the substance by either natural elimination or by the person attempting to reduce or stop the substance. With the imbalance in the body that is created by substance reduction by either means, the body begins to crave the substance more vigorously as it is expressed by whatever means that a particular substance signals a state of withdrawal.

Addictive Substances

Each substance has specific effects that users may find to be an artificial solution to a particular area of personal vulnerability that they had suppressed previously with the use of substance only to make the difficulty worse than when they began. The DSM-IV-TR divides the criteria for diagnosis in regard to each substance between abuse and dependence. Substance abuse is defined as an earlier stage of addiction that may seem fairly innocuous at first because the person does not deem the use of substance as anything more than an escape. Other than the unwanted changes in behavior while using the substance that may result in legal and/or social problems and in the loss of interest in formerly enjoyed activities, the person's life has not been so severely interrupted. Dependence is a later stage of use, where the addicted person's purpose for use is to maintain homeostasis due to symptoms of withdrawal and for wanting to feel normal again. In dependence, using substance has developed an obsessional preoccupation with the substance. Dependence occurs in circumstances where the person is using the substance even though there is no longer much of a perceived benefit. And despite many dire consequences for doing so, the person continues to use the substance. The following is a list of many of the potential substances of addiction:

1. Alcohol is the one of the most toxic of substances that one could use because of its easy distribution through the body due to its chemical structure: C2H6O is a very small molecule with low molecular weight. Its small size enables the molecule to penetrate the blood-brain barrier that protects the brain as it also penetrates many other soft tissue organs of the body. Unmetabolized alcohol will destroy neurons upon contact, and chronic long-term use of alcohol may result in Korsakoff's psychosis that is a permanent condition where short-term memory is so reduced that the user may not be able to remember events that happened just seconds prior (Hildebrandt et. al. 2004). When alcohol does metabolize, it metabolizes into narcotic like substances. Its toxic effects also threaten all of the vital organs of the body, except for the kidneys.

    The scriptures indicate that strong drink is a deceiver (Proverbs 20:1) and possibly this passage is recognizing this property of the drug in at least three ways. One deception is that alcohol gives the sensation of warmth when alcohol actually reduces the core temperature of the body (Brasser & Spear 2002). This is a critical problem for the alcohol dependent person who lives on the street when outside temperatures drop to near freezing. When temperatures drop, this person may drink to feel warm but the person is deceptively disposed to hypothermia. Another significant way that alcohol deceives is the sense of euphoria that users seek from its use, but alcohol is actually a general central nervous system depressant reducing heart rate and respiration (Eiden et. al. 2004). Another dangerous deception of alcohol is its direct correlation with violent crime because alcohol reduces the person's normal inhibition. One study indicated that the probability of violence co-occurring with a social event of alcohol use is 21.7 percent (Mulvey et.al. 2006). And yet, alcohol is the substance chosen for its anxiety reducing effect in social situations when the person attempts to fit into certain social roles. Alcoholism represents the natural adaptive means that human beings seek in order to reconcile the difference between how they want to be regarded in these social roles and relationships and how others truly assess their behavior. Feeling defeated in this attempt, they turn for help in alcohol. For a while at least, alcohol can deceive the person into becoming ambivalent to his perceived deficiencies regarding this social dilemma rather than finding spiritual solutions for his character development from them.

2. Sedatives-hypnotics (barbiturates) were once used as sleep medications, but because of many serious and dangerous side effects, they are seldom prescribed for this purpose. As sleep medications, they were only superficially helpful because of their ability to sustain a quantity of sleep, but these drugs inhibit rapid-eye-movement (REM sleep, making these drugs counterproductive as a sleep medication. Brain waves during sleep appear to slow down their wave-like motion from stage one to stage five sleep until the person reaches the level of REM sleep that occurs about three to four times during a given night's sleep. REM waves are very active waves similar to the activity of waves when the person is fully awake, even though the person in REM sleep is in a deeper stage sleep. REM is thought to have a rejuvenating effect for the person, making his feel more rested and invigorated for the next day's activity (Stepanski et. al. 2003. Sedatives-hypnotics are a class of drugs that block REM sleep waves, as are alcohol and many other drugs. The user may have eight or more hours of sleep but feel tired and not at all refreshed. The worst effect of this class of drugs is the effect of respiratory arrest when overdosed or when combined with alcohol to create a synergistic increase of effect in their distribution in the body. Benzodiazepines are sedative type drugs of the tranquilizer variety that are still being prescribed for anxiety and sleep deprivation. Drugs like Valium, Xanax, Klonopin, and Librium have been used for a variety of anxiety and sleep conditions. However, many of

these drugs have found their way into the street trade probably from left-over or stolen prescriptions. They have the same effects as barbiturates on REM sleep waves, but they are less potent in the blockage of REM. Benzodiazepines do have a problem with what is called the "rebound effect" that is experienced by users when they attempt to stop taking the drug, even with individuals who have been prescribed the medication (Gosselin et. al.2006). The anxiety symptoms and restlessness rebound to greater severity than they were prior to first using the medication. Taking benzodiazepines without prescription and without sound medical guidance would not be recommended for this reason. The sedation effect of barbiturates and benzodiazepines is also very high and a person overdosing with benzodiazepines may appear to behave like one who is drunk with alcohol. The scriptures speak of the rest that is given to those who accept his invitation to come to him, who offers his followers a lighter burden in comparison to the one that is already self-imposed by attempting to resolve stress through one's own means (Matthew 11: 28–30). However, effective sleep may not be so readily obtained by any means if the underlying health issues that would require greater medical investigation are not sufficiently understood and remediated.

One woman who struggled with depression told the story of her former husband who had died from an overdose of cocaine and other multiple substances and had also managed to get her involved with using cocaine as well. She had stopped using many years prior to counseling even while he was yet living, but she began to use another substance through excessive smoking. Current to her counseling process, her physician determined that she would be benefited from a combination of Welbutrin and Klonopin, the latter of which is a short-acting benzodiazepine. This drug seemed to cause her to vacillate from extreme depression to extreme nervousness. In an effort to reduce anxiety, benzodiazepines also depress mood and follow a pathway in the brain known as the pleasure pathway. For her, the benzodiazepine prescription medication was another drug of abuse as it had enabled her to escape many of the haunting memories of the past to replace them with a mood less anxious. However, she sought so vigorously for this passive state so that she overused the benzodiazepine, and the benzodiazepine has a moderate ability to tolerate quickly that increases the need for more drug to gain the same effect after repeated administrations.

3. *Narcotic drugs* are the pain-relieving drugs that are either opium derived or synthetic narcotic medications. Codeine, morphine, percodan, and heroin are some examples of narcotic drugs. Codeine suppresses cough in the form of the over-the-counter cold medications, but it is also found in the possession of those who intend to use it for a very different reason. Morphine is a much stronger opiate medication than codeine, and morphine is used as an injectable surgical medication because of its potency in relieving surgical pain and for its ability to slow the peristalsis of the gut while relieving pain that makes it a primary choice for gastrointestinal surgery. But for this reason, it also causes constipation. Morphine is a favored drug for those who intend to use it illegally for reasons other than for the pain experienced in surgery—often pain in this case is emotional in nature. Heroin is likely the drug that is in the greatest demand for illegal use in this class. It is mostly used in an injectable form that makes it a risk for secondary infections such as hepatitis and HIV. The paraphernalia of syringes and needles are also illegal when in a person's possession without a prescription for their use. A narcotic drug relieves pain by its similar molecular structure that is nearly identical to the body's own pain-relieving neurotransmitters. Therefore, narcotic drugs are agonist drugs that mimic the action of these neurotransmitters called enkephalins and endorphins. Endorphins are so named because they are "endogenous morphines." The problem with taking these drugs is that they build tolerance quickly, creating a craving for the drug. This is caused by the presence of the exogenous substance of the drug that is introduced into the body that causes the activity of endorphins or

the endogenous neurotransmitter substance to almost completely cease their residual activity. After chronic use, the person cannot maintain painlessness without using the drug. These effects increase exponentially over ti me. In the end, the person cannot get enough of the drug to feel normally pain free. In full-blown addiction and withdrawal, the person develops flu-like and respiratory symptoms along with more craving for the drug. There seems to be more than just a physiological reason for taking these pain relievers. The body's endogenous morphines seem to be depleted for reasons that are not merely physical in nature (Palfai & Jankiewicz 1997). It has been established that endorphins also remediate emotional pain (Lekander, 2002), as endorphin receptors are also found in the brain's limbic area that is the brain's emotional center. This perspective also supports t he assumption that was previously stated that opiate drugs are the faulty substitute for conflict resolution that ultimately creates greater emotional pain for the person. Fentanyl is a very dangerous powerful form of this class of opiate drugs.

One couple was referred to counseling by their physician after he had discovered that they were receiving pain medication for alleged back pain problems from two different doctors. However, after some investigation, it was found that there may have been as many as four or five different doctors that were prescribing for them—each one not knowing about the other except for the doctor that sent them there. Their pain was very real because their endogenous pain relief neurotransmitter systemhad been compromised and ceased to function with the presence of so much exogenous substance in their system.

Another heroin addict attempted to avoid rehab by seeking outpatient counseling, but she came bearing the marks of one who was in need of such rehabilitation. Without seeing the "tracks" on her arms and legs, most observers would conclude that she had a very bad case of influenza. She wore slacks and long-sleeve shirts to cover any of those telltale marks. It was evident that she was in a withdraw state. However, unless she entered the hospital for rehabilitation, she would likely use again to relieve her pain. Parallel to the physical and in most cases more prominent is the internalized emotional pain produced from failed or difficult relationships.

4. Stimulant drugs, such as cocaine and amphetamines, continue to represent some of the classic substances of addiction. The so-called designer drugs, such as ecstasy, are analogs of the amphetamine drugs that produce stimulant-hallucinogenic effects. Ecstasy has a similar chemical structure to both hallucinogen drugs and amphetamine drugs (Nichols, 1994). The danger of the MDMA or ecstasy is that it has grave irreversible neurotoxic effects (Rivas Vasquez & Delgado 2002). The effect of stimulants amphetamine and cocaine is the upregulation of brain activity that increases alertness and other vital functions. With the effect of overstimulation and quick rise and rate of brain activity, there is also a crash and burn experience in the aftereffects of th is initial overstimulation experience. Am phetamines are quickly tolerated so that the person would need to procure a sufficient amount of the drug for several runs to be used during a two to three-day period only to binge by increasing the dose for each run. In the aftermath, the person becomes seriously depressed and likely suicidal, which may also be accompanied with visual hallucinations in this withdrawal state. Often, the chronic user of amphetamines ends up in an emergency ward with symptoms of depression and psychosis. The psychosis involved in amphetamine toxicity may be distinguished from the psychosis of schizophrenia.

The difference is that amphetamine withdraw is typically characterized by visual hallucination whereas schizophrenia is typically characterized by auditory hallucinations. Amphetamines are taken in a tablet form, typically a methamphetamine.

Cocaine is a very addictive substance as well that is made from the cocoa leaf and cured until it can be made into a white powder. The difficulty with cocaine is that it has a different rate of tolerance for its various effects. It also lowers the seizure threshold, initiating a higher potential for seizures upon withdraw. Its most dangerous effect is the cardiac effect of tachycardia and vasoconstriction that is less tolerant than other effects of cocaine that produces the potential for cardiac arrest (Liska, 2004). Cocaine is taken in a powder form and is used by snorting it into the lungs and nasal cavity; it is also used intravenously when it is liquefied, known as mainlining, and it is smoked in a manner that is known as freebasing.

Cocaine blocks the reuptake of the neurotransmitter DA at the presynaptic membrane, preventing DA from entering the DA transporter system. This makes DA more available to attach to DA receptors on the other side of the cleft on the postsynaptic membrane. This upregulates the activity of DA, and therefore, the drug creates greater internal consciousness and greater demand for personal gratification from its pleasure-producing effect. Amphetamines act as agonists for NE, block reuptake for NE, potentiate the release of NE and DA, facilitate the synthesis of NE and DA, and block the enzymatic degradation of NE and DA (Liska, 2004). NE is the neurotransmitter of increased activity and alertness. Ironically, it is a lower potency of amphetamine known as Ritalin that is widely used as a prescription medication for Attention-Deficit-Hyperactivity-Disorder (ADHD). Some of the Ritalin prescription medications have been used for other purposes inhaled as a powder by teenagers to give it a greater, cocaine-like effect (Bromfield, 1998). Cylert was manufactured as a response to this problem of misuse, making it difficult to grind the tablets into this powder form, but Cylert was withdrawn from the US market in March of 2005 because of the dangerous hepatic side effects. DA is the neurotransmitter of visceral mental powers that also leads to a delusional state of mind and hallucinations. The DA pathway in the brain is known as the pleasure pathway, making cocaine a highly addictive substance. Galatians 5 gives an interesting contrast that may help to explain the foundational spiritual formation principle and to clarify the personality dynamics of addiction and for amphetamine and cocaine addiction in particular. The passage is well-known for its teaching about the "fruit of the Spirit" in verses 22–24, but it is not as well known for the contrasting thought of the "acts of the sinful nature" in verses 19–21. The context of this discussion is very important because it is the topic of legalism vs. grace, or more succinctly the issue of self-help vs. God's help to establish righteous living. The "acts of the sinful nature" are not purposed for the development of sinful behavior but are focused on human attempts to live righteously by means of human effort. The method of "human effort" that is used to obtain righteousness is found to backfire in the words of Paul, the author of this passage.

One of the elements that appears on the list of "acts of the sinful nature" is the term translated "witchcraft" (NIV). The early Greek manuscripts use the term φαρμακεια anglicized as pharmakeia. This term, while correctly translated witchcraft, but carries the nuance involved in the protocol of the witchcraft trade, namely, inducing their subjects to an altered state of mind by using the common psychoactive drugs of their day. The interesting feature of these "acts of the flesh" is that they represent faulty attempts to attain righteous living that result in an opposite set of consequences from what is intended. This indicates that drug use, among other extreme pleasure-motivated actions, provides a short-term false sense of personal goodness that has a quite opposite result in the longer run. Although the reasoning may be somewhat convoluted, observation of those who use amphetamine and cocaine are often exemplified by certain individuals who have lived in environments that have attempted to prop up their public image while secretly using the chemical cop-out of stimulant drugs. It is a head for right living without a heart to sustain this path that eventually gives way to the total disillusionment for even continuing to try to be a good person. In the end, users of these drugs often appear to have little or no conscience for what they are doing to themselves or to others by this means.

5. Marijuana is either smoked or eaten as hashish. It inhibits nervous system activation generally by inhibiting the production of Adenosine Triphosphate (ATP), an enzyme that is an intermediary link in the chemical chain reaction that causes G-proteins to open calcium channels in the postsynaptic membrane that activate the neuron (Liska, 2004). Marijuana also blocks brain DA that controls appetite and sleep and is very similar in chemical structure to natural steroids in the body, such as testosterone and estradiol (Palfai & Jankiewicz 1997). It produces a response of amotivation so that it is a reinforcing drug to those who fall behind in achievement or the accepted level of performance in comparison to the level of achievement attained by peers of the user's related field. In this manner, the drug provides an escape from the compelling pressure to achieve. It blunts the user's affect and replaces conviction that the user would ordinarily feel in the face of imminent failure with a sense of euphoria. It is the favored drug for many middle class high school and college-aged students and has had great popularity among the peace movement of the 60s and 70s (Palfai & Jankiewicz, 1997). Marijuana has been the favorite anti establishment drug. It validates and reinforces the position of those who "sit in the seat of the mockers" who pretend that they are not a part of the conflict that exists between the established forces of this world and their own personal convictions as was explained by Psalm 1:1–2 previously. As it was popular during the peace movement of the 60s and 70s, marijuana tends to endorse the same perspective on the world—artificially removing the person from any sense of conflict that really exists. Substrates of marijuana without the active form of marijuana may give relief for chronic pain.

    A young adult male had entered into counseling to deal with his inability to manage his life in general, and although he had not used drugs since high school, he had used marijuana very heavily at that time. His current mood was light but readily given to bouts of anxiety and despair. He wanted to get ahead in life but when time came to make his move, he lacked the motivation to take the initiative, follow through and succeed. His mental process seemed to be unclear and he seemed to lose track to make the mental associations necessary to follow complex instructions, and so was relegated to a life of simple blue-collar employment. Although he was considered to be a promising student in high school bound for an excellent college career, he did not seem to be able to construct more than simple three to four word sentences at the present time. Another high school student used marijuana regularly knowing that his father used the same drug when he was in high school. While his father had stopped using for a number of years, his son continued the tradition. There was more than one reason that motivated him to use. He disliked school very much and his school counselors and administrators were frustrated with his incorrigibility to engage in any meaningful learning activity. He would come into class pull his hooded jacket over his head and if anyone, student or teacher, came near him he would moan and groan. The school in cooperation with his parents eventually referred him to a boot camp for high school students that would resist learning in the mainstream. Marijuana assisted him in his oppositional behavior to the environment that was urging him to achieve in a not very encouraging manner using motivation by guilt. He also was acting on marijuana as a protest to the impending divorce between his parents.

6. Hallucinogens such as lysergic acid (LCD), psilocybin (hallucinogenic mushrooms), peyote (hallucinogenic cactus), and phencyclidine or phenylcyclohexylpiperidine (PCP) are partial 5HT agonists/antagonist drugs. This means that these drugs mimic the action of serotonin but do much more negatively to affect the user. The manufacturer of angel dust uses mint leaves, parsley, or low-grade marijuana laced with PCP, because PCP in full strength, although a much more inexpensive product, produces greater mental confusion and dysphoria than other hallucinogens (Liska, 2004). These drugs are chosen for their euphoric hallucinogenic effect. However, "acidheads" or "heads" (users of LSD) have been known

to be cruel and unfeeling in their residual state of addiction. PCP has also reportedly been the source of violent behavior (Palfai & Jankiewicz, 1997).

Serotonin, when bound to its respective receptor sites, is responsible for dream states and altered states of consciousness. The specific receptors for 5HT2A along with DA2 are involved in the production of auditory and visual hallucinations in relation to schizophrenia (Stahl,2000). The blockade of these two receptors by antipsychotic medication has produced the best results for alleviating the positive symptoms of schizophrenia (Stahl, 2000). LSD is known to bind with at least fifteen serotonin receptor subtypes and to two dopamine receptor subtypes (Liska, 2004). Professor at Harvard University, Timothy Leary, believed that LSD and psilocybin enabled him to be much more creative (Liska, 2004), but perhaps his work was creative in his eyes only as others view his writings while under the influence of these drug as mostly incoherent and incomprehensible.

The residual state for heavy users of this hallucinogenic class of drugs may experience brain burnout. The anti-drug campaign that shows an egg placed into a frying pan with the comment made that "this is your brain on drugs" depicts well what happens to the chronic user of hallucinogens. The motivation for using these drugs may be understood by considering the person who has grown weary of the logical conclusions drawn from mundane conventional thinking and now seeks a very tantalizing cognitive process through the use of hallucinogenic drugs. The user of hallucinogens may be seeking to be free from what he considers to be the bondage to sound thinking. In the practice of witchcraft in Central America, shamans use the hallucinogenic cactus peyote to allegedly make contact with the spirit world that is thought to be inaccessible through the ordinary focus of innate mental ability. Could those who use hallucinogens be having their own type of "Tower of Babel" experience, seeking their own determined way to reach their spiritual high? While this may not be the expressed intention of the users of these drugs, it is apparently the underlying implication to their motivation. Mastery of one's own destiny and mind to be free from any common sense is the heart cry of the user of these drugs, but their bid to procure this freedom by this means leads them to greater mental confusion and personal destruction.

7. *Sexual addictions* mix the innate chemistry of the body with other substances that they may deem as providing them with aphrodisiac effects. The paraphernalia used for these effects involved in sexual addictions may be very extensive, such as various levels of pornography as well as drugs and alcohol. Nitric Oxide (NO) is one such attempt to remove the ordinary guilt involved with such incredible behavior. Many other attempts to use wine and other substances may have been effective for removing inhibitions, but they also lose some of the essential consciousness to achieve their intended thrill of the experience. So, the abuser of substance finds creative ways to link substance addiction with obsession for sexual experiences by gravitating to drugs like ecstasy and NO. NO is a vasodilator (dilation of capillary walls) and by this means, stimulates blood circulation in the brain as well in the genitals. As a result, the sought-for altered state may distress the capillary walls in the brain and also incur permanent brain damage (Wright, 1995). The brain has its own NO receptors in the entorhinal cortex (behind the nose) of the hippocampus that is located in the midsection that is responsible for the potential development of short-term memory (Carlson, 2004). The exponential growth of these receptor sites of the hippocampus is indicative of the human being's ability to remember complex details of thought and emotionally labeled material. Perhaps, this is the source of brain stimulation sought for from the exogenous substance.

    Sexual addictions can exist without comorbid addiction to exogenous substances. Apparently, the body has sufficient chemistry of its own to develop an addiction that is entirely sexual in nature. It is Paul the Apostle's contention that this behavior is tantamount to sinning against the body (I Corinthians 6: 18). The innate substance, perhaps adrenaline, gives a quick, shortcut, sensational stimulus to replace the arduous process of finding lasting gratification with the relationship between a man and a woman. Alfred Adler, who followed Freud as the leader of the psychoanalytic society, wrote to the effect in his self-help book on marriage and family relationships that masturbation confirms isolation (Adler, 1982). Several ideas may be taken from this comment. One is that sexual addictions are intended to be a shortcut to the cheap thrill apart from sacrificing self needs. This shortcut to sexual pleasure gives only a short-term sense of fulfillment in relationships as well without a long-term unselfish commitment to the relationship. The passage of Romans 1:26 also indicates that homosexuality is an example of how other sinful passions exist as a desire for intimacy; however, it is a desire that is out of the context of God's plan for intimacy in marriage between man and woman. It is held out in this passage as a general condition of the human race of which homosexuality is an example of how out of step and misdirected human passion has become in general, but it is being applied to the larger heterosexual population. A second idea that may be derived from Adler's comment is that there is an inherent deception that is posed by this tantalizing effect. While seeking intimacy by means sexual addiction in whatever way, the final result of unchecked sexual desire produces greater isolation than the person had intended and, as a result of these actions, a real loss of intimacy. But like other addictions, this short-term thrill is what also maintains the addiction. But in the final analysis, the person is left alone with no real relationships but with only more opportunities to seek cheap thrill after cheap thrill to gain some modicum sense of intimacy. This is also why there is no real contentment with the simplicity of sexual experiences among those so motivated; instead, the addicted person will seek more and more bizarre sexual experiences to satisfy a need for a more tantalizing form of intimacy that he cannot attain by this means either.

In contrast, the passage in I Corinthians 7:4 indicates that in marriage, personal gratification should not be the primary motivation when seeking intimacy. Paul addresses the Corinthian believer and states that the husband does not have authority over his own body, but that his wife does have this authority. Likewise, the wife does not have authority over her own body, but the husband has this authority. This is a direct application of the general principle of spiritual formation that Jesus proposed to his disciples, "Whosoever loses his life for my sake shall find it" (Matthew 10:39). The partners should not be primarily concerned with their own self gratification that ultimately eludes them and leaves them isolated and dissatisfied. The husband's sexuality exists primarily to gratify his wife, and the wife's sexuality primarily exists to gratify the husband.

The act of caring unselfishly for on e's spouse brings the greater gratification than self gratification could ever bring. As Jesus also taught, "Whoever wants to be first must be a slave" (Mark 10:44). The servant's heart is crucial for healthy relationships and for the development of one's personal spirituality.

One woman could not take a break from My Space and other chat forums on the Internet long enough to spend time with her family. She would spend hours every evening after her husband went to his evening shift at work. She would rather bring her children for "psychological help" than to admit her lack of attention was the reason for most of the disturbances felt by her and the family. On the Internet, she profiled herself as a single woman and posted a picture that portrayed her as available and seductive. Her husband read the profile and saw the picture and felt betrayed by her. She excused these portrayals as just fun and games. Two affairs later she continued to deceive her husband using alternate forms of media. Once a new method to make contact with the outside world was discovered, she would feign repentance and find another.

8. Eating Disorders may also be classed as a substance of a addiction; however, it is addiction to an everyday substance of use, namely

food. There may also be some remote connection of the so named "eating disorders" with that of anxiety conditions, such as Obsessive Compulsive Disorder especially when it is viewed in this socio-spiritual nuance. There are three major types of eating disorders: overeating, anorexia nervosa, and bulimia nervosa. Overeating may find its root in the history of responses that a person gives to perceived unrequited love and affection. It is a motivation to gain the instant gratification from food that the person has grown hopeless to find in relationships. Overeating suffers the consequence of weight gain that occurs when eating is the unlikely substitution for pleasure and acceptance from the same history of responses that overeating has, but rather than finding solace in eating for gratification, anorexic people attempt to use an obsessive prohibition against eating as a means to compel others to love them—compulsively viewing fat as ugly and unattractive. The obsession to prohibit eating soon borders on being delusional regarding the person's view of his own body and physical self concept. Bulimia nervosa is an attempt to have the best of both worlds. Bulimia carries out the goal to substitute instant gratification for the loss of pleasure in relationships without having the effect of gaining weight from increased food intake.

A woman in her late thirties came for counseling because of a problem with her weight. She was a dedicated Christian and worked as a secretary for a foreign missionary agency. Her family has had its share of struggles including the oldest daughter's drug use and sexual relationship with her boyfriend. Her two teenage sons seemed to know Christ but also seemed to be more attracted to the ways of the world than to living for Christ. Her husband, though given to bouts with anger, genuinely loved the Lord and supported the mission agency where she worked. She didn't know why she could not stay trim and queried if this might not be a genetic problem. However, when gathering data about her family of origin and present family, some other clues emerged. She told a story of her parents being very poor because of her father's lack of diligence with work. Although he did not drink regularly, he came home drunk on one occasion when no one else was at home and raped her when she was about thirteen years of age. Although the details about the rape were foggy to her, she did believe this has been a major problem for her self-esteem. She was a wild teenager after the rape, and she became pregnant to a young man who quickly left the town to join the armed forces when he learned that she was pregnant. She had gone out with the man who was now her husband before this time, but he considered her too worldly for him to pursue. She went to him after learning that the father of the child had left town and her present difficulties in life. Even ordinary bantering that went on between husband and wife could impact her as rejection—this was the clinical deja vu from the past. She would eat constantly while at home, especially when she was preparing meals for the family. She would also eat "junk food," which her husband attempted to hide. Although she may not have been feeling particularly unloved or rejected at the time, she did feel relief from sadness when she would enjoy food. Her in-laws were very manipulative toward her and the families of their adult offspring. This often became a point of contention between her and her husband, who attempted to avoid them rather than confront them with their attempts to manipulate her.

The family seemed to play a big part in her problem with eating, but the counselor managed to see her husband on only one occasion. The counselor did manage to set up a family conference in their home where she more openly expressed her feelings, fears, and concerns to them. When it came to communication, she became very adept in expressing herself more openly and fully than her husband could express himself. She decided to go to a hospital on her own for the treatment of eating disorders, which turned out to be a disaster. Through counseling she was more courageous in communication and her identity problems improved significantly, but the weight issue was changing little.

The weight issue would be an on-going battle. Although the "love-hunger" interpretation is probably an accurate one, the removal of that impetus for eating would not automatically cause her to eat less. While her improvement in other areas would certainly expedite her weight loss eventually, old patterns for eating would have to be remedied more directly. She attempted to find the elusive tenderness in her relationships, but responses to her seemed so inadequate that she found more immediate satisfaction with food.

Intervention Strategies for the Addicted

Efforts to help addicted people have focused mainly on the efforts of the support group strategy. Each person must at least minimally commit to attend these support groups according to this method of intervention.

There are several principles that are extracted below that seem to guide the methodology used in the Alcoholic Anonymous (2001) (AA) group process that have been applied to other group strategies for various addiction categories:

1. The individual person is helpless to recover on his or her own ability
2. Each person needs a higher power to recover effectively
3. Each person needs the help of the support group (perhaps for some this is the embodiment of the higher power)
4. Each person needs constant accountability to a sponsor
5. Each person needs to acknowledge that once addicted always addicted
6. For each person recovery is an ongoing process that is never finished
7. Total abstinence is required because the person is only one failure to abstain away from total addiction.[1]

These above principles have compatibility with Christian formation concepts such as the need for a higher power, a sterling endorsement for a Christian spiritual formation methodology. However, this principle is lacking for specifics regarding who this higher power really is. For this reason, some have used the AA steps and applied their specific doctrine of God along with these basic principles. Another compatible idea of AA is the use of constructive social relationships to replace the relationships that were formed around the addiction. This is a principle need to be examined for its dynamic effect on the addicted person in both respect to its facilitation of the addiction and for the treatment of addiction. However, the critical principle of needing the support group to continue abstinence has been one of the major criticisms of AA due to the perception of fostering dependence on group support. Some clinicians have forwarded another concept for intervention called "harm reduction" that disputes the AA step of total abstinence (Wetermeyer, 1994). They contend that total abstinence may be too dangerous in withdraw. They also indicate that the major part of the user population will only elude and resist treatment protocols with this requirement at the beginning of treatment. AA approaches are also cited for their obvious substitution of dependency—first a dependency on the drug and then on the AA support group with a danger in the break of affiliation. However, there are also inherent dangers involved with harm reduction methods that may reinforce the user's deception of self and others in regard to the denial of continued drug abuse that is common among substance abusers in general.

While a support group may provide a fresh start socially for a person who is abusing drugs, eventually the counselor will need to counsel the addicted person individually. Polcin (2003, 165–184) recognizes the need for a personal "confrontation" in drug and alcohol treatment, but the researcher wishes to rethink how the confrontation is traditionally carried out by recognizing that it cannot be done as a one-size-fits-all approach for the addicted person. He modifies such steps in confrontation by considering four different aspects to it:

1. A focus on behaviors and thinking that is related to the substance of misuse
2. Implementation of confrontation within the context of a trusting relationship
3. Consideration of the nature of the treatment setting and characteristics of the client/recipient of the confrontation

4. Avoidance of extreme expression of emotion that can detract from the content of the confrontation

His work recognizes the complexity of confrontation, and in general, his call for looking at each case individually to determine how to conduct effective intervention is commendable. Confrontations work best when you observe contradictions in what the person says or does. It also has a prophetic function of warning the person of consequences for persistence in the wrong course of action, providing for a certain negative consequence. More specifically for the alcohol and drug abuser, the focus of the intervention should be on the developmental aspects of the social and relational under-pinnings of the addiction long before and throughout the growth of addiction process. This indeed places the assessment of the person's addiction on the relevant aspects of the person's life. There may need to be some attention paid to the substance itself and to how it fits into that person's developmental context, but effective strategies for dealing with the inner conflict and the concomitant conflicts found in relationships will pay huge dividends for the purpose of intervention. Regardless of whether or not the person has accepted total abstinence as the path to recovery, the person's approach to recovery should motivate the person to want help or the counseling relationship in a group context or conducted individually would not be very effective. If there were no openly expressed motivation for addiction by the addicted person, the counselor should implement measures that are described in a previous chapter for the unwilling counselee. There may be little or no motivation on the part of the counselee or benefit for the counselee to begin speaking about the problem of drug or alcohol problems until the counselor observes how dynamic relationships have impacted the person's social and cognitive development. Without understanding the role that drugs play in the person's life, as futile attempts to rectify significant problems in relationships, the intervention may lose its principal effect. From this context of understanding, four basic levels of analysis of confrontation will be useful for the counselor as explained below:

1. The first level of inquiry related to addiction is to find the counselee's significant set of reactions to those failed or difficult relationships of the past. As Jesus said, "It is necessary that trouble must come, but woe to him from whom it comes" (Luke 17:1). Trouble is ubiquitous to life, and it can complicate life for so many people. When children do not sense sufficient care, they will not simply change course to find a different form of care but will crave a greater level satisfaction of love and care than is commensurate to their true need. They will desire satisfaction of this unmet need too much. Later on in life, prospective addicted persons will seek for care from others in ways that may make it impossible for them to be satisfied. Addictions become the crossroads of decision where the person switches from finding satisfaction in significant relationships to that of finding satisfaction for relationships through the abuse of substance and addictive behaviors. This is like the little girl who was paid a quarter every time she practiced her violin. She was doing so splendidly in her progress that her parents thought it was no longer necessary to pay her a miserly quarter because she was having so much enjoyment from its practice alone. Shortly thereafter, she was not only practicing one hour, she was practicing two hours. Her parents were genuinely impressed until suddenly she stopped playing the violin completely. Her parents inquired about the reasons for her sudden resignation from the instrument that prior to this time she seemed to love. She expressed that she was very upset at their question, "You used to pay me a quarter when I only practiced for one hour. I thought that you would surely pay me at least 50 cents when I practiced for two, but you paid me nothing at all. So, I quit because it is not worth it anymore!" This little girl shows not only how a total misunderstanding within intimate relationships creates such bitterness, but also how behavior may be motivated and initially increased by a symbolic offering of appreciation until all hope for that type of appreciation is lost. When all hope is dissipated, the child often self-destructs with behaviors that block the potential for further disappointments. What is missing in the understanding

of this episode is the dynamics of the relationships. The parents thought she really enjoyed playing the violin, but she did not enjoy it nearly as much as she enjoyed the token of appreciation that her parents gave her for doing so. She thought that she played the violin because she was being paid a quarter, but the amount of displeasure that she expressed after not being paid indicates that she valued the contractual relationship with her parents more than the fund itself.

It is important for the counselor to take a history of family and relationships where the dynamics may be found that may contribute to the on-set of addiction. Then, trace the addiction to its very root, a craving for satisfaction in relationships that is exaggerated by the dissatisfaction that was created by being denied satisfaction during those formative years of life. The pain of the person's suffering will not be sufficiently abated by the desired effects of the chosen substance or behavior, and the earlier trauma of failed relationships would have been enough of a significant source of difficulty for the person without adding another problem to the person's life, namely, the addiction itself.

2. But before drugs are ever used to artificially satisfy these needs, the person craves satisfaction in relationships that are well beyond what is essential to satisfy this craving as in the case of the little girl practicing her violin for two hours. Negative affect has long been studied in its relationship to addiction, and it is also assumed that the negative affect links with the person's social relationships that may also be understood to impact addictive behavior (Measelle et. al., 2006). The precedent behaviors that lead to substance abuse may involve similar extraordinary measures to secure those previous expectations in regard to relationships. So much of what the person has experienced has been so sensationalized that the ordinary life experiences that should bring satisfaction and resolution through simple relationships no longer seem to give enough satisfaction to the addicted person. The person wants too much satisfaction from relationships when it is further withheld or denied them so that

they then want the wrong thing in its place. Helping the person find contentment in the common, everyday experiences of life and relationships would enact some stability for the addicted person. However, the extreme craving for substance and/ or its concomitant behaviors often interferes with any attempt to find contentment in everyday experiences.

3. Ultimately, the person cannot find sufficient satisfaction from the wrong thing that is intended to abate the original dissatisfaction with relationships. And early in this search for faulty substitutes, the prospective addicted person may not be fully apprised of what a given drug will do for him toward this superficial goal. Eventually and perhaps serendipitously, the despair of not finding satisfaction in relationships will lead the person to find the substance or behavior that best substitutes for the specific deficits in relationships that had previously produced this craving for satisfaction. In the current context of addiction, the whole circle of the person's life and relationships needs to be considered in order to conduct such a comprehensive strategy for recovery. Addiction is not just to a substance but it is an addictive lifestyle where substance is used to support the role that the person would like to play in relationships and a role that the person desperately attempts to reproduce from the use of this particular substance or behavior.

4. The next area of concern is to consider what appeal a given substance might render for the person seeking satisfaction. Marijuana reinforces those who wish to resist the urgency of obligation to achieve. Opiates give something in return for people who wish to resolve their unrelenting physical and emotional pain. Eating is the more acceptable and accessible means for gratification when relationships seem too remote to give the gratification of being sufficiently loved. Illicit sexual experiences are the shortcut to the tantalizing sense of fulfillment in relationships without the problems associated with building a relationship with another

person. Alcohol emboldens a person to overcome the trepidation of his inadequacy in relationships that the user would not want to ordinarily to feel. Hallucinogenic drugs help the person to live in a sense of altered euphoric state of unreality to avoid the reality of failures in relationships. Uppers like amphetamine and cocaine lift the person from mundane existence to make the person feel exciting and wonderful even when he knows that his life is often mundane and simple. Sedatives reduce the sense of stress that the person feels without having to face or solve any of the problems that causes this stress. *Substance seems to be chosen for the specific effects that the user intends to achieve, which effects are linked to the deep craving associated with an individual's peculiar desire for satisfaction that was unresolved in past relationships.*

A woman in her mid-thirties became alarmed with a recent development in her husband's behavior when another woman drove him home late at night from the neighborhood barroom. It was not unusual for him to be out late and not uncommon for someone to drive him home, but she was not going to tolerate a woman who was also a regular attendee at the bar herself spending more time with her husband than she had. She demanded that they go to counseling and he was obliged to comply but with the protest that he did not know this woman who had brought him home. The counselor inquired about the history of alcohol abuse and he described that he had started drinking at a very early age of preteen years. His father was an alcoholic and kept a rather large stash of a variety of the beverage close at hand in the home. He revealed what was a very sad tale of his father's absence and that when his father was present, he was usually not of sound mind or body to do any of things a father and son might do together. The man who had come for counseling just got by with passing grades in school, graduated and married the woman whom he now joins in counseling, and together they have one daughter who is the preoccupation of her mother. The counselor inquired if there was a time from the beginning of his use of alcohol when he had ever stopped using. This man responded by indicating that he had started drinking when he was eleven years old and he had stopped only once just after they were married when he attended AA meetings for a period of about two to three months. When asked about his progress with AA, he said that he was miserable the entire time that he had abstained from alcohol for those two to three months of time. He said, "All that I could think about was when am I going to get my next drink." He worked in construction and against workplace standards, kept his own stash of alcohol inside the water cooler hidden from everyone except for a few of his buddies. He was able to function at work but would immediately head out to the bar after work where he would drink until he literally passed out. This was the expressed reason for others driving him home late at night. He had stopped drinking two weeks prior to coming for counseling and he felt as miserable this time as he did when he quit drinking the first time that he attended AA. He did not wish to return to AA for fear that it would fail to make any difference in his life, as he had tried it once before. To move in a positive direction with his addiction, the counselor began to assess more closely his background in addiction and recognized that his relationship with his father was a key to his addiction story. Moreover, his current relationship with his daughter was greatly impacted by his use of alcohol as well. It was incredible how much he did not know about being a father and husband and what he could do to enhance these relationships. His wife was content to focus on her daughter rather than to face the discouragement of her husband's addiction, and so she was resistant at first about him making any changes in his relationship with her or with their daughter. Not only family counseling but also marital counseling became the order of the agenda in this counseling process. Several weeks later, the counselor evaluated his progress in maintaining sobriety. His newfound involvement with his daughter and with his wife was very exhilarating to him, reinforcing his attempt to remain sober. He said, "This is the first time in my life that I feel like I can live without drinking and be okay; I no longer have the strong desire that I once had—that I would always need to have that next drink." However, he did recognize that he was one drink away from "falling off the wagon," and so the elders in his church committed to be his accountability partners as he continued the counseling process. Continued efforts to rebuild the marriage and family relationships that had been neglected through alcohol abuse continued to be the topic of counseling. He came to future sessions more upbeat, excited about his newfound role of being a father to his daughter and a husband to his wife. When he invested time and effort into these roles, his desire for alcohol was vanquished to the degree that he had preoccupied himself with these efforts. However, it was a difficult adjustment for his wife who had been used to a home without a husband and a father. She was a little reluctant at first to share her daughter with her husband and to assume a role that accepted his presence in the home that was equivocal to her role. At times when he would be stymied in his progress by her more reluctant reactions and by his own lack of consistency, he would begin to feel depressed and was in danger of resuming relief through substance. However, he did not yield to the urge to drink by remembering the benefits of these more recent changes.

SECTION FOUR

THE HOLY SPIRIT AND HIS IMPACT ON CLINICAL PRACTICE

The Christian counselor should be a practical theologian, especially in regard to the work of the Holy Spirit and should be wise to the basic motivations related to human nature known in formal theology as theological anthropology, harmartiology, and soteriology. The role of the Holy Spirit in the counseling process should be valued and understood so that the counselor can harmonize with efforts that the Spirit initiates long before the person appears before the counselor. There has been a growing interest in "Spirit work" in recent decades. These interests in the work of the Spirit have exceeded the role of the charismatic movement that focuses on the work of Holy Spirit in an experiential sense with faith in the miraculous power and the sign gifts that God gave to those who were identified as his people of the first century church (Trask & Goodal, 1998). Some perceive the Spirit of God to be the means through which many other world religions are better able to relate to Christian theology (Yong, 2003). In this frame of thinking, pneumatology is the common denominator for the development of a more transient religious diversity. It is also, according to this thinking, understood to be the means for a renewed revival of interest in historic denominational churches that want to see

God as having a more feminine presentation through the person of Spirit (Karkkainen, 2002). In their mind, this idea makes the worship of God more inclusive and acceptable to the entire feminine and masculine church. The current non-Christian culture has also embraced spirituality that is distinct from organized religion. As Elaas (2005, 1) indicates by his opening comment quoting a common mantra of those who subscribe to this cultural perspective on spirituality, "I wouldn't call myself religious, but I'm very spiritual." He further indicates the contemporary postmodern spirituality that often disengages spiritual experience from any consequent moral behavior. However, Elaas rightly asserts that the Spirit of God and revelation of truth of scripture are intimately connected. It is just such aberrations from biblical doctrine that often obscure and misconstrue the truly valuable elements of the Spirit's work. To summarize the concepts set forth in the first chapter of this written work regarding the preconditioning of the Spirit, the convincing work of the Spirit will be evidenced in every person's life, even when the person is not responding by the acceptance of his message. Majorly, responses to the convincing work of the Holy Spirit are fraught with the natural and adaptive human response that minimizes rather than utilizes the Spirit's work. The adaptive responses of self-effacing, blame shifting, denial, and pleasure seeking generate wide-spread effects in the various personality domains of self-concept, prevalent behaviors, social interactions, and

Figure 4.0.1

Style of Relief	Pleasure-seeking	Denial	Self effacing	Blame shifting
Self concept	Helpless	Autonomous	Inferior	Justified
Social Interaction	Selfish	Shallow	Avoidant	Aggressive
Behaviors	Addictive	Rationalizing	Blaming	Controlling
Emotions	Despair	Worry	Fear	Anger

Two responses, self-effacing and blame shifting, are the accusing type of responses that involve both surrendering control to others and controlling others as a defense against being controlled. Two responses, pleasure seeking and denial, are the excusing type of responses that involve both internalizing interpersonal conflict and thus consequently developing more interpersonal conflict or likewise from inter-personal conflict developing chronic, unresolved internal conflict.

The Personality of the Holy Spirit

The most important element of this discussion is to understand that the Holy Spirit is a not an influence or an energy but a person of the trinity. The relationship between the other two persons of the trinity with the Spirit of God provides a dynamic description of the distinctive identity of the personality of the Spirit of God. Hawthorne (2003) recognizes that the Spirit is specifically the Spirit of Jesus. As he explains, while Jesus obeyed the Father he depended on the Spirit throughout every phase of his human life. Jesus did not, according to Hawthorne, rely on his own deity to enact his miraculous power, but Jesus depended on his fellow member of the trinity to enact these miraculous wonders. It is the same Spirit that Jesus then gives to his followers that enables them to live with the same presence and power of the Spirit. Walvoord (1956) recognizes that a greater number of references regarding the Spirit in scripture are in the context of the revelation of God's wisdom and knowledge. There are basically two themes that the scripture emphasizes the Spirit's work in the believer's life. They are his work of empowering and his work of giving knowledge and wisdom to the believer.

> **Asking God to fill you with all spiritual wisdom and understanding. And we pray this in order that you might live a life worthy of the Lord and may please him in every way: bearing fruit in every good work, growing in the knowledge of God, being strengthened**

with all power according to his glorious might so that you may have great endurance and patience and joyfully giving thanks to the Father. Colossians 1: 9–11

There are some in the church of today who may primarily emphasize the Spirit's power and others who primarily emphasize his wisdom. But the scriptures describe the two ministries as having one purpose. Every act of obedience must utilize the Spirit's power or every attempt to obey God's Word would ultimately turn into the hypocrisy and rebellion (Galatians 5: 16). Any attempt to grow spiritually would also require a learning experience where the disciple of the Spirit experiences a transformed mind that is encouraged both by the hope for solutions to problems and by the vision for a new direction in life. Spiritual growth is not simply the result of learning the wisdom of God alone, but it is also the result of learning from life experiences that reveals to the person his fatal defects and contrasts that personal liability to God's person of goodness and holiness as seen in Jesus Christ so that the person might be also empowered to do and be what that spiritual wisdom instructs them to be and models for that believer to enact (I Corinthians 13: 11–12, James 1:22–25).

With this idea, a concern arises concerning: what to do with counselees who are not believers in Christ. Does the Spirit have anything more than a ministry of condemnation for them? Turner (2000, 431–432) recognized the contrasting perspectives on the Spirit's work that is different in the Old Testament Judaism perspective that he called the "the Spirit of prophecy" from the New Testament Christian perspective that he noted as "the power of preaching." The latter of which was deemed as the "empowering for mission" to restore and to convince the hearer of the message. From this, there appears to be a dual purpose of the Spirit in one work. As he empowers and gives wisdom to his witnesses, he gives comfort to his people and convinces the lost of his message. Don Howell (1997, 39) of the Evangelical Missiological Society said that the apostle Paul recognized that it was the empowering presence of the Spirit "that gave this new covenant ministry its glorious character."

The Trinitarian God best illustrates the mission of God to the world as understood by how it might connect these two vastly different realms, one human and the other divine. Between the two (i.e. God and man), there is a great chasm fixed (Luke 16: 26). The Father is the standard bearer for the holiness of God who sent his Son, the heir to the throne of God, into the world to a cross instead of a throne, and the Spirit empowered him to minister to the world as a man even though he was God, but he, as a man and yet God, worked to redeem man by his death and as a mortal man was raised from the grave by the work and assistance of the Spirit. And by the enabling Spirit, he was victorious over death and was enabled by the Spirit to give the promise of his Spirit to those who believed so that God might also declare those who are sinners righteous. As in all covenanted relationships, that is, between God and man, God, in all three persons, becomes at once both the executor as well as the recipient of God's promised covenant that is readily shared with those who belong to him.

The Relevance of the Spirit's Work to the Counseling

A name given to the Spirit by Jesus himself is, in its various translations, the Counselor (NIV), the Helper (NASB), or the Comforter (KJV) that is translated from the term παρακλητοσ, anglicized as Paraclete (John 16:7). Here, his name describes his primary purpose in the Trinity, in particular to help and comfort Jesus when he was in a human form on earth. It is this Spirit that Jesus also promised and gave to those who belong to him. The Spirit not only affords to the believer the benefit of Christ's presence to guide him with counsel and help, the Spirit that he gave also gives a personal responsibility to multiply the effort that Jesus initiated. Moreover, those attuned to the Spirit are also called to conduct their spiritual responsibility, as the Spirit himself has done for them, that is essentially spiritual restoration:

Brothers, if someone is caught in a sin, you who are spiritual should restore him gently. But watch yourself, or you also may be tempted. Carry each other's burdens, and in this way, you will fulfill the law of Christ. Galatians 6:1–2

First, the term "caught" carries the nuance of those who are being trapped in their circumstances that they are unable to escape, the consequences of their own failures. The spiritual one should "restore" or mend another who is so trapped. The term καταρτιζω, translated "restore," is the same term used to describe what the disciples were doing in a physical way when Jesus found them "mending their nets." The physical task of mending nets was a good object lesson for what he intended them to do in a spiritual way in their future ministry. For he said, "Come and follow me, and I will make you fishers of men" (Matthew 4: 19). Mending carries the nuance of restoring an item for what was that item's original purpose or repairing what was broken. When considering the activity of repairing fishing nets, it is the tedious work of finding each broken strand and tying it to the unbroken other in a way that will bind the broken part to be strengthened by the unbroken part. The physical activity of mending nets carries the implication for the spiritual work of restoring that requires a careful and sometimes tedious work of tying each broken strand to the other, but the spiritual one cannot begin to repair the life of another unless he has been mended in his own life as well. The responsibility of that the spiritual one is found in carrying the burden of another who is overtaken in a fault, and by this work the spiritual one fulfills the law of Christ. The implied contrast is between law that is fulfilled by observing the collective summation of the law that says, "Love your neighbor as yourself," and the law of Christ that says that his disciples should love others in the way that Christ has loved them (Matthew 19:19 cf. John 13: 34). The intended contrast indicates that the spiritual one is to go the extra mile by loving those whose lives are broken in the manner that is most similar to way that Christ has loved those same spiritual ones whom he has already redeemed. He loved them to the extent of dying for them rather than to ascend to the throne of an earthly kingdom. Such was and is the measure of the extent to which the Christian counselor should care for those regarded as counselees. For the Christian counselor, the Holy Spirit is central to the counseling process, and the Spirit's presence in the counseling process is much like the hand inside the glove. The passage found in I Corinthians 2 presents a perspective that might support this "handing love" analogy. The passage largely radiates the truth that the believer has received the promise of Jesus, the gift of the indwelling Spirit. The chapter ends with verse 16, and the topic of the indwelling Spirit transitions to the topic of contrasting the spiritual to the carnal Christian in chapter 3. Verse 16 starts out with a quote from Isaiah 40:13 that says, "For who has known the mind of the Lord that he may instruct him?" Presumably the answer to this rhetorical question is that no one knows the mind of the Lord except for the Spirit of God, as it was previously indicated in this passage in verse. 11. However, this verse adds a postscript to the quotation, "But we have the mind of Christ." Certainly, there is some limit to what human beings, even those who have received this promise of the indwelling Spirit, will know and/ or understand. How does the Spirit reveal his counsel to mere mortal human beings? Does he roll back the clouds and write his directives in the sky? Would he offer more miraculous signals to highlight his truth to his people? This passage strongly indicates that the believer's mind is the conduit of God's revelation/illumination of truth that can make one free and help that person sustain a Christlike life and meet his most daunting of challenges to do so. As enlightening as this perspective might be, it is not altogether clear how this might work. The hand-in-glove analogy might lend some degree of clarity in how this concern might be addressed. For in the analogy, the glove may be seen to be the first responder, but without the hand or the Spirit in the glove, it would be powerless and limp to carry out its work. The hand may also purpose to work without the glove or to work bare-handed, and so the work of God is not dependent on the complete compliance and faithfulness of the glove to be present on the hand of God. But when the glove is firmly on the hand of God, the glove seems to carry out feats that are only possible for the hand of God to do and the glove experiences God's work firsthand when it is firmly placed on the hand. The Spirit is necessary and a vital part of this operation for the functioning and energizing of effective Christian living and essential to Christian counseling.

CHAPTER SIX

IMPLICATIONS FOR THEORY AND METHODS IN CLINICAL PRACTICE THE PROFESSION

Since the early days of our modern era when counseling theory was initially formulated, there has been a multitude of ideas set forth about how to conduct the task of helping people through a talk therapy format, dating back over a century of time. Since then, the avid interest of Christians who understood the benefit that could be found in learning how to counsel effectively began to set forth their own ideas for professional and pastoral counseling. This was a subsequent and late start at a venue of helping others despite the foundation found in scripture for such a means of ministry. Rather than finding their origin solely in the faith, almost all Christian counseling theories strikingly resemble historic and secular counseling theories and methods. Even when the proponent of the "Christian" counseling concept claims to be independent of such ideas, the similarity continues to exist.

Much of this distinction may be attributable to the fact that whether the person is a Christian or not, the person seeking the best information on a particular topic will certainly be rewarded for his effort based on the universal appeal of natural revelation that the Spirit brings to all of God's creation regardless of their religious or philosophical orientation. However, this universal appeal of natural revelation is still limited by the tendency of human beings to resist the acknowledgement of their personal culpability and their need to yield their life to God through Jesus Christ. Such resistance could bias the person from knowing the best perspective of what is accurately true of human beings when formulating a counseling theory. However, there are additional difficulties for human beings to be receptive to a perspective that is uniquely God's perspective, but it is by God's sovereign choice to choose that which any human being might be receptive. The proof of the best method is found in the effective practice. When the Spirit makes something that is divine known to mere mortal beings, the person is not any more intelligent or knowledgeable in an academic sense about how or what counseling method to use, but it does orient the person to be receptive to the Spirit's leadership in making wise choices as he pursues knowledge and wisdom regarding how to counsel others effectively.

Even before formal ideas of counseling practice were forwarded in the halls of academia, perspectives and ideas on personality theory were the first matter to be addressed. One major concept as ancient as any is that the clinician should understand the person and problem before applying any given counseling or therapeutic method or technique—echoes of scripture that one should not answer a matter before hearing it. Every method has its pretext related to what that given theorist believes is the major problem that human beings face before that theorist espouses any given clinical method to help. In other words, the interpretation of the person drives the selection of the method. Therefore, no practitioner should espouse a method to be used hook, line, and sinker that is based on a solitary and/or inaccurate theoretical concept or one that does not recognize comprehensively the unique ways human beings adapt, behave, and relate to themselves and to other human beings. The scriptures have indicated a basic concept of human beings long before any of these theories existed, but the scriptures also recognize the diversity of God's creatures and the variety of ways human beings adapt to their fallen human nature and to the fallen world around them. Method selection is not a rigid task to be found solely through a formal study of a variety of methods in textbooks, but it involves a careful understanding of both what the person has in common with others and what the person may possess that is unique to his personal characteristics. Each person has a unique story to tell about personal experiences that, in turn, impact that person's development of character, involving aspects of self-concept, behavior, affect, and social functioning.

Common counseling theories may have either a strong theory of personality without as much practical application in method or a strong practical application of method without out as much depth to theory. The derived spiritual formation counseling method from theology or theory should not be so simplistic that it becomes a one size-fits-all approach. It should attempt to base its ideas on scripture where the scriptures give insight into the nature of human beings and their diversity of difficulties. However, the spiritual formation theory of personality cannot simply explain human character in isolation apart from the person's relationship with his Creator and Redeemer. Scriptures do not simply help with the development of a theory of personality in this way, but there are, contained in scripture, elements that help the Christian counselor relate to how the "spiritual one" should help others that are no less applicable to counseling practice and methods. When ideas about human personality are based on spiritual formation concepts, there is just as much potential for methods to be derived from them that may be applied to everyday life as well as to counseling practice.

As the formation categories were already discussed in the previous chapters, historical counseling theories and methods will also be evaluated on this same basis in the following sections. There will be some beneficial elements of traditional theories that will survive the test of spiritual formation analysis that could be useful. Any spiritual formation counseling strategy must be understood from the people who are being counseled, viewing them through the lens of formation thinking. Many of the traditional theories and methods continue to show some resilience over time and benefits of their use because they likely share an affinity to the truth found in Christian formation thinking. Needless to say, not all of the traditional theories and methods in their entirety conform to the standards of scripture. In fact, there are very few, if any, traditional theories and methods that are practiced exclusively or comprehensively by practitioners from any given perspective. And no historic theory or even modified theory should be practiced without first assessing its applicability to the person being counseled and understanding what such an approach would mean to that person in order to maintain an ethical and effective practice, regardless of the counselor's theoretical orientation.

Counselors may differ in their theoretical orientations to counseling in several respects. There is the counselor's educational orientation—secular, religious, and variations of each. There is the counselor's ethnic orientation with all of its potential subgroups. There is also the counselor's unique personality orientation, cognitive style, and thought process. Christian Formation counseling does not eclectically embrace all orientations as an aggregate whole but provides a standard by which any given idea may find a common denominator with the principles of Christian formation. Other elements that do not richly convey a contradiction to spiritual formation doctrinaire may amount to the counselor's personal preference that may or may not be judged to be essential for practice at a later date. Effective development of practice principles that is based on sound theory will not happen if the counselor is not accepting of the challenge to strategize from a Christian formation perspective and/or is not impacted personally to believe in the sovereign care of God regarding its development. The question is, Why should one bother to evaluate traditional theories and methods? Or, Why should we just not start from scratch with a methodology that is derived from a more superior means and point of view? To answer the above question, it would be prideful to suggest that Christian counselors cannot learn from those who do not share the same faith values as evangelical Christians do, especially when these secular theorist and practitioners are spending a lifetime focused on pursuing knowledge that will enhance their ability to counsel effectively. Second, the demands placed on the counselor require that counselors, and Christian counselors in particular, be knowledgeable in every way possible because the future will demand more from the counselor's knowledge and ability rather than less. Third, if Christian counselors believe in the sovereign care of God's provision, they will also recognize that the truth of scripture will prevail against all opposition from every quarter throughout time. As an example, Freud, not at all a friend to Christianity, thought that the church represented the outworking of the superego and that the superego in the individual person enterprises repression that strangulates normal development. Instead of lastingly disproving God's work in the church, he unwittingly confirmed the truth about the sinful nature. However, he did not endorse a biblical idea about the sinful nature. To him, guilt was repressive rather than helpful to the person, and the source of guilt was merely psychological rather than spiritual in origin. Some credence to Freud's thoughts must be noted. Without the remedy of repentance and faith, guilt does negatively impact the whole of human personality, and the manner that institutionalized religion of Freud's day attempted to portray the Christian life made the church of his day seem more than just a little repressive. It is those elements of secular theory that endure the test of time and scripture (e. g. "the Word of the Lord endures forever," I Peter 1:25) that may provide some useful information for the practice of counseling even when the basis of the original theory is propositionally flawed and opposed to the truth of scripture. Lastly, any given concept must be tested against the application of the truth of scripture in the real-life situations at hand. For example, psychological research provides a greater understanding of the comprehensive effects of abuse upon the person that aligns with Jesus' reaction to those who would "offend" a child. Jesus orients his listeners to understand the serious consequences of this abuse by stating that it would be better if such an offender, long before any research on abuse was conducted, have a millstone hung around his neck and be cast into the deep. Actually, two issues are handled by this same example. One is the viability of social science research for the development of Christian counseling theory and method, and the other is preemption of the development of potential error in theory through a consideration of the applicable biblical truth. The important balance for the Christian counselor is to hold onto personal conviction while being open to learning more. The work of defining a Christian counseling theory and method is a work in progress, and the obligation of the effective Christian counselor is to follow the leadership of the Spirit in his own personal life before taking leadership in the counseling session. There may be much more in scripture that has not yet entered the understanding of the practitioner regarding its applicability to counseling theory and method. These vital perspectives may be found from a study of scriptures, and the study of scriptures is essential before any assumptions can be made about formation theory and practice—if the practitioner wants to counsel from a spiritual formation framework. However, some concepts may also be indicated or validated through other avenues of human observation, experience, and research that can open the door to a greater understanding of the scripture as well. I have often pondered on a certain passage knowing its basic interpretation, but it became more dynamic in its application as I came upon some struggle in my life or a difficulty in my practice. The light dawned (the Spirit's work of illumination) on my mind about how a particular scripture might be richly applied. In addition to this, I have often observed the echoes of these same types of discoveries may be found as scriptures when reading scientific, psychological research. The varied and sometimes contradictory conclusions made by various Christian practitioners regarding theory and practice may be the product of the varied levels of validity and bias found in the research on which they rely or in one's flawed attempts to accurately interpret and apply scripture. The scriptures themselves are, however, immutably fixed forever, and the Spirit of Christ brings greater assurance and unity to our understanding of the truth in these proposed conclusions by the continued work of the Spirit in our lives. As the scriptures themselves state, "Let God be true and every man a liar" (Romans 3:4).

Typical Theory for Affective Difficulty

Historically, Freud focused his work on attempts to psychoanalyze those suffering from anxiety, but he had little to offer the more delusional type of person in these early days of his medical intervention model. It was not until the middle of the last century that much of any of these ideas changed for clinical practice from these early ideas of Freud. The psycho-dynamic approach in its more recent evolution of Freud's original ideas has continued to be used for affective difficulty, mainly in the modified form of ideas advanced by Heinz Kohut who related to the concept of the loss of a love object (Ivey, 2006). The later psychodynamic concepts reduced the rigidity of Freud's constructs related to his ideas of the sexual instinct that, to him, was the seed to all anxiety issues. These later psychodynamic theorists searched for a more varied and dynamic way to explain human behavior (Rychlak, 1981). The church before this era supplied the village priest or parson who offered his listening ear, but a truly Christian approach to counsel parishioners was mostly left obscure in application and either relied heavily on church tradition or on the individual parson's knowledge of scriptures, employing them as he saw fit.

The most enduring concept of psychodynamic ideas is *object relations and self-psychology* based in part on Kohut's theory. It is an idea that has held wide acceptance, even among those of evangelical clinicians in various modified forms (Jones & Buttman, 1991). And it is quite understandable that a loss of a love object could be understood to have great compatibility with theological concepts of faith or even that of the anti-faith objects, such as idolatry. However, idolatry is not exactly what object relations theorists have in mind. Object relations would be applied to the person who has suffered the loss of a love object to explain his current distressing mood of the present. And who in the circumstance of mood disturbance could not relate to a past loss? However, while seemingly very relevant to human experience, this perspective does not readily address the personal culpability of a given client that is already present in the person with a mood disturbance. And psychoanalytical theories, such as object relations, are heavy on the theoretical end, but they appear to be weaker in their methodological structure for assisting the therapist/counselor to help the client find ultimate wholeness in respect to their mood. The method of object relations may be assumed to offer some form of a replacement for the loss of a love object or a relationship from the past with the current therapeutic one and with the insight that this might provide.

Later on, in the history of systems there were three principal movers of secular theory and practice that were used to help those who were considered to experience difficulties in mood, affect, and self concept—Carl Rogers, Albert Ellis, and Aaron Beck. Also, this was the era when the support group was experiencing widespread use in therapy. Pharmacotherapy has also been used to significantly reduce affective difficulty that targets the reduction of affective symptoms within the person's neurological environment more than it targets the personality dynamics involved in affective problems, thus it is typically practiced in conjunction with one of the other talk therapies involved in self-reconstruction.

1. *Carl Rogers* seemed to focus more on counseling technique than theory, but his renowned approach to therapy is not without a profound basis in theory. The summation of his theory is that the therapist should have "faith in the capacity of the individual to deal with the psychological situation" (Rogers 1951, 23). His foundational principles for counseling practice are that the counselor should possess genuineness, empathy, and unconditional positive regard for his counselees. Rogers grew up in the midwestern United States where the frontier spirit still thrived, and neighbors were trusted to help others when the need would arise. His mother was apparently an evangelical Christian. In this environment, Rogers eventually attended a seminary in New York City. At one point in his educational endeavors, he went to China on a short-term mission's trip, and from this experience he disavowed much of his religious upbringing, stating that it is untenable to believe that there

is only one way to be saved by trusting in Jesus if most of the people in China had never heard his name (Monte, 1991).

However, his *person-centered therapy* is classic to the counseling profession, and he is considered by many to be the father of the modern-day counseling movement (Monte, 1991). He left a liberal seminary and enrolled in the psychology program at New York University sometime after his trip to China. He was never satisfied with the predominate perspectives of psychoanalysis or with the clinical use of behaviorism that nearly cost him a university post to teach later in life. He finally landed at the University of Wisconsin where he pioneered the new profession of counseling. In philosophy, he was an existentialist, but not after the order of post-World War II European existentialist had a more pessimistic outlook on human nature after their experiences with Adolph Hitler. His roots in the Midwest appear to make him perhaps too optimistic, as his concepts are thought to be unworkable for those who are less intelligent, incapable of self-reflection, controlling personalities, or sociopaths (Raskin & Rogers, 2000). For Rogers, personal identity could not exist outside the social context of the person and for him a person's true self was immutable and an invariable component of therapy that is mostly accessed by the person's feelings. Everything counts on one's social environment being conducive to the expression of the true self for the person's positive development.

Specifically, his six theoretical principles are consistent with his theory (Prochaska & Norcross 1994, 129–133):

Introjection–the indulging of another's experience on self that obscures the true self from being expressed.

Projection–assuming that another's experience is the same as the experience of self—obscuring an accurate perception of others.

Subception–that feeling about what one may think is true before it is formulated into a perception.

Perception–a meaningful and accurate perspective on self and the true self in another.

Congruence–occurs when the true self is freely expressed within the social environment.

Experience–living in congruence with the true self without introjections and projections.

Rogers comprehends that the true self is deep within the clutter and debris of human existence that would shine through if the person could unload all of the barriers to its expression. Such barriers to living in the true self occur when the person is living vicariously for what others have superimposed upon the person; some barriers are also self-inflicted and others due to the insistence of others. A counselee's detection of the true self is based on little more than just a feeling or a hunch. As the hippy would say when encountering the more conventional wisdom of a matter, "I've got some bad vibes, man." This means that the hippy cannot be his true self in the environment where he encountered these contrary elements. Rogers was a big advocate of what is true in life is also true for therapy and wrote his book, On Becoming a Person (1961), for that specific purpose.

His counseling techniques involve his very basic concept of total unconditional positive regard for the person of the counselee. In general, the technique that he used is called reflective listening, and consistent with his theory, there is no need for the therapist to do anything more than to carefully listen because the therapist's task is to release an already existing capacity for competence in this individual (Prochaska & Norcross, 1994). Reflective listening involves several tasks. Not even the stronger separatists of the

Christian counseling movement can argue with Roger's ideas about reflective listening for the purposes of gathering data about the counselee. First, he set forth the practice of using open questions that was already explained in chapter two. Second, the clarification is a simple rewording of the client's statement to assure that the counselor understands what the counselee is saying and that the counselee understands that the counselor understands what the counselee is saying. A reflection continues to advance data gathering because in reflection, the counselor verbally captures the counselee's emotional expression. The use of silence supports the theoretical overtones of his theory. Rogers is extremely careful not to project the counselor's perspective or give advice to the counselee that would further obscure the true self, upholding the idea that this person has already an existing capacity for competence. He will offer interpretations to the counselee, but such interpretations must be religiously based on exactly what the counselee has previously expressed. An empathetic response is used as an encouragement to strengthen the true self in an environment of unconditional acceptance.

Reflective listening may be helpful for data-gathering methods, but the total concept lacks other significant aspects, such as the element of instruction that distinguishes Christian counseling from this secular counterpart. The level of instruction in Christian counseling, however, is not so didactic in nature as an exposition of scripture. Instead, it is woven into the fabric of the counselor/counselee exchange in a more Socratic style of instruction. This critique reveals why reflective listening alone is ineffective for the delusional and oppositional counselee. Rogers' assumption that all of the barriers are superimposed rather than inherent to the person is also erroneous precluding the need for instruction. This may also indicate that directive techniques are often more applicable to the more greatly disturbed person. Rogers' idea that the counselor should have faith in his counselees that they are capable of handling their situation would be true but mostly in those cases where it is apparent that the Spirit is successfully assisting the counselee to have this capability.

2. *Albert Ellis* espoused a theory and method that is in sharp contrast to Rogers' person-centered therapy and reflective listening because Rogers' great care to protect the true self is not so evident in *rational-emotive behavioral therapy* (REBT). Ellis believes that emotional problems directly stem from magical and empirically unvalidatable thinking (Ellis, 1980). Because in REBT the stimuli for these emotional responses are more cognitive than physical, and the responses are as much emotional as they are behavioral, REBT is understood to be a modification in the cognitive direction of the more comprehensive form of behaviorism. In direct contrast to reflective listening, REBT did not think that a warm relationship with the counselee is essential for good therapy. The simple steps to therapy are outlined and illustrated below (Prochaska & Norcross 1994, 315– 319):

Figure 4.6.1

A	Activating Cause	"My girlfriend broke up with me."
B	Irrational Belief	"This is the worst thing that could happen to me."
C	Consequent Emotions	"I am depressed."
D	Disputation	"Losing my girlfriend was hard, but I will survive!"
E	Effective new philosophy	"I feel somewhat better now."

Therapy begins with the step of disputation and the previous three steps are the simple observations that are made during the REBT style of data-gathering method. However, several problems are associated with this method. REBT minimizes the need for warm relationships when it is just such a warm relationship that the scriptures indicate, as it was discussed by the passage of Galatians 6 in the introduction to this section. Yet some loosening of the construct to maintain warm relationships invariably in counseling could free the counselor to be more natural and open with the counselee. Could not some of the elements of REBT be useful by the inclusion of warmth in counseling, as William Backus seems to propose? (Backus, 1985). This idea may be only one part of the consideration before presuming that this would take care of the matter. By changing irrational beliefs to more rational and/or biblical ones, the Christian counselor would gain a considerable advantage, but people do not merely make cognitive mistakes that set off chain reactions to enslave the whole being of the person. REBT forgets that people often repeat their cognitive mistakes even when they know they are making them. People are passionately motivated to continue to hold onto cognitions or their beliefs or misbeliefs, behaviors or misbehaviors, and/or cognitive mistakes because of what they purpose to gain from them disparaging whatever negative consequences may be comorbid to making them. They may wish to escape the more unpleasant results of these so-called cognitive mistakes, but they are no less passionately tied to the most enduring consequences of these behaviors and effects in the end. As a result of this analysis, it may be understood that there are many layers or slices to the problems that people have that need to be addressed, but within each element there may be these irrational beliefs involved that would also need to be addressed. 3.

In the middle of the last century when psychoanalysis was nearly in sole possession of the preferred ideology for clinical psychology, behaviorism was mostly confined to research psychology. Shortly after Carl Rogers presented a major shift in thinking for clinical work, behaviorism started to look for ways to make their research more applicable to clinical work as well (Dobson & Dozois, 2001). The various behavioral theorists aroused by this new direction initiated the development with a hard determinism of the stimulus response model for human personality and later theorists softened this hard determinism of behaviorism to include variables of human cognition. Behavior therapeutic approaches found an alliance with psychiatry because their model was nearly congruent with studies of human behavior as they relate to neurology and neurochemistry that also found great compatibility with psychopharmacology. In this same vein, Aaron Beck presented a cognition-to-affect theory after the order of Albert Ellis and these latter behaviorists that became known as Cognitive-Behavioral Therapy (CBT). Beck (1976) believed that people's suffering was due to their restricted perception of reality. This idea represents a significant variation to the ideas of REBT by defining in greater detail irrational beliefs and cognitive distortions and mistakes in a more dynamic way and by cataloging specific rectifications for thesedistortions (Leahy, 2003). It is used widely for a number counseling issues and special populations (Satre, et. al., 2006). Further, Beck (1976, 233–234) recognized three sources of this restricted perception of reality:

1. Sensory functions that are malfunctioning, as in the case of psychosis
2. Possible drug influences
3. Interpretations that are based on fallible cognitive functions

The last of these three sources of restricted perceptions is the main focus of Beck's discussion.

There are two main interventions for cognitive distortions that are pivotal for CBT. Beck (1976) believed that distancing distinguishes the hypothesis from the fact, indicating that the development of one's belief system is not often factually based but distorted by irrational thinking. Certainly, taking action or making conclusions based on one's perception of some significant matter before one is certain of its veracity could have devastating results if the assumptions turn out to be untrue. Decentering enables clients to disengage themselves from being the focal point of all events. This harmonizes with the previous discussion about attributional theory in chapter two. However, clients may be motivated to make themselves the focal point of all events for what they perceive to be gained from doing so as much as they are aware of the possible negative results from it. Though more sophisticated than REBT, the mistake of CBT is similar with the assumption that the basic source of one's difficulty is this restricted perception when restricted perception has a deeper root source of difficulty itself, namely the sinful nature. While CBT has a perceptive benefit in the short run, it may not always observe the deeper context of the issues. Secondly, similar to REBT, CBT uses a unidirectional, two-dimensional view of human personality and cognitive process that may not embrace the complexity of fallen human personality. Human beings develop lifestyles that are based on the passions of their hearts that involve cognitive distortions that are not always or solely the original sin for the distressed person. Beck's focus in therapy was on the cognitive process that he had labeled self-observation techniques. The benefit of this activity is to engage the counselee in a therapeutic process beyond the therapy session itself and to commit the counselee to take greater responsibility for their therapeutic process. He mentions specific types of homework assignments that may be used to continue a better cognitive process for the counselee and thus enhance the therapeutic process (1976, 270–273):

1. The graded task assignments are used to bolster the counselees flagging sense of worth by listing tasks in an order from the least difficult to the most difficult and then prioritizing the least difficult to start activity.

2. Parallel list of activities in two columns of mastery and pleasure are used to help balance the counselee's life by recognizing the possible imbalance between the two and then helping the counselee to commit to a more balanced activity.

3. Cognitive appraisal is a very basic way of self-observing one's thought-to behavior process to obtain the appropriate result.

4. Scheduling of activities helps the counselee to sort out how much activity may be possible in one day, how to prioritize these activities, recognize the purpose for such activity, and to give the counselee a sense of accomplishment rather than to feel overwhelmed by the sheer number of uncompleted responsibilities that a counselee might have.

5. Alternative therapy involves the exercise of considering what changes in cognitive process might bring to the person's life to bring about a more positive result.

6. Cognitive rehearsal involves the practice of a newly acquired cognitive set to implement that change.

7. *Homework assignments* involve a variety of specific assignments that are tailored for the person's specific needs and problems.

Many ideas may be gathered from Beck's concept related to self-observation assignments, but none are more useful than the seventh because the assignment should naturally follow the data gathered and interpretation based on those data. Beck's model has been deemed as effective for difficult personalities as for the affective distressed persons (Beck, 1991).

Positive Psychology offers a positive alternative that focuses on human assets rather than focusing on the liabilities on human cognitive dysfunction (Karwoski et.al. 2006). Self-System Therapy utilizes the setting of goals in two areas, giving balance to prevention of negative outcomes and to the achievement of positive outcomes (Vieth et. al., 2006). Emotion-Focused Therapy (EFT) presents another interesting contrast to CBT (Greenberg, 2002). EFT does what it says it does with human emotions in much in the same manner that CBT does with cognition. Rather than maladaptive cognition being at the helm of resulting emotion, EFT therapists want their clients to recognize their maladaptive emotions and institute more adaptive ones in their place. What is striking about this new wave of thinking is that it gives greater balance to both cognition and emotion that recognizes the circuitry of the brain that involves both elements in a different sequence than is clinically applied by CBT.

The core of the brain is largely responsible for placing a chemical tag on any of the thousands of items of information that travels through sensory areas of the brain on its periphery. The core area of the brain tags these items for their emotional significance that in turn are cataloged in memory from this central portion of the brain to be stored in the frontal area of the brain for the purpose of behavioral organization, planning, and the assigned personal meaning of external stimuli. The person's plan the reaction to these chemically tagged sensory items is then generated from the frontal lobe to the area posterior and adjacent to the frontal lobe and above this central portion of the brain for the purpose of activity. Furthermore, major neurotransmitters found in the brain flow in the same direction described above, suggesting that the appropriate sequence is affect-cognition meaning-behavior. In effect, the brain's organization supports the idea that primitive emotions are established prior to the higher order thought process that CBT claims to be prior to these emotions. However, the brain is not organized in a simple sequential manner as EFT may suggest but has many feedback loops therein. Therefore, EFT does not so much contradict and replace CBT completely, because CBT may act a means to evaluate the meaning of a given emotional result. Nonetheless, the organization of the brain does suggest that there are probable missing links in the evolution of both theories.

Emotion Focused Couple Therapy has been utilized for PTSD victims in several stages (Johnson, 2002. Stage one is the stabilization phase of the victim accomplished by finding a safe place. Stage two is the restructuring of bonds phase where the relationship must rebuild personal identity and potential for relationships. Stage three is the integration and consolidation phase that circumspectly works to provide the PTSD sufferer self-efficacy.

Scriptures recognize the role of cognition, behavior, and emotion in several passages such as I John 3: 19–20 and Philippians 4:4–10. John writes,

> **This then is how we know we belong to the truth, and how we set our hearts at rest in his presence whenever our hearts condemn us. For God is greater than our hearts, and he knows everything.**

The scriptures contend that EFT and CBT are incomplete as they stand because they lack for having an ultimate objective. Are emotions maladaptive if you despair over the triumph of wrongdoing and the unpopularity of right living? Is your thinking irrational if you are saddened for an indefinite period of time because your wife of twenty years has decided to leave you for another man or another woman? By what standard do we judge our emotions to be maladaptive and our belief system to lack common sense? This passage gives a spiritual focus that can help the affect-ridden person. John indicates that a person can set his own emotional goals without a complete cognitive makeover as CBT suggests. However, this also includes an affective/cognitive evaluation that is based on their knowledge of God and its relationship to affective/cognitive states. Affect and cognition are so closely linked that it is difficult to distinguish them as separate elements when they are united into the one human being. The brain's organization suggests that emotions and cognitions are more complexly systematic than sequentially related. However, these ultimate emotional goals cannot be set without the characteristic of transcendence that enables the person to think and feel a reality that is beyond the reality of his physical being or that is confined within the person's mind and emotion, a reality that can be only revealed to the person by God. As Paul writes in Philippians 4: 4–10,

> **Rejoice in the Lord always. I will say it again: Rejoice! Let your gentleness be evident to all. The Lord is near. Do not be anxious about anything, but in everything, by prayer and petition, with thanksgiving present your requests to God. And the peace of God, which transcends all understanding, will guard your hearts and minds in Christ Jesus. Finally, brothers, whatever is true, whatever is right, whatever is pure, whatever is lovely, whatever is admirable—if anything is excellent or praiseworthy—think about such things. Whatever you have learned or received or heard from me, or seen in me—put into practice. And the God of peace will be with you.**

Typical Theory for Difficult People

Several theories have been developed and designed to treat personality disorders, including the combination of various psychotherapies with pharmacotherapy. Psychodynamic therapy was the first therapy to be used for personality disorders. One such recent study has considered the use of the analytical aspects of psychodynamic therapy with the clinical treatment protocols of behaviorism (Bornstein, 2006. This study also indicated that one cluster of personality disorders is more readily helped by the psycho-dynamic approaches and that behaviorism is given a more central role for a different cluster of personality disorders. Psychodynamic therapeutic approaches are thought to be better for dependent, narcissistic, histrionic, obsessive compulsive, paranoid, and borderline personalities presumably because of the disorders' characteristic of anxiety and perceived loss. Whereas, behavioral therapeutic approaches are thought to be better for antisocial, avoidant, schizoid, and schizotypal personalities because of the characteristic cognitive distortions related to their self-concept. Aaron Beck (1991 has brought CBT to the treatment of personality disorders. The common cognitive disorders are categorized according to their respective personality disorders. The analysis of these cognitive distortions reveals that there is quantitative rather than a qualitative difference between personality-disordered people and those who are "normal." Support-expressive therapy (SE used in group therapy sessions is a blend of ideas more practically applied to the support group setting where the client is assisted to express previously forbidden emotions that have become hardened into personality characteristics. In another study, those diagnosed with obsessive-compulsive personality disorders were found to reduce symptoms more quickly than those with avoidant personality disorders using SE (Barber et. al. 1997). In regard to avoidant and obsessive-compulsive personality disorders, another empirical study indicated that depressed patients with obsessive features were helped by the interpersonal approaches and that depressed patients with avoidant features were more helped with the cognitive behavioral approaches

(Barber & Muenz, 1996). Interpersonal approaches involve helping the counselee become more competent in relationships by means of reenactment and role play to modify relationships troubled by the person's behavior and communication. Probably both interpersonal and cognitive issues are present in all of these personality diagnostic categories, but one issue may be more immediate than the other in a given person. Behaviorism has also contributed to other branches of therapeutic models such as Multimodal Therapy (MT) and Reality Therapy. These therapeutic approaches did not become as popular for use as other approaches have. CBT, MT, and Reality Therapy are worthy of mention because of their applicability to the controlling type of counselee. MT is the premier eclectic model that has something for everyone regardless of theoretical orientation, making it applicable to almost any person's orientation, such as the case with the various personality disorders. Much more, it has the flexibility to adjust to the particular forte of the counselee. At minimum, this approach recognizes that theory and methods are not a one-size-fits-all proposition, but for the therapist to make these important decisions must be based on a coherent evaluation of the counselee (Dengrove, 1972). But the theory itself lacks an absolute directive in its means to make these decisions and relies largely on the individual theorist's knowledge of these historic behavioral theories and ideas about clinical methods to decide. With the resistant counselee who would carry his penchant to be controlling in his relationships with others will no doubt attempt the same in the counseling relationship as well, MT may prevent the counseling process from going into lockdown mode by the design of the counselee's central character.

1. The MT counselor may pursue the outline of possible avenues that are listed in the acrostic BASIC I.D. However, the first step would be to carefully assess the mode that is most prevalent in the person's orientation or what mode might be used most often in crucial areas of the person's life (Lazarus 1989, 163–164):

Behavior: a focus when the counselee demonstrates a predominately learned behavioral response that is evidenced by past reinforcement.

Affect: the issue when a person has difficulty in accepting and owning his own feelings.

Sensation: a focus for the person that seeks stimulus as his most significant motivation.

Image: the issue for the person that views his circumstances as mostly reflecting his self-image.

Cognition: the focus of cognitive process regarding the need to correct the person's cognitive frame of reference

Interpersonal: the main issue when relationships are the most prominent problem.

Drugs and Biology: the focus when drugs and biology are the basic issues for the person.

None of the therapies for these various modalities take on the appearance of a historical therapy comprehensively, but there are similarities to these historical therapies when represented as one. The therapy for behavioral mode would resemble Behavior Therapy that will be covered in the last section of this chapter. The therapy for affective mode would compare closely to Rogerian reflective listening but would be less existential and more directive in nature (Friedman, 1972). The therapy for the sensation mode would tend to be similar to Behavior Therapy focused on how the person may be reinforced through this mode. The therapy for the image mode would be most similar to CBT in therapeutic practice (Brown, 1972). As well, the therapy for the cognition mode is basically a cognitive-behaviorists approach that may be exactly described as Beck's CBT. The therapy for the interpersonal mode would utilize the current family systems therapies that will be covered in the following sections (Friedman, 1972). Drugs and Biology would use the traditional drug treatment models and pharmacotherapy for biological problems and/or consider the influence of drugs upon the person's life and being.

2. Reality therapy was developed as very simple approach that was initiated by William Glasser, a psychiatrist who questioned the validity of psychoanalysis and its seemingly outlandish interpretations. As a result, he began what may be considered a no-nonsense type of approach. His theory of human personality was simply expressed—that the main problem that people face is that they use faulty attempts to control the world around them (Bassin, 1980). People are upset that they have a problem, that they have a problem they cannot solve, that they need to see a counselor to solve a problem that they cannot solve, etc. His treatment plan starts with the development of a warm relationship where the person may have the opportunity to be relaxed when conversing with the counselor to the point of the counselee being able to freely express his problem. After a relationship is established, the process begins with the total acceptance of counselee so that the counselee feels comfortable to express what they want to say. The counselor does not argue with the counselee but accepts the goal that the counselee wants to accomplish in life. As the counselee describes what he is doing to acquire his desired goal, the counselor inquires of the counselee, asking the counselee if the steps that he or she is taking is accomplishing this desired goal or effect. Based on this evaluation, a new plan might be considered as the counselee thinks through his options with the counselor's assistance. When an idea is considered to be valid, the counselor elicits a commitment from the counselee for this new plan. In the follow-up phase, the counselor challenges this person to be accountable to the counselor and to show some proof of compliance to this plan. The counselor will not waste time listening to excuses about the person's lack of compliance but asks for

a new commitment instead. Also, the counselor does not reinforce the person who uses the fear of punishment to be successful or those who continue to fail because they are content to fail (Bassin, 1980). It seems that the reality therapy approach assumes that the tragedy of human difficulty lies within that person's will-power to succeed. However, reality therapy is nearly as non-directive as reflective listening when it requires the client to be highly motivated, enabled, and intelligent to make these decisions and meet these challenges. And it appears to be as simplistic as REBT, indicating that it may not be as effective for those whose problems involve mild to severe cognitive distortion or mental confusion. However, it outlines two elements that make counseling the resistant client more effective by emphasizing the importance of gaining a commitment to implement resolution to problematic personality characteristics and holding that counselee largely responsible for the ultimate outcome of counseling.

Typical Theory for Defensive and Abused People

The defensive and abused counselees are not readily disposed to receive treatment and may identify counselors as those who may add to their sense of internal conflict and loss of autonomy by allowing the clinician to unscramble and reconstruct deeply-rooted, seemingly irreversible difficulties of highly personal nature that have been well guarded for a long time.

1. Existential theorists, such as Rollo May, Irvin Yalom, and Victor Frankl, provide some ideas that might be helpful to reduce defensiveness and help to open the doors that create an environment of openness for the person who has been heavily criticized or, at worst scenario, abused. Existentialists seek for higher meaning to life beyond the simple concrete expressions of survival and the basic needs for existence. While it is not often used for this purpose, the creeds of Christianity also attest that a human being's ultimate purpose for existence is to "glorify God" (Routley, 1962. The

psychodynamics of existentialism are elaborated in the following order: guilt, death, isolation, freedom, and meaninglessness (Corsini & Wedding, 2000. Guilt is defined as the failure to live up to one's potentials. The fear of death is the pathological effect that is the primary source to anxiety. Freedom is found in the tension between one's responsibility to procure and maintain freedom and isolation so that freedom is little more than selective bondage. Isolation is the gulf that exists between oneself and other people. Meaninglessness is the constant struggle of human beings to resist satisfaction in reaching the goal of meaning-fulness that ultimately eludes every person. Existential concepts are similar to Christian Formation concepts about human existence. But they are only true insofar as they are defined, but in their original definition they exist apart from any real hope. These concepts of existentialism are assumed to be a product of a human endeavor to strive for what seems to ultimately elude everyone. However, the existentialists do attempt to help their adherents think outside the box of human limitation. Victor Frankl, a victim of a WWII German concentration camp, observed that it was the person who recognized that he had a purpose for life outside the concentration camp that was able to survive the same exigencies that cost others their very lives. He survived such an experience himself and developed what he called logo-therapy that he wanted to replace psychotherapy, but it never did under that name (Prochaska & Norcross, 1994). He thought that the emphasis on psychology would void the reality of the person by the objective of classifying every psychological aspect of the person rather than accepting the person as a reality. He wanted to purge psychotherapy of these *psychologisms*. There is a strong application for Frankl's ideas in light of his own past experiences in the concentration camp, both to his development of theory and to its applicability to victims of abuse.

2. *Gestalt Therapy* parallels the philosophy of Kant more than it does the philosophies of Locke and Hume, and in particular it parallels the

Kantian philosophical concept of phenomenology. Phenomenology carries the idea of holism, indicating that the part is configured into the whole. Individual difficulties do not happen in isolation from other significant relationships (Prochaska & Norcross, 1994). Fritz Perls formulated his therapy to be very directive that would confront every mistake of the counselee that did not recognize these holistic ideals (Perls, 1959). The central concern of Gestalt is introjection, the same term used by Rogers but with a different effect on therapy. Subtly, introjections of significant others enter into the person's self-concept to create an inner conflict of a clinical deja vu. The language of the counselee is strictly analyzed for possible evidence of these introjections, such as the use of "should" or "must." Corrective measures are taken to maintain psychologically correct language that is oriented to "here and now" rather than "there and then." Questions are also examined that emphasize what and how rather than the "Why me?" Gestalt techniques rely on the reenactment of a significant, typical past event (Prochaska & Norcross, 1994). This may involve sculpting that sets the scene with the positioning and the assigning of verbal comments to these significant others that involve the dynamic circumstances of the past. Sculpting guides the steps to formulate the group experience of psychodrama where many others in the group play those roles assigned that are identified through sculpting. Other simpler reenactments involve the empty chair technique that involves the imagination that the empty chair is occupied by a significant to which the counselee addresses his communication (Stevens, 1980). The two-chair technique permits the counselee to continue the conversation by sitting in the empty chair to respond as the significant other would respond. Loosening involves the removal of any emotional barrier that would *prohibit the counselee from free expression of emotions related to these significant relationships. Synergy* involves therapeutic touch to relieve stress converted to a physical area of the body (Rubenfeld, 1980). Depth therapy is a group technique that has its origin with ideas forwarded by Otto Rank (Rapoport, 1980). This group technique involves members to form a womb where a given member who is in need of a new start in life is given new birth. The difficulty posed by the pure use of Gestalt is that it is a very direct style of therapy that may entrench some clients into greater defensiveness, especially the ones who are already defensive in the beginning. In the case of depth therapy, it is remarkable that the therapy recognizes the need to be born again, but there is a more effective means to accomplish that task than Gestalt seems to provide. The imaginary elements of Gestalt techniques may not be so appealing to the less abstract thinking person. However, Gestalt clearly recognizes how the intimidated, abused, and/or defensive person is stuck in the past without much realization for hope of a future. The confrontation of the irrationality of the client's behavior alone will not excise this person from these obsessive and compulsive tendencies. Christian Formation indicates a twofold response of a turning from our past practices and a turning to a new way of believing and thinking with an object of faith in the person of Christ who offers a gentle touch and a lighter load to carry (Matthew 11:28–30).

3. Eric Berne formulated Transactional Analysis (TA) that is, in keeping with its name, heavy on the assessment side and light on the method side. The analysis is of the social and family structure that is incorporated within each individual. Each person in their ego state contains five aspects: nurturing parent (NP), critical parent (CP), adult (A), adjusted child (AC), and free child (FC) that looks similar to the example found below (Prochaska & Norcross, 1994):

Figure 4.6.2

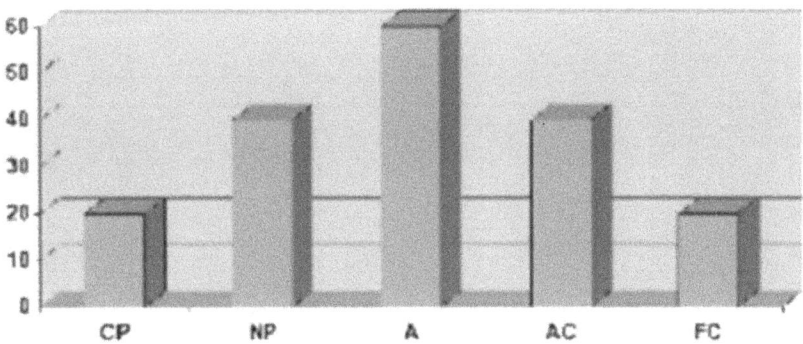

The above example would depict a normal psychologically healthy person whose CP and FC are limited in their influence while the NP and AC are greater proportionately in their ability to influence personality construction while the adult aspect is maintained at the highest possible level. TA is a pop-psychology version of Freud's original theory of structure of human personality involving the id, ego, and superego with the split of the lower and upper portions in TA. Another example, as seen below, would show the abnormal configuration of a person whose FC and CP are greater influence, even greater than the adult aspect of the person, that might represent the depressed and suicidal person whose emotional response is indicative of his position in the family from early in development that has greatly impacted this person's internalization of these interpersonal relationships:

Figure 4.6.3

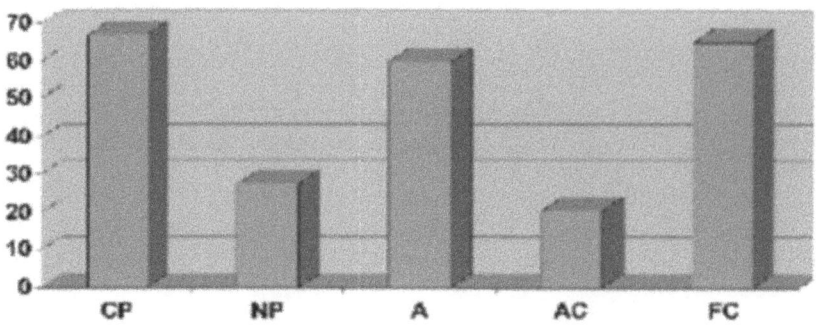

Berne (1977) also proposed ego games involve the elements of each person, parent-adult-child, to demonstrate the typical games that people play with each other. The normal interaction is where two people interact in adult-to-adult communication, described by TA as complimentary. A crossed interaction is where each person is speaking condescendingly to the other person as from parent-to-child. An ulterior interaction on the surface seems to relate matters to one another as adult-to-adult but underlying that exchange are subtle and sarcastic put downs that are not intended as more than a joke. Such as the owner of a small business might comment to his administrative assistant, "If we could get good help for this office, we might make even more profits." To which she might reply, "So when are you going to hire a new CEO!" A symbiotic interaction would tie the parent aspect of one person to the adult and child of another person. An example of the symbiotic relationship might be how the adult daughter feels obligated to stay on the phone with her mother for over an hour each day, even though her mother never listens to what she says and is afraid to confront her mother with her desire to change or limit their conversation on the phone. TA, similar to Gestalt, recognizes the human tendency to idolize relationships from the past that makes the person ineffectual in present relationships. However, TA is an entirely defensive perspective on human personality, assuming that evil is out there that presently has come inside the person. According to TA, the responsibility of the person is to keep all impersonal elements out of his own formulation of personality, but the contrasting formation thinking perspective would place greater emphasis on what might be inherently wrong inside the person and how that person should responsibly confront these problems.

4. Goulding and Goulding (1979) wrote the book entitled *Changing Lives Through Redecision Therapy.* The title almost sounds evangelical! Redecision Therapy (RDT) combines elements of Gestalt and TA. Injunctions are those statements made by significant others in the past, and the recipient of these messages is seemingly injured for life by the way that this person continues to react to this relationship long after there is no contact with the person giving these injurious remarks. An injunction is a disturbing comment from a significant other made to the person of the counselee in the past that the counselor uses an example to track the counselee's development during the assessment process. It might be the comment or the implied meaning of words of a father to his son, "You'll never amount to anything!" Scripts are the past decisions of the son to respond to those injunctions that are implied or openly stated. An impasse is a script that continues to be repeated, even when there is no direct contact with the person who gave this disturbing injunction. A first-degree impasse might be, "I'll show him, I will never stop working hard until I retire." A second-degree impasse might be, "I will not let him ruin my life, but even my recreation is so competitive that it seems like work to me." A third-degree impasse might be, "I am hopeless, and I will never amount to anything." A redecision is where therapy begins for RDT and involves therapeutic contracts that are appropriate to counter past ineffective and unrewarding *decisions, scripts,* or impasses. The strategy of RDT is appropriate for those who are intimidated, abused, and/or defensive counselees. However, it is an appropriate goal without as much means to reach that goal. The goal of countering past ineffective and unrewarding

decisions does not guide the person to know what decisions will be rewarding or effective. Most defensive and intimidated people will not be motivated to change much by the mere assertion that these past decisions are not efficacious so that the ultimate goal of RDT is not laid out in a way that causes the person to abandon old decisions and make new ones. They may feel that they need to hang on to what they have!

Typical Theory for Addicted People

While there are numerous approaches to consider for the addicted person, none have been as significantly utilized as combinations of behavioral therapy, group therapy, and family systems therapy. Cognitive impairment has also been implicated in the outcome for addictions by indicating that excessive drinking may have a better outcome by rectifying specific cognitive impairments through therapy (Bates et. al., 2006). Behavior therapy emphasizes how behavior is reinforced based on the philosophies of Locke and Hume who perceive of human beings as blank slates (tabula rasa) that learn through environmental stimuli (Rychlak, 1980). Group therapy developed with the beginning of Alcoholics Anonymous (AA) and branched out, being used in psychiatric care and also into the community as support groups for almost any distinctively different human malady that anyone could identify. Family therapy has relevance to both addictions and to the group method.

1. *Behaviorism* also has several branches of development beginning with Watson and Pavlov's concept of classical conditioning where the unconditioned stimulus (US) produces an unconditioned response (UR). When a conditioned stimulus (CS) is introduced, such as in Pavlov's experiment the rattling of buckets or the light that is turned on in the Siberian winter, it produces a conditioned response (CR) of salivation by the dog and unless salivation is not soon reinforced

with the unconditioned stimulus of food pellets in the future, the response will deteriorate (O'Donoghue & Krasner, 1995):

Figure 4.6.4

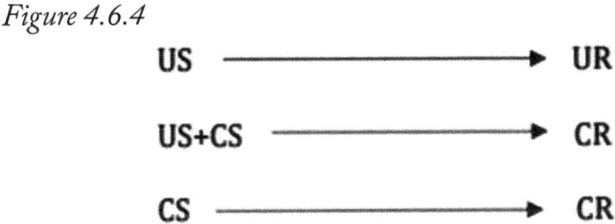

The difficulty with the continued use of the CS alone is the development of extinction of the CR, as the response deteriorates with offering the CS alone. However, behaviorists think that this phenomenon can be used to their advantage. Learning theorists have long held this approach to control child and adolescent behavior by what is known as timeout. However, timeout may only foster a sense of isolation when the child misbehaves rather than helping the child resolve those behaviors. Behaviorism also often compliments psychiatric interventions both in theory and practice. The next stage of development involved four major figures of behaviorism: Joseph Wolpe, B.F. Skinner, Stampfl, and Albert Bandura. Wolpe defined the role of the central nervous system in anxiety (Wolpe, 1973). He said that the higher cortical nervous system where thought and decision is carried out is reinforced by operant conditioning that B.F. Skinner had described in greater detail (Skinner, 1971), but the autonomic nervous system where knee-jerk responses were processed is reinforced through a classical type of conditioning. However, Bernard Brucker (1996) insists and vividly demonstrates that even reflexes can be relearned through EMG biofeedback after profound injury and a period of healing in the spinal nerves. Operant conditioning is described by the use of a different animal illustration; rather than dogs, a bear will be used to illustrate operant conditioning. The bear freely emits a response before any condition is given, such as rolling logs over to see what is underneath them. In some cases, he finds little or nothing, and in other cases he is rewarded for his effort. The bear's behavior is freely emitted and occasionally reinforced to make this behavior more rewarding for the bear. The interesting connotation related to the animal illustrations for the two types of conditioning is their inference for human personality. The dog illustration for classical conditioning infers that the environment masters the person, whereas the bear and operant conditioning infers that humanity is wild and free to prey upon his environment. This is exactly the point that Skinner (1971) makes in his seminal work, Beyond Freedom and Dignity. Trial and error learning is another way to express the concept of operant conditioning. Skinner came up with a schedule for reinforcement, fixed and variable intervals along with fixed and variable ratios (Rychlak, 1981). An example of a fixed interval would be payday to reinforce working behavior. An example of a variable interval would be the weather as reinforcement to how one clothes himself for the current weather. An example of fixed ratio would be pay based on piecework as reinforcement to working behavior. An example of variable ratio would be the gambling slot machine as reinforcement for gambling. Experiments to find which type of reinforcement schedule would rate from the most difficult to the least difficult schedule to extinguish was found to be the order listed as follows: variable ratio, variable interval, fixed ratio, and fixed interval (Silverstein et. al. 2006), with the behavior reinforced by variable ratio being the most difficult to extinguish. Logically, this makes sense because the behavior of work would cease as soon it is announced that employees will no longer be paid with this fixed interval of reinforcement while gambling behavior is not so readily extinguished and becomes addictive with its variable ratio of reinforcement. Wolpe (1973) also championed aversion therapy that was indicated by pairing of an unpleasant stimulus with a behavior that the counselee wishes to eliminate so that it might change that behavior. There is both overt aversion that uses a physical stimulus and covert aversion that uses a cognitive device, such as labeling pornography as "sugarcoated strychnine." The difficulty with this approach is that the counselee quickly becomes wise to the therapeutic conditions and avoids the conditions outside of that therapeutic setting in order to continue the behavior. If the counselee really believed that pornography was in fact sugarcoated strychnine, there might some merit in this practice, but a more comprehensive aversion to pornography would be necessary for complete change. Moreover, Wolpe (1973) recommends the use of systematic desensitization by pairing the aversive emotional state with systematic relaxation that may also have some limited value, as described in chapter two. The difficulty of systematic desensitization is that it lacks direct relevance to the source of the person's despair and subsequent addiction. A little more relevant would be the use of in vivo exposure as opposed to the former in vitro exposure. The former, in vivo exposure, is an exposure to the real-life situation and the latter would be exposure to the idea or to the imagery of the circumstance. An example of the former idea would be the practice of taking gradual steps of exposure toward a real-life experience to reduce the aversive stimulus. Related to heroin addiction, Siegel et. al. (1987) used what he called compensatory conditioning to reduce the craving that the person had for heroin by exposure to a life-like environment similar to the one where the person had used heroin. During the exposure to the lifelike environment, the person would not, of course, use heroin. This exposure would create hyperanalgesia that involved the physiological triggers of pain reduction without the use of an exogenous substance. Hyperanalgesia would extinguish craving after a period of exposure. The problem with this approach is that the inherent reason for using heroin was not addressed in these cases, namely the wartime conditions of Viet Nam.

The assertive training model is in part reflective of the self-control model found in several figures in this textbook starting with Figure 1.2 (Wolpe, 1973). It is a social interaction model that recognizes that people are on a plane where they feel like they may be treated like the doormat on one hand or that they may need to respond to that treatment with the angry defiance.

Figure 4.6.5

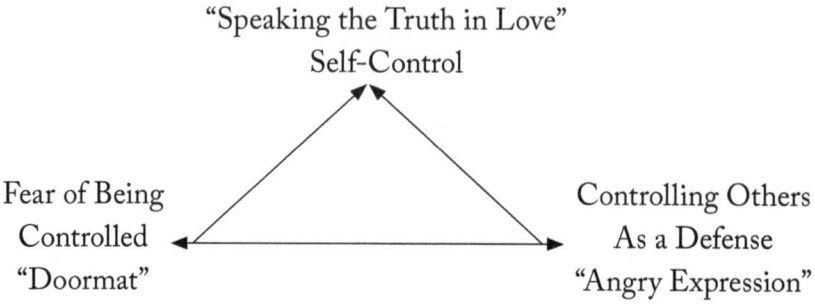

"Speaking the Truth in Love"
Self-Control

Fear of Being
Controlled
"Doormat"

Controlling Others
As a Defense
"Angry Expression"

Assertive training is a social skills management training that seeks a middle ground between the two extremes. However, to describe exact nature of this middle ground is very difficult indeed. With far greater insight, the scriptures clearly assign the better alternative that is neither to control others as a defense against the fear of domination or to become that proverbial doormat, but rather that one should be "speaking the truth in love" (Ephesians 4:15, NIV). Stampfl brought the concepts of flooding and implosion to the discussion of behaviorism. He believed that pairing aversive stimuli with relaxation was not always effective for anxiety. Instead, he proposed that either in vivo exposure or an exposure to anxiety invoking stimuli through fantasy in therapeutic conditions would reduce subsequent anxiety. While the counselee is in a safe environment, the counselor asks this person to close his eyes and imagine progressive scenes of contact with the source of the person's greatest fear. At certain points, the person is not instructed to conduct systematic relaxation, but instead these counselees are simply assured that they are in a safe place to extinguish anxiety responses. When the client is not permitted to experience the full-orbed anxiety condition, anxiety is inadvertently reinforced. This part of the technique is called flooding (Foa, 1980). The broader description of the therapy that is called implosion involves the occurrence of childhood images in the abreactive phase of flooding interpreted in the manner of psychoanalytic interpretations (Wolpe, 1973). Behaviorists themselves have recognized the dangers of the flooding technique that is very similar to psychodrama. It is not particularly difficult to achieve an abreactive response from its use, but it is not as apparent what to do with these reactions in a way that is beneficial to the client.

Albert Bandura (1986) gave some very practical ideas to behaviorism that could as well be helpful to the entire counseling effort. He integrates the standard behaviorist approaches with the consideration of human cognition. His key concept is called modeling. Indeed, it very important for the counselor to live in a manner that is conducive to the way the counselor instructs his counselees to live. Bandura indicates that learning could involve indirect contact with the stimulus, such as by the observation of another's experience. He was a strong advocate of the careful review of children's TV programming. He believed that when violence was glorified and the negative consequences of violence were not revealed or portrayed accurately, the child would naturally want to emulate these behaviors. He analyzed feedback systems in larger social context that developed ideas of learning theory known as contingency management. Carroll et. al., (2006) found that contingency management combined with CBT was more effective than CBT alone rather than CBT with motivational enhancement training for the remediation of marijuana dependence.

Traditional and cognitive behaviorism has some validity for the development of a therapeutic model for addictions as it relates to the Christian formation perspective. The scriptures indicate that behavior and cognition of the believer must consistently follow faith in order for the individual to experience what he professes to believe. This is the perspective that indicates that the complement experience to faith values a fully committed human effort to obey God's Word. That idea may seem paradoxical as the human effort to obey also believes and depends on what God can do for them rather than what the human beings can do for God because even human effort to obey is yet divinely given and provided by the promise of God (II Peter 1: 3). In application to addictions, addicted people need to understand the destructiveness of addiction in their lives and recognize their apparent motivation to abuse substance. With this knowledge, the addicted person would need a genuine change of heart and mind to resolve addiction through socio-spiritual solutions before a change of behavior can be lastingly valid. The Christian term for "heart" indicates a true commitment to change, not just a mere change in thought process. James said that the doer of the Word would be blessed in his deed, indicating that a change of heart would not be validated or really sensed by the person without an implementation of action (James 1:25). And action should not simply focus on abstinence but on constructive action to replace and rebuild their lives in a manner that resolves the life issues that instigated the addiction in the first place. However, behaviorism has varied objectives that would mostly yield to the counselees' decisions of what they would like to change without as much meaningful redirection of their goals in life in that specific spiritual formation direction. Amodeo 1995) agrees that the therapist should avoid the premature introduction of the need for immediate behavioral change, driving the substance abuser back into denial and other defenses. While the consummate resolution to addictions will involve a follow through on specific behaviors, addiction may at times be at the tip of the iceberg with other dynamic issues beneath it that may be more significant than the specific addiction itself. This is indicated by the recent rise of interest among clinicians regarding concepts of dual diagnosis. Perhaps, addictions are mostly secondary to other more personal struggles, and treatment that is focused entirely on substance reduction may be too limiting in scope to be effective.

2. *Support Groups* are the conventional method for addictions recovery in the current addiction's recovery culture, utilized in both residential and outpatient treatment protocols. It is consistent with the contention of this text that addiction is closely associated with significant failed relationships of the past. While groups by their very nature provide a forum to address the role of relational issues in addictions, it may not so specifically deal with the relational issues of the past that are closely associated with the source of the addiction and the type of addiction utilized. It is possible that the current circumstances are such that these significant relationships of the past cannot be addressed directly. Relational issues of the past may not be readily addressed because the significant persons of the past may be deceased or are too intimidating for the addicted counselee to contact directly. However, the addicted person will eventually need to do more than avoid the issue—an action that would likely result in giving more impetus to addiction. Within the general class of group methods, there are many ideas about how to conduct groups. Support groups began with addictions in mind through the concept of a New York stockbroker and an Ohio doctor who, through their own alcohol dependence, began the movement called Alcoholics Anonymous (AA). Their premise was to use the support group for those whose problems seem to be "unsolvable," adopting a medical model for addiction recovery (General Service Staff of AA 1980). It is a medical model because it proposes that the problem is virtually unsolvable from a human standpoint. It's compatibility with Christian Formation ideals is remarkable (as it has already been addressed in chapter five) because the group concept fosters a dependence on a "higher power" that some, however, might assume to be the group itself. The same connotation has been assigned to various religious sects and churches where group dependence is fostered to a cultic level in the name of spirituality. Personal responsibility may have been somewhat eroded by the emphasis with the concept of the "unsolvable" problem, and thus creating greater dependence on the group. Harry Stack Sullivan, an American

psychiatrist, was thought to be the father of American psychiatry (Rychlak, 1981). His major theoretical concept was based on the idea that pathology is largely socialized. He believed that self-concept and behavior is reinforced by one's social environment. If one is regarded to be weak, incompetent, and incapable, then people are impressed to act the part as though they are what others believe they are. The theme of his analytical group work was that members should be led to catch their true self through the guidance of the group and their leader (Goldman, 1980).

Drama therapy is also concerned about the socialization of the person, but uses various role-playing techniques (Johnson, 1980): *role reversal* is a technique that involves another group member playing the role of member on whom the approach is focused while that person plays the role of a significant other of the past, the double is a technique that involves a member of the group who plays the role of another group member as that member remains in his own role identity, the *mirror* is an imaginary technique of group members looking at themselves in the mirror and describing what they see. Moreno also developed *psychodrama* that is a more elaborate soliloquy and a form of role play where each group member has the opportunity to "confront his or her auxiliary egos" (Yablonsky, 1980). The first step of psychodrama involves positioning significant others by drawing the member's childhood family on a piece of paper that is called sculpting and then assigning the other group members to play these roles of childhood family members, positioning them in the room where they were drawn on the paper. Each member is also assigned a posture and a verbal statement that is indicative and symbolic of the relationship that these individual family members had with the group member in focus. The effect can be very emotionally disturbing for the group member in focus and this person may need to have a period of discussion that might be considered to be a follow-up debriefing. The approach can pull apart the person's long-held defenses. The nursery rhyme of poor "humpty dumpty" who had at one time sat high on the wall but in the end "all of the king's horses and all of the king's men could not put humpty dumpty back together again" might serve as a good analysis of the impact of this method. If the counselor attempts to bring a counselee to a cathartic self-reflection such as this through this or any other given method, the counselor must also be sure that it will result with a benefit for the group member and have a plan for resolving the brokenness that may result from it.

Psychoanalytic groups utilize any opportunity to identify transferences and projections of the group members (Aronson, 1980). Bio-scream group psychotherapy focuses on the analytical elements of primal emotions and the expression of such emotions that are repressed deep within the person (Saltzman, 1980). Existential groups or meta-groups would be consistent in their activity with existential therapy to assist group members in finding meaning to their lives (Smith & Smith, 1980). Group analytic utilizes a free-floating discussion as it would utilize free association in individual psychotherapy occasionally unplanned slips of the tongue to capture insight into the unconscious level of the person (Foulkes, 1980). Jungian groups use creative fantasy and dream analysis to obtain information about the universal archetypes that is the marquis for Jungian analysis that are also deemed by Jung to be the determinants of human personality (Greene, 1980). As it was formerly stated, insight alone does not always drive the therapeutic course to real change, and the insight provided by such analysis may not be consistent with the insight provided by spiritual formation principles. The greater popularity is reserved for the support group rather than the therapy group, but there is also the encounter and T-group that has been very commonly used. The "T" in T-group does not stand for "therapy" but for "training" for learning social or behavioral skills (Golembiewski & Miller 1980). Guided Group Interaction is to attempt to remove as much structure from the group as possible to promote the well-being of the group rather than the individual (Stephenson, 1980). Integrity Groups developed by Hobart Mowrer (1980) is quite oppositely posed to make the individual more responsible by taking guilt more seriously, but in other ways it is more similar to the Guided Group because it is a member-operated group. Marathon groups are so named because of their length of time that they are conducted. Sleeping and eating are optional, even though the group may last for days—usually over a weekend in time (Bach, 1980). This method attempts to break down the stamina of its members in order to work behind the person's defenses. Group work most likely provides the initial step for helping a person to develop openness about his addiction. Group approaches can be used for other diagnostic categories other than addictions to foster responsiveness to treatment paving the way for the ultimate steps of recovery. There is potential to use art and other forums that provide a neutral activity that could provide some projective personal data about the member and to help the member to be more constructive and relaxed to be more open to the therapeutic process. Yalom (1995) recognizes that group efforts are so very disarming to the person's ordinary defenses and that the individual group member is often surprised at how much and what he reveals in the various group activities, often denying that these revelations could be really true after they have been dispatched.

Yalom indicates that it is not sufficient to have such catharsis and acceptance leads to the completion of the process. However, the intimate sharing that may develop in a group setting may also unintentionally dis0parage other relationships that members have outside the group. While this may be a certain counterproductive danger while counseling a person individually as well, the level of intimacy that can develop in a group that is cohesive may be so intense that the person could escape from the realities of relationships outside the group rather than face them. Only the group and its leadership could identify this potential and attempt to rectify it. What is evident from this review of group methods is that relationships with other human beings are paramount to the treatment of addictions. The scriptures are replete with instruction and wisdom regarding how human beings can improve their relationships through the Christian Formation nuance.

3. Family Systems is another relevant approach in regard to treating addictions. Obviously, family systems have many other purposes for helping marriages and families to grow and adjust in the midst of the many possible difficulties within marriage and family that exist apart from the problem of addiction, but the focus of this section is on how seminal theories of family intervention might be helpful to understand the family member(s) with an addiction. Family assessments have been created to gain greater information on the best means of intervention for numerous clinical problems (Cook & Kenny, 2004). In the Handbook of Family Therapy, edited by Gurman and Kniskern (1981), historical family systems are outlined starting with the influence of psychoanalysis, and after that initial influence of intergenerational concepts regarding family therapy, the formal development of family systems began. The handbook outlined six domains for family systems therapies: Intergenerational View of Family Therapy, Structural Family Therapy, Strategic Approaches to Family Therapy, Functional Family Therapy, Problem-Centered Systems Family Therapy, and Integrative Family Therapy. These domains or categories embraced a wider range of specific therapies are distinguished into specific family therapies enlisted by another text Family therapy: Concepts and Methods by Michael Nichols (1984).

The first mention in Nichol's chapters on family systems therapies is Psychoanalytic Family Therapy that lays the foundation for object relations. In theory and practice applied to family therapy, the child and his mother object are centrally important to this theory. The relationship between child and mother is the context for personal identity as well as for the direction and intensity for that purpose. The early orientation provides an unconscious bent for the person's future growth and perception of others. With this idea, it would be easy to recognize the relevance of object relations to addiction as it was considered in the previous chapter. The psychoanalytic family therapists trace their origin to Bleuer's analysis of the schizophrenic's bizarre mental state as the dynamic process of early experiences (Stierlin, 1977). However, the field of family systems represents a variety of theoretical paths with some of the later theorists having roots in psychoanalytic theory. The major difference between psychoanalytic approaches and the later family theorists is that the focus of therapy is mostly on the family itself instead of the individual within. Therefore, some would not include psychoanalysis as a family "systems" therapy at all. Outside the United States, Group Family Therapy is thought to have had more influence on family therapy than either psychoanalytic theory or general systems therapy (Nichols, 1984). Group family therapy simply recognizes that families are groups and applies principles of group dynamics to families in therapy. Group cohesion eventually involves open communication so that cohesion assumes to resolve problems by encouraging greater openness among its members. The therapist takes a less directive function but is more of a facilitator for the ensuing discussion. The goal is to increase the function of communication rather than to focus on the content of the discussion and to analyze the meaning of various behaviors that occur with reference to a certain type of events and reactions during the group process. Experiential Family Therapy is based on concepts of humanistic psychology, such as Gestalt psychology (Nichols, 1984). The sculpting and psychodrama techniques described in the section of group techniques would be applied to family therapy groups. Again, the predicament of unraveling the emotions of any given person of the counselee does not necessarily reach the goal of the resolution of the addictive behavior or any other problem. Behavioral Family Therapy would apply behavioral concepts of extinction, reinforcement, shaping, etc. to family relationships, especially in the parent to child relationships (Nichols, 1984). The concept of extinction used with the use of timeout for children may have an unwelcome side effect that is not intended. As previously indicated, this may teach a child to use isolation as a means to continue poor response behaviors, and addiction does seem to thrive in a world of secrecy.

Extended Family Systems have developed largely from the work of Murray Bowen. Murray Bowen is most known for the concept of triangulation (Nichols, 1984). Another key concept is the concept of emotional fusion that involves the explanation that what one family member feels about another member is readily assumed to be the emotion that yet another member feels so that one member is triangulated in a relationship that the significant other has with that third person. *Differentiation* is the reciprocal response to this emotional fusion. The therapist would work to extract the identity of the person from these fused relationships. A common triangle would be the circumstance of a child who runs to his mother because the father has been cruel to him. The mother gives comfort to the child and intercedes with his father to protect her son. The child grows up, marries and finds the urge to be abusive to his wife so that he might have the renewed experience of having the same woman both receive his abuse and then simultaneously receive comfort from her. This concept of family therapy represents the potential for intergenerational transmission of addiction. Communications Family Therapy is based on a more anthropological and social psychology framework than on clinical theory. Gregory Bateson, an anthropologist whose study with schizophrenics and their families was funded by psychiatry, indicated that the interchange of messages given between family members determined the nature of their relationship (Nichols, 1984). Analysis and evaluation of these terms used in communication may also be used to change those relationships that may also hold the dynamic for the interdiction of addiction.

Strategic Family Therapy involves elements of brief therapy, problem-oriented, and solution-based family therapy. Jay Haley is one of the major contributors to this systems approach to family therapy (Nichols, 1984). The identified patient is not the real patient, according to this point of view. When behavioral problems arise in one member of the family, many will ask, "What is wrong with this person?" However, strategic family therapists will instead ask, "What is going on in this system of interaction that maintains this problem?" To be fair, the concept does not altogether eliminate personal responsibility, but the idea of the "identified patient" leans in the direction of family systems rather than the individual. Thus, substance abuse may be considered a family problem.

Structural Family Therapy arises from the work of Salvador Minuchin who held that the family structure related to the emotional bonds between its members (Nichols, 1984). It was a treatment designed for families in therapy that seem stuck for a lack of alternatives. Therapy is designed to unfreeze members from their former responses and interactions that have been maintained through the difficulty so that the family circumstance appears to be without remediation. Concepts of structural family therapy range in a spectrum from *disengaged* relationships with strong boundaries to that of *enmeshed* relationships with diffused boundaries and are evaluated openly with the presence of the clients. Minuchin agrees with Bowen and Haley on the conceptual relationships of triangles within families, but he believed that the therapist might triangulate with family members to produce a therapeutic result, whereas Bowen and Haley did not (Minuchin, 1974). This approach supports the concept of how helpless to change addicted people may assume that they are. The scriptures attest that family therapies have the validity by their support of the idea that individuals may be in a bondage to a family perspective on what they believe to be the truth about themselves. The passage of Exodus 20:5 indicates that the sins of the father will be visited upon future generations. And while the book of Judges records the wrongdoing of Achan whose sin of taking booty at Jericho, in direct violation to God's specific command, presumably caused the defeat at Ai, no mention of wrong-doing was recorded of his extended family that also were punished to death along with him. The question is what God understood about his family that brought this judgment upon them for his misdeed. On the other side and in support of personal responsibility, Ezekiel 18: 1–4 records the comments of people living during the time just prior to the time of final judgment on the nation of Judah. Their plea was recorded in the form of a proverb, **"The fathers have eaten sour grapes, and the children's teeth are set on edge?"** (Ezekiel 18: 2). They were worried that the impending judgment was due to what their fathers had done in regard to idol worship. Ezekiel rebukes these people to stop saying this proverb, indicating that they also bear personal responsibility for the impending judgment. The implication is that rather than personal responsibility being at odds with the responsibility of the community for others' misdeeds, the two issues are very compatible. No one should ever deny that either perspective is contrary to the other, as it may often seem. It was Paul the apostle who challenged a Corinthian man who chose to live with his father's former wife to take responsibility for his transgression and change his ways, while at the same time he also rebuked the church for not recognizing the transgression in their midst as a signal to at least grieve over this horrible circumstance in their church.

CHAPTER SEVEN

THE ULTIMATE OBJECTIVE

Modern day methods and theories are subjected to rigorous training in theory and methods and lengthy internships to deal with the biological and psychological mechanisms that present the person as having some personal abnormality and/or grave difficulty in his most of their intimate relationships. Although the information produced from the research in abnormal psychology is very useful, they implicate interventions without a well-defined alternative objective for what might be considered normal. Normality as a modern concept has lost its way. Posing the question, "What does a fully functioning adult human being look like?" most consider normality as a relative concept—relative to what any one given person thinks normality is—and to follow this trend of thinking, abnormality may be considered to be simply anything that the person is unwilling to endure or what others are not willing to endure in another person. However, without a true goal or target for what is considered to be the best outcome for the helping process, how can anyone in the clinical profession really effectively help anyone? The model illustrated in chapter one that relates the coping strategies that one uses to minimize the work of Spirit, namely blame shifting, self effacing, denial, and pleasure seeking, can be extended to show the way that one might be fully impacted and changed by the Spirit's work without minimizing his work. This response or strategy would also show the characteristics of the "spiritual person" that would complete the model for the ultimate spiritual formation outcome that would also provide some insight into what should be the ultimate objective in the counseling relationship.

Figure 4.7.1

(A bonafide) Style of Relieving Guilt and Conviction	Repentance and Faith (as opposed to denial, blame-shifting and etc.)
Self-Concept	Forgiven (as opposed to other methods of self-justification)
Social Interaction	Caring about others before self
Predominant Behavior	Giving sacrificially out of a full contentment with life
Primary Emotions	Fruit of the Holy Spirit as described in Galatians 5:22-24

Before explaining the ultimate characteristics that would be the ultimate goal of Christian formation counseling, it would be wise to speak of the means that would be used to reach that goal. Repentance and faith have been much trivialized by the world around us. Repentance is often viewed as an escape route that one might use when he is caught in one of life's most embarrassing moments. Faith is often viewed as the avoidance of taking responsibility for one's mistakes and without a realistic plan to change one's future behavior. These perspectives may be the result of not knowing the true object of faith, Jesus Christ, or how repentance or faith cannot be experienced—one without the other. Ultimately, the true nature of repentance and faith cannot be understood without their objective of justification, and justification is not justifying one before others or before the church, but it is the justifying of one before a holy God. Justification has been another source of great discussion and controversy in its relationship to repentance and faith. It is important to recognize that these ultimate objectives for self-concept, social interaction, behavior, and emotion of the spiritual formation outcome cannot be exactly attained or accomplished in this life of a human being because human beings as sinful creatures ultimately fail to achieve such perfection. This is perhaps why many do not even attempt to improve and react to this perception of this need by living for as much self-gratification as they can consume or by living in denial that one needs to be motivated to achieve these ideals. The balance of the two ideas is to live in a tension between what the person obviously perceives to be true of self and what the person aspires to become. Faith, like joy, provides the energy for human beings to believe that they do not need to default with the presumption of abject condemnation when they are challenged by the Spirit to identify their nature for making mistakes, committing grievous offenses, and possessing specific shortcomings. And righteously living is not a benefit that people bestow in service to God, but it is an opportunity for human beings to experience their ultimate capacity to live as God's perfect creation. It is, after all, the **"broken and contrite heart"** that God will not despise (Psalm 51: 17). Theologically, justification and sanctification have been distinguished from each other by the understanding that justification is an imputed righteousness, where sanctification is a process of achieving greater consistency in righteous living (McCormick, 2000). Some present-day liberal theologians would like to completely disparage the need for personal justification from their theology (McGrath, 2005). Contrary to this thinking, Lovelace (1979) indicated that sanctification and justification are nearly identical in their means and end so that the goal for justification and forgiveness is ultimately to improve one's personal functioning in life. By this spiritual formation ideal, the Spirit may continue the work of sanctification in human beings by the same means and end that starts with justification. Many object to the idea of any association being made between sin and the person's struggles in life (Lovelace, 1979), such as the struggles that counselees often present in counseling. This is, perhaps, the thinking that sees sin as an intentional act to commit some wrong, which it is, but this concept of sin is a very narrow view of sin and a view that may obscure a more complete understanding of sin, making this view a very wrong view of sin in the end. Sin is the common denominator of human existence, a circumstance for all people who are already separated from God, but sin also places human beings in a tension between having an understanding of their shortcoming on some level and yet creating in them a desire to have a greater fellowship with God and to achieve a higher ideal for their lives on the other (Zacharias, 1998). On the other side of these matters, some may think rigidly that one's personally committed sins are the source to every particular malady. Contrary to this presumption, a committed sin is the evidence of human pathology, but a committed sin may only coexist through and in reaction to one's personal struggles. However, helping others involves placing the person who is struggling in a position to be empowered in their mind and motivation and to bring about the activity that may resolve these struggles. Job's sufferings did not find their source in his own personal sin, but God did answer his complaint about his suffering with a rebuke. God did so rebuke him so that he could resolve his sense of misunderstanding about God's relationship with him in the midst of his suffering and from this idea ease his sense of suffering as well (Sproul, 1988). In a sense, Job did not sin so that he suffered, but when he suffered, he was tempted to sin. This is likely the case with many counselees. Likewise, the man who was born blind did not cause his blindness by any particular sinful act nor was it caused by his parent's particular sin, but Jesus explained that his blindness from birth had occurred to show the great work of God in him. Jesus took this example of physical blindness to show how spiritual blindness could also be used to reveal his presence and power in this person's life.

A sense of exasperation grows within when human beings consider seriously what God wants and expects of them. That is a very common human response, but when one realizes the truth of II Peter1: 3–8, another response is made possible. The passage starts out by stating,

"His divine power has given everything that we need for life and godliness through our knowledge of him."

Through his provision, the believer has opportunity to acquire the aspired to "divine nature" (verse 4). The divine nature may be synonymous with the previously expressed, "fully functioning human being" as God created that person to function. What is this "divine nature" in Peter's words? Fortunately, he enlists the virtues that describe this divine nature in the following verse:

> For this very reason, make every effort to add to your faith goodness; and to goodness, knowledge; and to knowledge, self-control; and to self-control, perseverance; and to perseverance, godliness; and to godliness, brotherly kindness; and to brotherly kindness, love.

The list of virtues that describes the fully functioning human being involves three categories. Faith, goodness, and knowledge are the virtues that are essential for beginning to live as a fully functioning human being. He asserts the idea that faith empowers the believer's motivation to hope and believe in the efficacious promise of God that will enable the person to attain the unattainable path to righteous living. To be forgiven and filled with goodness is one thing, but the virtue of goodness is also the means to accomplish genuine acts of goodness that are acts motivated more out of gratitude and the freedom to act without the bondage of the obligation to act. Knowledge is also significant to normal formation in terms of the type of information being conveyed—recognizing that attempts to help oneself directly only tend to recoil in the opposite direction of the futile attempts to a self-focused righteousness. Knowing Christ intimately enables the adherent to acquire an unselfish attitude and behavior because the Savior takes the burden of self away from its bearer. Self-control, perseverance, and godliness are the virtues that are *necessary for living optimally under stress*. Self-control is optimal for living in control of one's mind, will, and emotion rather than becoming the stimulus response animal to one's environmental stressors. Perseverance is the ability to live with a positive faith by prevailing with acts of kindness, even when there is no apparent relief to the continued distress. Godliness is ability to see matters in the adherent's life from God's perspective, even when the human senses related to stress are contrary to that perspective. Brotherly kindness and love are the virtues necessary to conduct strong, fulfilling relationships. Brotherly kindness is the virtue of sensitivity to others' needs and concerns without being critical of their shortcomings and offenses. Love is a sacrificial act that loves in a manner that is not as much concerned about how much one is being loved by others but more about how much one loves others. The virtue of love considers loving others as his first priority above being loved by others. Human beings are made in the image of God, but that image has been tarnished and corrupted by each person's separation from God. Christ, as the Word of God, bears the **"life"** in his being according to John 1:4, and Ephesians 2:1 indicates the Spirit gave this "life" to his followers, after Jesus had long left his earthly counterparts that were deemed to be spiritually dead previous to this act. However, John 1:4 also indicates that this spiritual "life" that Jesus possessed was a **"light to men."** Interesting, the very word that is translated **"Spirit,"** or Πνευμα, is the word for "breath of life," suggesting the very life that was breathed into Adam at creation was the work of the Spirit of God (see Genesis 2: 7). From this idea and other evidence, the person of Jesus is understood to have universal appeal. He is not just a remote figure from a bygone era in a remote part of the world, but he is the aspiration of all of the various cultures of world for spiritual vitality, his inherent quality of **"life"** that is still disseminated by his Spirit to the believer, and he is also the universal **"light"** to all people who remain spiritually dead. In the person of Jesus, life is the ultimate objective for human life as Hebrews 1: 3 attests that he is the "exact representation" of God's person in the flesh, God's Son. It, then, follows that he should serve as the ultimate model of a fully functioning human being as God intended for human beings to function.

The Ultimate Self-Concept

As renewed image bearers of Christ, the ultimate profile that would be a light to every human being is of one who does not accede to the common aspiration of achieving some superhuman status. It is, rather, the self-appraisal of having worth that is based on God's forgiveness. The fully functioning human being should be one that regards oneself as a servant that is consistent with the model of Christ. Jesus said the, **"Son of Man did not come to be served, but to serve and give his life a ransom for many"** (Mark 10: 45). As he was called to pay the ultimate sacrifice for others, he admonishes his disciples to be servants who are no greater than their master—to suffer the same rejection that he had suffered in this world (John 15: 20–21). James also promises a **"crown of life"** to those who persevere under such circumstances (James 1: 12). The general and basic principle of life that Jesus gave was not given so that his followers might glorify themselves in their suffering as though there was some masochistic virtue in this accomplishment, but this major concept was conveyed to set his people apart from the evil that is already present in them and in the world. People in the world are not so wary of the evil that is in the world until the **"light"** dawns in their spiritual being that enlightens and enlivens them spiritually. The true purpose for spiritual awakening is not to produce a negative self-concept by making them more aware of evil within self as much as it is to give the person hope for changing those more troubling aspects of their human condition. Without spiritual formation, the average person would not even like to acknowledge this inner condition, let alone understand it. Paradoxically, with the guilt that is produced from conviction, the adherent to faith finds greater and greater security that does not come from a confidence welling up within self but comes from the security of a relationship with God. One very basic principle of Christian formation that is aligned with the previous one is the principle of other-centeredness. The principle that was taught by Jesus is found in several places in the Gospels and is utilized more specifically by Paul in passages like I Corinthians 7: 3–4 and Philippians 2: 1–5.

Mathew 10: 39 records Jesus' words, **"Whoever finds his life loses it, and whoever loses his life for my sake finds it."** One implication found in this passage is related to the condition of basic human motivation. They are found to be searching for something that would lead to their ultimate satisfaction for self, which goal ultimately eludes the person of this motivation. Self-satisfaction is the principle motivational paradox or oxymoron. To live completely for self is a hollow victory and does not assimilate into the model of Christ. However, when people are hurting or desperate for satisfaction, they become all the more self-interested and self-focused by its shear inertia. This describes the futility of the human motivational condition. On the other hand, Jesus instructed his followers to lose their lives in order to find it. Earlier in the book of Matthew, Jesus instructed them to give without an ulterior motive of what might be given in return as much as they should give appropriately to needy persons in a private manner. He added that one should not let the right hand know what the left hand is doing (Matthew 6: 2–3), so that one's motivation to give might not appear to be for one's self-gratification and the warning is for a person to not so cunningly devise giving as to fool others into thinking that it is an unselfish act when it is not.

What would one find by losing one's life? A whole new world awaits the person who can be relieved of the burden to satisfy self. It is a life that can afford to any person the ability to see others clearly and to have the priority of a concern for and profound insight into others that would ordinarily be blocked by pressing personal needs of self. And because of these pressing needs to satisfy self, the person's desire for God and spiritual life would also be often circumvented and replaced with inadequate objects of faith, known in scripture as idols. How can one be so content that he is not driven by personal needs to satisfy self? The potential to be able to lose one's self is found through the means of being completely comforted and consoled by the Spirit's presence in one's life. The Spirit intimately connects the life quality that he gave to Jesus and gives that spiritual life to those who follow him. It is like the man who was born blind who could only attest that he was once blind and that now he sees. He knew of no feat or trickery of his own that procured such a glorious result other than his contact and compliance with Jesus' miraculous work.

The Ultimate Behavior

The natural outgrowth of the ultimate self-concept of the identity of a servant is to be other-centered in relationships and is the concomitant behavior that advocates much more giving than consuming from others. The ultimate functioning of human beings must not only imitate Christ in his self-concept but also in his behavior (Ephesians 5: 1–4). There are many descriptions in scripture about what this imitation does not mean and many descriptions about what this imitation does mean. Outside of specific activities that one should avoid seems obvious, the scriptures also describe the general propensity and motivation behind worldly activities that the imitator tor should avoid. Ephesians 2: 1–2 reads,

> *As for you, you were dead in your transgressions and sins*
> *in which you used to live when you followed the ways of*
> *this world and of the ruler of the kingdom of the air, the*
> *spirit that now works in the children of disobedience.*

The contrast here is between that of following the spirit of this world and the Spirit of God. The ultimate deception noted in this passage indicates that those who follow this course of the world do so because they are following this course in life in an anti-spiritual manner. They are religiously engaged in an activity that they suppose might be based on their own desire to follow the right course when they are actually captivated by forces that they do not realize are in charge and engage them to do things that they never conceived to do on their own. Also, the spirit of this world acts as a counterpart to true religion so that they are not just acting independently but fall in compliance with these other spiritual forces that are not from God. John announces that believers also face opposition to their faith in the trilogy of the world's assault by the cravings of sinful man, the lust of the eyes, and the pride of life (I John 2: 16). Cornelius Plantinga (1995, 56–57) recognizes this corruption progresses and infects every human being,

> ...psychological explanations of family violence often focus on the dynamics of precedent and imitation within family systems or in character disorders of arbitrary and domineering parents. Sociological interpretations, on the other hand, focus on such factors as poverty, ignorance, class and racial status, and powerlessness— factors that may dangerously raise the family's stress level. The predictable truth is that people living sorry lives often hate their lives, and people who hate their lives often hate the most intimate reminders of their lives, including their parents and their children.

In contrast to this line of thought, the activity of following the Spirit of God involves a similar circumstance but a propensity in another direction. And instead of deception being the means to direct the course of the person's life, it is the influence of the Spirit that sheds light on the path to this ultimate activity. The Psalmist declares, **"Your word is a lamp unto my feet and a light unto my path"** (Psalm 119: 105). The activities of those who follow the Spirit are those who **"live in accordance with the Spirit"** so termed by Paul (Romans 8: 5). Further, he establishes that the only means to be compliant with God's law is to be spiritually minded, producing life and peace. In contrast to this, the carnal mind is a "slave to fear" (Romans 8: 15). The by-product of living in accordance with the Spirit is that each person may truly engage in taking full possession of his own will and behavior. Philippians 2:13 so informs, **"It is God who works in you to will and to act according to his own purpose."**

Behavior is also more appropriately activated and motivated when the person lives in the Spirit. The first impulse of human beings when challenged to be good and righteous is to do something to become a good person. In contrast, John admonishes, **"Dear children do not let anyone lead you astray. He who does what is right is righteous, just as he is righteous,"**(I John 3: 7). In other words, directing one's behavior in the appropriate manner does not make one a good person, but only when that person has a solid foundation in righteousness will the person give evidence of righteousness by his behavior. As well, any good effort that is attempted should have its own inherent rationale for its attempt. One motivated to achieve or prove personal goodness or virtue by sponsoring such initiatives may be blinded to the true nature of its benefit. John Piper (1986, 93) confirms, "One thing is for sure: Love cannot be equated with any action!" Piper does not think action is unnecessary for love's expression, but defies the idea that the love's full expression is found in the act of love without impacting the whole heart of the person who "loves" another or without having a total and unselfish focus on the person whom that person loves. This last comment will serve to introduce the next section.

CHAPTER EIGHT

THE ULTIMATE RELATIONSHIPS

Difficult and broken relationships are the type of malady that counselors often encounter in their counseling practices. While their counselees often complain of the unfairness, inequity, and the inadequacy of their relationships, their travail is often focused on how their own expectations have not been unfulfilled in these relationships. It is not that their disappointments are illegitimate or that their anguish is without a genuine cause, but their focus is often one-sided and out of sequence for what would produce a foundation on which to build those relationships. Philippians 2 is a key passage that, in principle, gives greater validity to this notion in the way that counselees typically process and analyze their troubled relationships and suffer from a lack of other-centeredness that would really provide the help that is needed in these difficult situations. Paul starts out in chapter 2 by using four first-class conditional clauses that indicate the personal criteria essential for building strong relationships. These conditional clauses serve as the gate through which one must pass so that the person may also apply the criteria of the main clause. Specifically in verse 1, he says, **"If you have any encouragement from being united with Christ, if any comfort of his love, if any fellowship with the Spirit, if any tenderness and compassion."** So, if a person meets the ultimate level of the conditions above, then the following statements in verse 2 would also apply or be made possible, **"Then make my joy complete by being likeminded, having the same love, being one in the spirit and purpose."** Verse 2 sounds way too ideal or even a bit naïve for many of the relational circumstances that counselors may encounter in their counselees. Before one assumes that this may not apply richly to couples or family members in counseling, continue to read verses 3 through 5.

> *Do nothing out selfish ambition or vain conceit, but in humility consider others better than yourselves. Each of you should look not only to you own interests, but also to the interests of others. Your attitude should be the same as that of Christ Jesus.*

In review of what has been already covered in previous sections of this chapter, several themes are found in this ideal for ultimate relationships that may help in the circumstances where relationships are more troubling. The potential for being so unselfish and other centered is enhanced by meeting the criteria of these four first-class conditions. The offended party in relationships whose disappointments are grave may take comfort and refuge in what they have in their relationship with Christ. Typically, partners in marriage are distressed about their commitment to a person who may not or will not reciprocate the same affection that they have given and therefore they might feel "ripped off." But in a relationship with Christ, the offer to love someone does not carry the same stigma of the ordinary unrequited love. When the person meets the criteria of these conditions stated in verse 1, the source and supply of love and what love this person is able to give to the other does not come from the prospect of the other's reciprocal act but comes from the fellowship of the Spirit and is therefore endless in supply. In another passage, Paul states, **"God has poured out his love in our hearts by the Holy Spirit, whom he has given to us"** (Romans 5: 5). Further, the order of a partner's relationship analysis is also reversed on this basis. Instead of distressing over how little the other reciprocates love or how much the other offends as the first priority to analysis, the concerned and distressed person relies on the almighty God to supply the necessary affection to proceed forward to a reconciliation with the other who loves so little. The flower petal study of "She loves me! She loves me not!" is placed on hold until there is a complete self-analysis of how much he loves the other first. This provides a break from feeling so victimized long enough to understand the other partner more objectively by placing the other's interests before your own. Ultimately, this process is incomplete until one accedes to the example of Christ. And how did he love us? It is clear that he did not exercise his thoughts about how unfaithful, disobedient, and unkind the world was toward him in order to derive a sense of affection for them. Instead, he glorified his father in heaven and derived his affection for the world from a relationship above, even as those in this world mocked him when he died on a cross for them.

The Ultimate Affect

Developing this ultimate self-concept, ultimate behavior, and ultimate relationships would advance the person to prospect of developing the ultimate affect. The first question to be asked, "Is the category 'ultimate affects' or 'the ultimate affect'?" With the multiplicity of emotional experiences, one might assume that the category should reflect the former rather than the latter heading. Just as each tree may bear a different fruit so each person may bear a different affect. But the emotions also represent a composite set of emotions that have dynamic relationships with each other. Anxiety and anger have a clinical relationship when observing those who become seriously agitated from an anxiety condition. Stress levels during serious anxiety often create a short fuse for anger to erupt more quickly. Anger and depression also have been closely associated, especially with bipolar depression. Antidepressant medications are often used for both conditions when in that clinical range. The ultimate affect also has many levels and aspects that are interrelated. The best summary of the ultimate affect is found in Galatians 5: 22–24.

But the fruit of the Spirit is love, joy, peace, patience, kindness, goodness, faithfulness, gentleness, and self-control, against such things there is no law. Those who belong to Jesus Christ have crucified the sinful nature with its passions and desires.

There are multiple aspects but only one tree on which this fruit may be found. The context of this passage is very important when attempting to understand how one might attain this ultimate affect. The letter that Paul sent to the Galatian churches had one overriding purpose that is clearly stated in the first chapter: **"I am astonished that you are so quickly deserting the one who called you by the grace of Christ and are turning to a different gospel—which is really no gospel at all"** (Galatians 1: 6–7a). Paul is writing about the teaching of some Jewish believers in Christ who were not content with salvation by believing in Christ alone and went from church to church, teaching that the believer should also keep certain aspects of the law to complete their salvation experience. Paul indicates that to do so would nullify the gospel message altogether. In his mind, faith plus the grace of Christ equals the gospel and faith plus the works of the law equals nothing. Surely there would be some merit in adding a good effort in keeping the law to faith in Christ, but not in the way that these teachers were going about it. They were at least inferring that one needed to consolidate personal merit for the award of salvation through their own personal efforts, thus nullifying the merit of Christ's efficacious act on the cross.

What does this have to do with the fruit of the Spirit? First and foremost, one cannot attain fruitfulness by trying to gain it through personal effort. When one reads that the fruit of the Spirit involves **"patience,"** should one attempt to try to be more patient as his primary method of gaining fruitfulness? To do so would be to turn the purpose of this book of Galatians on its head! Certainly, the objective of fruitfulness (the enlisted elements of Galatians 5: 22–23) should be understood in order to know what is the goal to be reached. Other than that, the appropriate manner in which one should utilize the profile of fruitfulness is found by using the list of fruit mentioned here as a litmus test. When anyone of these elements are missing from one's personality profile, the follower may be sure that something is out of focus in regard to his direction in life and relationship with Christ. It is a more pleasant way of keeping his followers on the task of measuring their devotion to him. Try to be more loving and it backfires. Try to become gentler, and it becomes more irritating. But when fruitfulness is not apparent, the follower needs not to take any further inventory or develop any greater introspection than to look at his relationship with Christ. This is the work of the Spirit and not a human work to create because a reliance on the Spirit produces the fruit of the Spirit most definitely.

CHAPTER NINE

SUMMARY AND CONCLUSION

The model that has been described above is based on the proposition of scripture that the Spirit sufficiently convinces everyone in the world of their very own personal need with respect to their ultimate self-concept, social relationship, behavior and affect that was exemplified in the person of Jesus Christ. Evidence of this work is seen in the contrasting examples of human beings that typically adapt to this convicting message, issuing responses of denial, pleasure seeking, self-criticism, and blame-shifting. The Spirit also empowered Jesus Christ to be and to do supernatural works evidenced by his miraculous birth, through his life, with his miracles, during his death, and in his resurrection even though Jesus had his own miraculous powers to perform these same acts and to do whatever feats he desired to do by himself. Instead, Jesus limited the expression of his divine attributes and relied on the Spirit to accomplish these works. For this reason, the Spirit is also named the Spirit of Christ. Based on the work of Christ, this same Spirit gives his life-giving form to the church initially at Pentecost after Jesus' resurrection. Thereafter, this gift of spiritual life is given (to those who believe in him) in a new and different way from the way he had already given life to the human race at creation.

The Spirit is able to find his way into the life of fallen human beings to whom, by Jesus' authority, were given his Spirit to make possible the impossible. The Spirit prepares these human beings to understand what God would want them to understand, to believe what they cannot see, and to develop a spiritual life that does not rely solely on human senses but paradoxically works through these same human senses. Even when the person is not compliant or is otherwise separated from this spiritual life, the Spirit has an immeasurable impact on the outcome of the lives of these human beings as well. His work accounts for much of what is seen in everyone's self-concept, social interaction, behavior, affect, and motivation whether or not they have acknowledged him as the standard bearer of this ultimate life exemplified by Christ. The Spirit does not work outside of the day today experiences as if he would have us live only in blissful realms of heavenly joy, but instead he works in and through the awful experiences of human existence. As J.I. Packer (1973, 221) had indicated, some misapply the purpose of the Spirit's work:

A certain type of the ministry of the gospel is cruel. It does not mean to be, but it is. It means to magnify grace, but what it does is rather the opposite. It scales down the problem of sin, and loses touch with the purpose of God. The effect is twofold: first to depict the work of grace as less than it really is; second, to leave people with a gospel that is not big enough to cover the whole area of their need.

Theories, models, and methods that do not account for Christian Formation perspectives are not so much completely wrong as they are incomplete. Many valuable ideas may be gained from a study of these ideas and especially as they are developed from a truly unbiased scientific research. The concepts and models of chapter 1 through chapter 5 are combined below to account for the entire spectrum of the potential responses of human beings based on these spiritual formation perspectives.

Figure 4.8.1

Style of Guilt Relief	Pleasure seeking	Denial	Self-effacing	Blame shifting	Repentance and faith
Self-concept	Helpless	Autonomous	Inferior	Justified	Forgiven
Social Interaction	Selfish	Shallow	Avoidant	Aggressive	Caring
Behavior	Addictive	Rationalizing	Blaming	Controlling	Giving
Primary Affect	Despair	Worry	Fear	Anger	Fruit of the Spirit

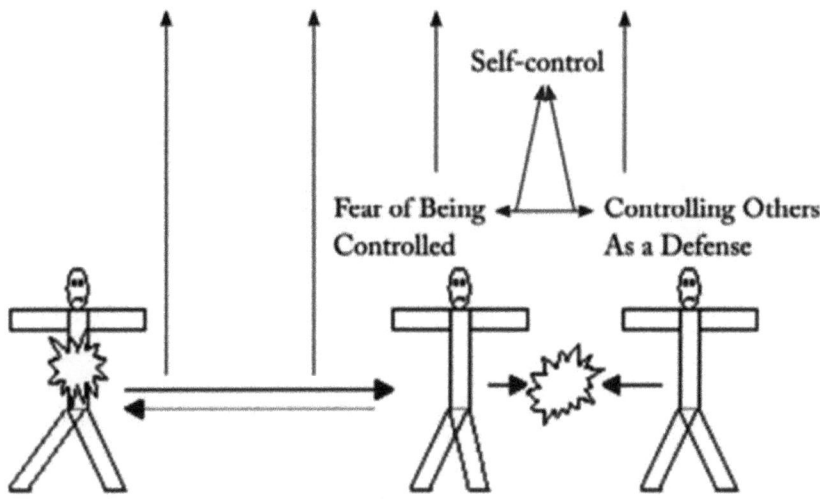

Pleasure seekers will mostly internalize conflict by forcing pleasurable stimuli into their lives regardless of the consequences for doing so. They attempt to overwhelm their sense of culpability with pleasurable stimuli, but this will only shatter their lives further for their attempt. Those who use denial attempt to use mind control to avoid the consequences or to stand for what they believe to be true by blocking their conscience mind from comprehending the reality of guilt in their lives and thus fail to take full responsibility for their own lives. Theirs is the tragedy of an unlived life. Self-effacing responders are the major source of the affective difficulties that are observed in clinical care. While they are most concerned with finding the person or persons who might be blamed for their most significant problems in life, their reason for not having control of their lives is that they highly suspect that they are mostly responsible for this unpleasant outcome. However, they are often afraid to acknowledge this openly. Blame shifters are very similar to the self-effacing responders because they also are concerned with blame, but they are determined to resist any such assertion to themselves by preempting this fear with a more-angry response to their circumstance. They magnify the faults of others, perceiving others as attempting to control them to justify their own aggression upon others. Those who adhere to the conviction of the Spirit are led by the same Spirit to believe in Christ because the Spirit is the Spirit of Christ. They do not need to remove every sense of culpability because they have found contentment and peace with the identity of needing constant forgiveness. Their knowledge of God's grace overshadows their guilt so that they have gained the basic resource of being other-centered and can also afford to care for others more than they care for themselves. However, by caring for others in a spiritual way, they do more than adequately care for another; they also find a better life for themselves.

ENDNOTES

Chapter One

1   The brain is organized in such a way that it gives values to certain sensory input received through sight, sound, touch, taste, and smell and then directs this input to midsection of the brain for labeling stimuli regarding their respective meaning. The brain is bombarded with thousands, if not millions, of particular sensory stimuli every waking minute. The midbrain, where short-term memory is stored, is also the area of the brain where certain stimuli receive a chemical tag that tells the brain where this input should be stored and how these stimuli should be used or perceived. It is eventually channeled to the frontal lobe for complex thought for what is called the executive functions of thinking and planning. The frontal lobe also carries other higher cortical functions, such as identifying what makes us feel good and what makes us feel bad or what is important and what is unimportant to us. Most of the sensory input received does not consolidate with long-term memory. It is a good thing that not all sensory input stimuli consolidate with long-term processing because the brain would be overloaded, unable to function, and would be unable to distinguish the significant parts of input received.

2   There are a number of theology texts that dispense a description of natural revelation that is traditional in nature: Chafer (1947) indicates that the source of natural revelation is mainly creation for the purpose of making man responsible for their spiritual state, whether or not any particular person is at all familiar with the

gospel message. The message of natural revelation is indistinct in its message, according to Chafer, so that any further distinction must wait for an understanding that can only be generated from the explanation of scripture. Berkhof (1941) indicates that the Reformers did not believe as the Scholastics that there is a dualistic relationship between natural and special revelation. According to the reformers, "… the handwriting of God in nature is greatly obscured, and is in some of the most important matters rather dim and illegible." Bancroft (1949) also indicates that God has revealed himself within the minds of human beings but also downplays the significance or utility of this concourse between God and man. While he supports the possibility of a scientific theology developed through natural revelation, he rightly indicates that natural theology is only possible by the quickening of man's mental powers by the Spirit of God. Hodge (1939) also indicates that natural revelation alone produces condemnation and judgment but special revelation pertains to redemption and hope. While these views are in harmony with the concepts that are espoused by this written work, they produce little interest in pursuing ideas about the manner in which human beings deflect the Spirit's work, as it is reflected in typical human experiences. Berkhof (1941) looks at John 16:7–11, but uses the passage as proof for the deity of the Holy Spirit. It is obvious that traditional theological writers were not focused on the topic of this written work nor should that be expected, but little has been attempted to find a theological framework for a personality theory that could be used as a basis for understanding how to conduct spiritual formation counseling. Even in other cognate disciplines of study, such as Christian counseling, little has been done to explore this important and relevant topic. There have been forums for papers at Wheaton College from which were published a compendium of papers on the topic (see Care of the Soul, edited by Mark McMinn). Larry Crabb (1992) has published his familiar work, Inside Out, that views human beings as polarized between what they are on the inside and what they are on the outside publicly. Other authors that I have cited have contributed some ideas about their view of spiritual formation concepts, but the topic has not been pursued so comprehensively in regard to how natural revelation may play a role in what Christian counselors do.

[3] Brown's alternative view to the one being expressed here related to the dual role of the Spirit's function, comforting and convicting. In this view, the Spirit is understood as having one function as the Paraclete, the term used to express the English word Comforter as it is used in John 16: 7–8. This view also changes other features of the passage from the view espoused here. The term for ελεγξει that is translated convict is rather translated "will prove wrong" and there is not object to this verb and the term κοσμοσ that is translated world is supplied. This instruction is directed to the disciples themselves according to Brown's view that indicates that the Spirit is given to carry out a patronal/broker function rather than a forensic function. Her interpretation of the passage is one that voids the idea of the Spirit having the function of ministry to the world and rather makes it an exclusive ministry to his disciples to make them more understanding of their role in the world (Brown, 2003). This alternative view is not very supportive of the features expressed in this written work, but it does, however, unify of these attributes of the Spirit.

Chapter Two

[1] Comorbidity is what occurs together in deference to one cause the other when that is not known.

[2] Benzodiazepines are agonist drugs for the neurotransmitter γ amino butyric acid (GABA) that is an inhibitory neurotransmitter that increases the influx of Chloride ions, thus inhibiting the stimulation of these neurons. GABA receptors are found alongside of benzodiazepine receptors in the limbic area of the brain. The limbic area of the brain is located in the midbrain and is responsible

for the anxiety state when its GABA receptors are not sufficiently stimulated. The brain does not produce benzodiazepine substance as a neurotransmitter, but receptors appear to develop for benzodiazepines, even though it is not an innate substance at these specific receptor sites (Preston et.al, 2001).

3   OCD–The DSM-IV-TR (2000, 217–218) lists the criteria for OCD as either obsessions or compulsions. Obsessions are defined by recurrent and persistent thoughts, impulses, or images that are experienced; at some time during the disturbance, the thoughts or impulses, or images are not simply excessive worries about real life situations. The person often attempts to ignore or suppress such thoughts, and the person does recognize that these obsessional thoughts, impulses, or images are a product of his own mind to distinguish the OCD condition from psychosis. Compulsions are defined by repetitive behaviors (e.g. hand washing, ordering, checking) or mental acts (e.g. praying, counting, or repeating phrases or words) that the person feels driven to do in response to an obsession. At some point during the course of the disorder, the person recognizes that obsessions and compulsions are excessive or unreasonable. The obsessions and compulsions cause marked distress and become time consuming and interrupt ordinary social activity and responsibilities.

4   Agoraphobia is a disorder that is diagnosed in conjunction with or without a history of panic disorder. Agoraphobia symptoms, aside from panic, are developed by the impending fear of developing panic like symptoms, but panic symptoms may not be sufficient to meet the criteria for panic disorder itself. The disturbance is not due to physiological effects of substance or medical problems. It is a fear of being in places or situations from which escape might be difficult, embarrassing, or in which help might not be available. Restricted travel or space due to fear of panic or panic-like symptoms are characteristic of the condition (DSM-IV-TR 2000, 212–215).

5   Social Phobia is a marked and persistent fear of one or more social or performance situation in which the person is exposed to unfamiliar people or to possible scrutiny by others. Exposure to the feared social situation almost invariably provokes anxiety, which may take the form of situational bound or predisposed panic attacks. The person recognizes that the fear is excessive or unreasonable. The feared social situation is avoided or endured with excessive anxiety. The avoidance, anxious anticipation, or distress in the feared social or performance situation interferes with the person's ordinary functioning with responsibilities (DSM-IV-TR 2000, 215–216).

6   PD–Panic attack symptoms are listed in this chapter. Further, the criteria define the condition of PD as recurrent, unexpected panic attacks. At least one of the attacks has been followed with a persistent concern about having other attacks, worry about the implications of the attack, and a significant change in behavior related to these attacks. There is also an absence of agoraphobia or the diagnosis changes to agoraphobia with panic attacks. The panic attacks are not due to the direct physiological effects of substance abuse or general medical condition (DSM-IV-TR 2000, 211–212).

7   GAD criteria also include the criteria for the overanxious disorder of childhood. Excessive anxiety and worry more days than days without worry for at least six months in course of duration. The person finds it difficult to control worry. The anxiety or worry is associated with three or more of the following symptoms: restlessness, being easily fatigued, difficulty concentrating, irritability, muscle tension, and sleep disturbance. The focus of the anxiety and worry is not confined to features of other anxiety disorders. The symptoms cause significant clinical distress or impairment in social, occupational, and other important areas of functioning (DSM-IV-TR 2000, 222–223).

8   PTSD criteria for diagnosis involve primarily an exposure to a traumatic event in which both of the following were present: the

person experienced, witnessed, or was confronted with an event or events that involved actual or threatened death or serious physical injury and the person's response involved intense fear, helplessness, or horror. The traumatic event is persistently experienced in one or more of the following ways: recurrent and intrusive distressing recollections of the event, recurrent distressing dreams of the event, acting or feeling as if the traumatic event were recurring in the present, intense psychological distress at exposure to internal or external cues that symbolize the event, physiological reactivity on exposure to internal or external cues to the traumatic event. Persistent avoidance of stimuli associated with the trauma ad numbing of general responsiveness as indicated by three or more of the following: efforts to avoid thought, feelings, or conversations associated with the trauma; efforts to avoid activities, places, or people that arouse recollections of the trauma; inability to recall an important aspect of the trauma; markedly diminished interest or participation in significant activities; feeling of detachment or estrangement from others; restricted range of affect; and sense of a foreshortened future. Persistent symptoms of increased arousal that were not present before trauma indicated by at least two of the following: difficulty staying or falling asleep, irritability or outbursts of anger, difficulty concentrating, hyper-vigilance, and exaggerated startle response. Duration of the experience is at least one month at length. The symptoms cause significant clinical distress or impairment in social, occupational, and other important areas of functioning (DSM-IV-TR 2000, 218–220).

9   Systematic Relaxation uses a step-by-step tensing and relaxing of muscles. Starting at the extremities and moving the legs to arm muscle and then to abdomen, neck, and facial muscles, the respondent will tense muscles, counting slowly from one to five and then will relax them gradually counting from five to one. Another more existential method uses an imaginary means to move more of the high oxygen blood from the extremities to the core of the body

for the heart, lungs, and brain to use. The counselee is to imagine that he is breathing alternately through the toes and the fingers and then exhaling by the same route.

10 Antipsychotic medications are used for schizophrenia. The classic antipsychotic drugs such as Haldol, Thorazine, and Mellaril block a select dopamine receptor, D-2, that by their excess, create the positive symptoms of delusions and hallucinations and by this action worsen the negative symptoms related to blunt affect and depression-like symptoms. They also have serious side effects, such as the involuntary tremors that will not be alleviated and may become permanent if the drug is not removed. The first-generation atypical antipsychotic medications, such as Risperdal and Clozaril, were less threatening with these movement side effects called Parkisonian symptoms, and these drugs also block selective serotonin receptors 5HT2a and many others. They were a little more helpful with mediating the negative symptoms, but Risperdal developed some serious liver problems among its users and Clozaril is responsible for the side effect of leucopoenia, low white blood count making patients susceptible to infections. The second generation of atypical antipsychotics that was designed to relieve both positive and negative symptoms, such as Zyprexa, was then found to induce diabetic neuropathy and is likely not to be used except in cases where it had been in se for some time without this symptom occurring. Other antipsychotics of this class have been found to be effective without as much side effect profile, such as Abilify and Geodon (Stahl, 2000).

Chapter Three

1 General attributes for personality disorders criteria indicate a deviation from ordinary expectations in the enduring patterns of two of the following areas: cognition, affectivity, interpersonal functioning, and impulse control. This enduring pattern is inflexible and pervasive across a broad range of social and personal situations.

The enduring pattern leads to considerable distress or impairment of social, vocational, and other areas of important functioning. These patterns are long in duration and stable over time with an onset that dates back to adolescence, or at least early adulthood. This pattern is not due to physiological disturbance of substance abuse or general medical condition. (DSM-IV-TR 2000, 287–288)

2 APD requires that the person so diagnosed be age eighteen or older and for its criteria, the characteristic of a pervasive pattern of disregard for and violation of the rights of others as indicated by three (or more) of the following:

1. Failure to conform to social norms with respect to lawful behaviors as indicated by repeatedly performing acts that are grounds for arrest.
2. Deceitfulness, as indicated by repeated lying, use of aliases, or conning others for personal profit or pleasure.
3. Impulsivity or failure to plan ahead.
4. Irritability or aggressiveness, as indicated by repeated physical fights or assaults.
5. Reckless disregard for safety of self or others.
6. Consistent irresponsibility, as indicated by repeated failure to sustain consistent work behavior or honor financial obligations. This pattern has been occurring since age fifteen and there is evidence of the onset of conduct disorder prior to that age. The criteria cannot be associated with symptoms of manic depression or schizophrenia (DSM-IV-TR 2000, 291–292).

3 BPD is a pervasive pattern of instability of interpersonal relationships, self-image, and affects and marked impulsivity beginning by early adulthood and present in a variety of contexts as indicated by five or more of the following:

1. Frantic efforts to avoid real or imagined abandonment.

2. A pattern of unstable and intense interpersonal relationships characterized by alternating between extremes of idealization and devaluation.
3. Identity disturbance: markedly and persistently unstable self-image or sense of self.
4. Impulsivity in at least two areas that are potentially self damaging (e.g. spending, sex, substance abuse, reckless driving, binge eating).
5. Recurrent suicidal behavior, gestures or threats or self mutilation (as a separate category).
6. Affective instability due to a marked reactivity of mood (DSMIV-TR, 2000, 292–293).

[4] HPD is a pervasive pattern of excessive emotionality and attention seeking, beginning by early adulthood and present in a variety of contexts, as indicated by five or more of the following:

1. The histrionic is uncomfortable in situations which he is not the center of attention.
2. Displays rapidly shifting and shallow expression of emotions.
3. Consistently uses physical appearance to draw attention to self.
4. Has a style of speech that is excessively impressionistic and lacking detail.
5. Shows self-dramatization, theatricality, and exaggerated expression of emotion.
6. Is suggestible and easily influenced by others or circumstances.
7. Considers relationships to be more intimate than they actually are (DSM-IV-TR 2000, 293).

[5] NPD is a pervasive pattern of grandiosity for admiration, and lack of empathy, beginning by early adulthood and present in a variety of contexts, as indicated by five or more of the following:

1. Has a grandiose sense of self-importance.

2. Is preoccupied with fantasies of unlimited success, power, brilliance, beauty, or ideal love.

3. Believes that he is special and unique and can only be understood by or should associate with other special or high status people.

4. Requires excessive admiration.

5. Has a sense of entitlement with unreasonable expectations if especially favorable treatment or automatic compliance with his or her expectations.

6. Is interpersonally exploitative and takes advantage of others for his own benefit.

7. Lacks empathy and cannot seem to largely identify with others.

8. Is often envious of others or believes that others are envious of him.

9. Shows arrogant, haughty behaviors or attitudes (DSM-IV TR2000, 294.

[6] SPD is a pervasive pattern of detachment from social relationships and a restricted range of expression of emotions in interpersonal settings, beginning by early adulthood and present in a variety of contexts, as indicated by four or more of the following:

1. Neither desires, nor enjoys close relationships, including being part of a family.

2. Almost always chooses solitary activities.

3. Has little, if any, interest in having sexual experiences with another person.

4. Takes pleasure in few, if any, activities.

5. Lacks close friends or confidants other than first-degree relatives.

6. Appears indifferent to the praise or criticism of others.

7. Shows emotional coldness, detachment, flattened affectivity (DSM-IV-TR 2000, 289–290).

7   PPD is a pervasive distrust and suspiciousness of others, such that their motives are interpreted as malevolent, beginning by early adulthood and present in a variety of contexts, as indicated by four or more of the following:

1. Suspects, without sufficient basis, that others are exploiting, harming, or deceiving him.
2. Is preoccupied with unjustified doubts about the loyalty or trust worthiness of friends or associates.
3. Is reluctant to confide in others because of the unwarranted fear that the information will be used maliciously against him.
4. Reads hidden demeaning or threatening meanings into benign remarks or events.
5. Persistently bears grudges and is unforgiving of insults or injuries.
6. Perceives attacks on his character or reputation that are not apparent/
7. Has recurrent suspicions, without justification, regarding of the fidelity of spouse or sexual partner.

This pattern of characteristics does not occur in the course of schizophrenia or other psychotic condition that is due to the direct physiological effects of that general medical condition (DSM-IV-TR 2000, 288–289).

8   STPD is a pervasive pattern of social and interpersonal deficits marked by acute discomfort with and reduced capacity for close relationships, as well as by cognitive or perceptual distortions and eccentricities, beginning by early adulthood and present in a variety of contexts, as indicated by five or more of the following:

1. Ideas of reference excluding delusions of reference.
2. Odd beliefs or magical thinking that influences behavior and is inconsistent with sub-cultural norms.
3. Unusual perceptual experiences, including bodily illusions.

4. Odd thinking and speech.
5. Suspiciousness or paranoid ideation.
6. Inappropriate or restricted affect.
7. Behavior or appearance that is odd, eccentric, or peculiar.
8. Lack of close friends or confidants other than first-degree relatives.

IV-Excessive social anxiety that does not diminish with familiarity. This pattern of characteristics does not occur in the course of schizophrenia or manic depression or with any other psychotic disorder (DSM-TR 2000, 290–291).

9   DPD is a pervasive and excessive need to be taken care of that leads to submissive and clinging behavior and fear of separation, beginning by early adulthood and present in a variety of contexts, as indicated by five or more of the following:

1. Has difficulty making everyday decisions without an excessive amount of advice and reassurance from others.
2. Needs others to assume responsibility for most major areas of his life.
3. Has difficulty expressing disagreement with others because of the fear of loss of support.
4. Has difficulty initiating projects or doing things on his own, presumably because of a lack of confidence.
5. Goes to excessive lengths to obtain nurturance and support from others, to the point of volunteering to do things that are unpleasant.
6. Feels uncomfortable or helpless when alone because of exaggerated fears of being unable to care for himself.
7. Urgently seeks another relationship as a source of care and support when a close relationship ends.

10   AVPD is unrealistically preoccupied with fears of being left to care for himself (DSM-IV-TR 2000, 295–296). AVPD is a pervasive pattern of social inhibition, feelings of inadequacy, and hypersensitivity to

negative evaluations beginning by early adulthood and present in a variety of contexts, as indicated by four or more of the following:

1. Avoids occupational activities that involve significant inter personal contact because of fears of criticism.
2. Is unwilling to get involved with people unless certain of being liked by others.
3. Shows restraint within intimate relationships because of feelings of inadequacy.
4. Is preoccupied with being criticized or rejected.
5. Is inhibited in new interpersonal situations because of feelings of inadequacy.
6. Views self as socially inept, personally unappealing, or inferior.
7. Is unusually reluctant to take personal risks or to engage in any new activities because they might prove to be embarrassing (DSM-IV-TR 2000, 295).

[11] OCPD is a pervasive pattern of preoccupation with orderliness, perfectionism, and mental and interpersonal control, at the expense of flexibility, openness, and efficiency, beginning by early adulthood and present in a variety of contexts, as indicated by four or more of the following:

1. Is preoccupied with details, rules, lists order, organization, or schedules to the extent that the major point of activity is lost.
2. Shows perfectionism that interferes with task completion.
3. Is excessively devoted to work and productivity to the exclusion of leisure activities and friendships.
4. Is over conscientious, scrupulous, and inflexible about matters of morality, ethics, or values.
5. Is unable to discard worn out or worthless objects even when they have no sentimental value.
6. Is reluctant to delegate tasks or to work with others unless they submit to exactly his way of doing things.

7. Adopts a miserly spending style toward both self and others; money is viewed as something to be hoarded for future catastrophes.
8. Shows rigidity and stubbornness (DSM-IV-TR 2000, 296–297).

[11] PDNOS meets the general criteria for this personality disorder mentioned in footnote #1 of this chapter but cannot be classified in any specific personality disorder. It may belong to a mixed category of two separate categories (DSM-IV-TR 2000, 297).

Chapter Four

[1] The DSM-IV-TR (2000, 240–241) criteria for DID are as follows:

1. The presence of two or more distinct identities or personality states (each with its own relatively enduring pattern of perceiving, relating to, and thinking about the environment and self).
2. At least two of these identities or personality states recurrently take control of the person's behavior.
3. Inability to recall important personal information that is too ex tensive to be explained by ordinary forgetfulness.
4. The disturbance is not due to the direct physiological effects of a substance (e.g. blackouts or chaotic behavior during alcohol intoxication) or in general medical condition (e.g., complex partial seizures). In children, the symptoms are not attributable to imaginary playmates or other fantasy play.

Chapter Five

[1] The 12 steps for Alcoholics Anonymous (AA) recovery are found in The Big Book (2001):

1. We admitted that we are powerless over alcohol—that our lives have become unmanageable.
2. Come to believe that a Power greater than ourselves could restore us to sanity.

3. Made a decision to turn our will and ourselves over to the care of God as we understand Him.

4. Made a searching and fearless inventory of ourselves.

5. Admit to God, to ourselves, and to another human being the exact nature of our wrongs.

6. Were entirely ready to have God remove these defects of character.

7. Humbly ask Him to remove our shortcomings.

8. Made a list of all persons we had harmed and became willing to make amends to them all.

9. Made direct amends to such people wherever possible, except when to do so would injure them and others.

10. Continued to make personal inventory and when we were wrong, promptly admit it.

Sought through prayer and meditation to improve our conscious contact with God as we understand Him.

Having a spiritual awakening as a result of these steps, we tried to carry this message to alcoholics and practice these principles in all our affairs.

The manner in which these steps are used is over a period of time.

Each step is to be successively accomplished as personal confession at a point of the accomplishment.

REFERENCES

Adler, Alfred (1982). Cooperation between the sexes: Writings on women and men, love and marriage, sexuality. Second Edition. Edited and translated by Heinz and Rowena Ansbacher (1982). New York: Norton Publishing.

Aharonovich, E., Nguyen, H. & Nunes, E. (2001). Anger and depressive states among treatment-seeking drug abusers: Testing the psychopharmacological specificity hypothesis. The American Journal of Addictions, 10, 327–334.

Alicke, Mark (2000). Culpable Control and the Psychology of Blame. Psychological Bulletin, 126, 556–574.

Allen, J., Coyne, L. & David, E. (1986). Relation of intelligence to ego functioning in an adult psychiatric population. Journal of Personality Assessment, 50, 212–221.

Alcoholics Anonymous (2001). Chapter 5: How it works. In The Big Book. Fourth Edition. Retrieved on November 20, 2006. http://www.aa.org/ bigbookonline /en_BigBook_chptr5.pdf.

Amodeo, M. (1995). The therapist's role in the transitional stage. In S. Brown & I. Yalom, Treating Alcoholism. San Francisco: JosseyBass Publishers.

Anderson, C., Miller, R,. Riger, A,. Dill, J., & Sedikides, C. (1994). Behavioral and characterological attributional styles as predictors of depression and loneliness: Review, refinement and test. Journal of Social Psychology, 66, 549–558.

Arbuckle, Douglas S. (1975). Counseling and psychotherapy: an existential-humanistic view. Boston: Allyn & Bacon.

Arndt, W. & Gingrich, F. W. (1957). A Greek-English lexicon of the New Testament and other early Christian literature. (A translation and adaptation of Walter Bauer's Griechisch-Deutsches Worterbuch zu den Schriften of urchrislichen literature). Chicago: The University of Chicago Press.

Aronson, M. (1980). Psychoanalytic Group psychotherapy. In R. Herink (Ed). The psychotherapy handbook: The A to Z guide to more than 250 different therapies in use today (pp. 511–513). New York: Meridian Books.

Bach, G. (1980). Marathon group therapy. In R. Herink (Ed). The psychotherapy handbook: The A to Z guide to more than 250 different therapies in use today (pp. 356–359). New York: Meridian Books.

Backus, William (1985). Telling the truth to troubled people. Minneapolis, MN: Bethany House Publishers.

Bassin, A. (1980). Reality therapy. In R. Herink (Ed). The psycho-therapy handbook: The A to Z guide to more than 250 different therapies in use today (pp. 553–557). New York: Meridian Books.

Baumeister, R. & Exline, J. (2000). Self-control, morality, and human strength. Journal of Social and Clinical Psychology, 19, 229–42.

Baumrind, D., Lazerlere, R. & Cowan, P. (2002). Ordinary physical punishment: Is it harmful? Comment on Gershoff (2002). Psychological Bulletin, 128, 580–589.

Bancroft, Emery (1949). Christian theology: Systematic and Biblical. Grand Rapids: Zondervan.

Bandura, Albert (1986). Social foundations of thought and action: A Social cognition theory. Englewood Cliffs, NJ: Prentice-Hall, Inc.

Barclay, L., Skarlicki, D. & Pugh, S. D. (2005). Exploring the role of emotions in injustice perceptions and retaliation. Journal of Applied Psychology, 90, 629–643.

Barker, G. & Graham, S. (1987). Developmental study of praise and blame as attributional cues. Journal of Educational Psychology, 79, 62–66.

Bates, M., Pawlak, A., Tonigan, J. C., & Buckman, J. (2006). Cognitive impairment influences drinking outcome by altering therapeutic mechanisms of change. Psychology of Addictive Behaviors, 20, 241–253.

Beck, Aaron (1979). Cognitive therapy and the emotional disorders. New York: Meridian Books.

Beck, A. & Freeman, A. (1990). Cognitive therapy of personality disorders. New York, Guilford Press.

Bergen, H., Martin, G., Richardson, A., Allison S. & Roeger, L. (2004). Sexual abuse, antisocial behavior and substance use: Gender differences in young community adolescents. Australian and New Zealand Journal of Psychiatry, 38, 34–41.

Berne, E. (1977). What do you say after you say hello? New York: Grove Press. Berk, M. & Dodd, S. (2005). Bipolar II disorder: A review. Bipolar Disorders, 7, 11–15.

Berkhof, L. (1939). Systematic theology. Grand Rapids: Wm B. Eerdmans.

Biederman, J., Petty, C., Faraone, S., Hirshfield-Becker, D., Henin, A., Polack, M., & Rosenbaum, J. (2005). Patterns of comorbidity in panic disorder and major depression: Finding from a non-referred sample. Depression and Anxiety, 21, 55–60.

Blanchard-Fields, Freda & Irion, Jane (1988). The relation between locus of control and coping in two contexts. Psychology and Aging, 3, 197– 203.

Bob, Petr (2004). Dissociative processes, multiple personality, and dream functions. American Journal of Psychotherapy, 58, 139–149.

Bowlby, J. (1982). Attachment and loss: V01.1 Attachment. New York: Basic Books.

Brasser, S. & Spear, N. (2002). Physiological and behavioral effects of acute ethanol hangover in juvenile, adolescent and adult rats. Behavioral Neuroscience, 116, 305–320.

Brenner, Ira (1996). The characterological basis of multiple personality. American Journal of Psychotherapy, 50, 154–166. Brown, B. (1972). The multiple techniques of broad spectrum. In Arnold Lazarus (Ed) Clinical behavior therapy: A guide to effective therapy in clinical practice (pp. 174–226). New York: Brunner-Mazel.

Brown, Tricia G. (2003). Spirit in the writings of John: Johannine pneumatology in social-scientific perspective. Journal for the study of the New Testament supplement series, 253,1–267.

Browne, A. & Finkelhor, D. (1985). The traumatic impact of childhood sexual abuse: A conceptualization. American Journal of Orthopsychiatry, 55, 530–541.

Brucker, B. & Bulaeva, N. (1996). Biofeedback effects on electromyography responses in patients with spinal cord injury. Archives of Physical Medicine and Rehabilitation, 77, 133–137.

Burke, K., Burke, J., Regier, D. & Rae, D. (1990). Age of onset of selected mental disorders in five community populations. Archives of General Psychiatry, 47, 511–518.

Carnes, P. (1991). Don't call it love: Recovery from sexual addiction. New York: Bantam Books.

Carroll, K., Easton, C., Nich, C.; Hunkele, K., Neavins, T., Sinha, R., Ford, H., Vitolo, S., Doebrick, C. & Rounsaville, B. (2006). The use of contingency management and motivational/skills-building therapy to treat young adults with marijuana dependence. Journal of Consulting and Clinical Psychology, 74, 955–966.

Chafer, Lewis Sperry (1947). Systematic theology Volume One. Dallas: Dallas Seminary Press.

Clayton, P. (1977). Bipolar affective disorder—Techniques and results of treatment. American Journal of Psychotherapy,13, 81–92.

Cook, W. & Kenny, D. (2004). Application of the social relations model to family assessment. Journal of Family Psychology, 18, 361– 371.

Coolidge, F., Thede, L., & Jang, K. (2004). Are personality disorders psychological manifestations of executive function deficits? Bivariate heritability evidence from a twin study. Behavior Genetics, 34, 75–84.

Cloud, Henry & Townsend, John (1992). Boundaries: when to say yes, when to say no, to take control of your life. Grand Rapids, MI: Zondervan Publishing.

Comino, E., Harris, E., Silove, D., Manicavasagar, V. & Harris, M. (2000). Prevalence, detection and management of anxiety and depressive symptoms in unemployed patients attending general practitioners. Australian and New Zealand Journal of Psychiatry, 34, 107–113.

Cowan, Eric & Presbury, Jack (2000). Meeting resistance and reactance with reverence. Journal of Counseling and Development, 78,411–419.

Dannon, P., Iancu, I., & Grunhaus, L. (2002). The efficacy of reboxetine in the treatment-refractory patients with panic disorder: an open label study. Human Psychopharmacology, 17, 329–333.

Davison, G., Neale, J., & Kring, A. (2004). Abnormal Psychology. Ninth Edition. New York: Wiley.

Delahanty, D., Herberman, H., Craig, K., Hayward, M., Fullerton, C., Ursano, R., & Baum, A. (1997). Acute and chronic distress and post traumatic stress disorder as a function of responsibility for serious motor vehicle accidents. Journal of Consulting and Clinical Psychology, 65, 560–567.

Dengrove, E. (1972). Practical behavioral diagnosis. In Arnold Lazarus (Ed) Clinical behavior therapy: A guide to effective therapy in clinical practice (pp. 73–86). New York: Brunner-Mazel.

Derlega, V., Winstead, B., & Jones, Warren. (1999) Personality: Contemporary theory and research. Second Edition. Nelson-Hall Publishers.

Diagnostic and Statistical Manual-Text Revision (2000). Fourth Edition. Washington, DC: American Psychiatric Association.

Dobson, K. & Dozois, D. (2001). Historical and philosophical bases of cognitive therapies, In K. Dobson (Ed) Handbook of cognitive behavioral therapies (pp. 3–39). New York: The Guilford Press.

Ebmeier, K., Donaghey, J., & Steele, J. D. (2006). Recent developments and current controversies in depression. The Lancet, 367,153–167.

Ecker, Richard (1985). The stress myth: why the pressures of life don't have to get you down. Downers Grove, Illinois: Inter-Varsity Press.

Eiden, R., Leonard, K., Hoyle, R. & Chavez, F. (2004). A transactional model of parent-infant interactions in alcoholic families. Psychology of Addictive Behaviors, 18, 350–361.

Elaas, Mateen (2005). The Holy Spirit: Foundation of Christian faith series. Louisville, Kentucky: Geneva Press.

Ellis, A. (1980). Rational-emotive therapy. In R. Herink (Ed). The psychotherapy handbook: The A to Z guide to more than 250 different therapies in use today (pp. 543–547). New York: Meridian Books.

Erickson, Erik (1963). Childhood and society. Second Edition. New York: W.W. Norton Publishing.

Erickson, Milton (1998). Christian Theology. Second Edition. Grand Rapids, MI: Baker Books.

Faiver, C., O'Brien, E., Ingersoll, R.E. (2000). Religion, guilt, and mental health. Journal of Counseling and Development, 78,155–161.

Foa, E. (1980). Flooding. In R. Herink (Ed). The psychotherapy handbook: The A to Z guide to more than 250 different therapies in use today (pp.233–235). New York: Meridian Books.

Folkman, S. & Lazarus, R. (1985). If it changes it must be a process: Study of emotion coping during three stages of a college examination. Journal of Personality and Social Psychology, 48, 150– 170.

Foulkes, E. (1980). Group-analytic. In R. Herink (Ed). The psychotherapy handbook: The A to Z guide to more than 250 different therapies in use today New York: Meridian Book.

Frazier, P., Mortensen, H. & Steward, J. (2005). Coping strategies as mediators of the relations among perceived control and distress in sexual assault survivors. Journal of Counseling Psychology, 52, 267–278.

Freud, Sigmund (1966). Introductory lectures on psychoanalysis. (James Strachey, Trans.). New York: W.W. Norton Publishing.

Friedman, P. (1972). Personalistic family and marital therapy. In Arnold Lazarus (Ed) Clinical behavior therapy: A guide to effective therapy in clinical practice (pp. 116–154). New York: Brunner-Mazel.

Garmezy, Norman (2005). Vulnerability and resilience. In D. Funder, R. Parke, C. Tomlinson-Keasey, & K. Widaman (Eds) Studying lives through time: Personality and development (pp. 377–398). Washington, D.C.: American Psychological Association.

Gaudiano, B. & Miller, I. (2005). Anxiety disorders comorbidity in bipolar I disorder: Relationships to depression severity and treatment outcome. Depression and Anxiety, 21, 71–77.

General Service Staff of AA. Alcoholics Anonymous. In R. Herink (Ed). The psychotherapy handbook: The A to Z guide to more than 250 different therapies in use today (pp. 21–23). New York: Meridian Books.

Gershoff, Elizabeth (2002). Parental corporal punishment associated child behaviors and experiences: A metanalysis and theoretical review. Psychological Bulletin, 128, 539–579.

Gilroy, P., Carroll, L., & Murra, J. (2002). A preliminary survey of counseling psychologist's personal experiences with depression and treatment. Professional Psychology: Research and Practice, 33, 402– 409.

Glasser, William (1981). Stations of the mind: new directions for reality therapy. New York: Harper & Row.

Glinder, J. & Compas, B. (1999). Self-blame attributions in women with newly diagnosed breast cancer: A prospective study of psychological adjustment. Health Psychology, 18, 475–481.

Goldman, G. (1980). Sullivan Group psychotherapy. In R. Herink (Ed). The psychotherapy handbook: The A to Z guide to more than 250 different therapies in use today (pp. 648–650). New York: Meridian Books.

Golembiewski, R. & Miller, G. (1980). T-group. In R. Herink (Ed). The psychotherapy handbook: The A to Z guide to more than 250 different therapies in use today (pp. 652–655). New York: Meridian Books.

Gosselin, P., Ladouceur, R., Morin, C., Dugas, M. & Baillargeon, L. (2006). Benzodiazepines discontinuation among adults with GAD: A randomized trial of cognitive-behavioral therapy. Journal of Consulting and Clinical Psychology, 74, 908–919.

Goulding, M. & Goulding, R. (1979). Changing lives through redecision therapy. New York: Brunner-Mazel.

Graham, K., Plant, M. & Plant, M. (2004). Alcohol, gender, and partner aggression: A general population study of British adults. Addiction Research and Therapy, 12, 385–401.

Greenberg, L. (2002) Emotion-focused therapy: Coaching clients to work through their feelings. Washington, D.C.: American Psychological Association.

Greene, T. (1980). Jungian group psychotherapy. In R. Herink (Ed). The psychotherapy handbook: The A to Z guide to more than 250 different therapies in use today (pp. 327–329). New York: Meridian Books.

Guitierrez-Lobos, K., Frohlich, S., Miller, C., Whitworth, A., Quiner, S. & Barnas, C. (2000). A comparison of patterns of tranquilizer intake, anxiety and Health locus of control between short and long term benzodiazepine users. Neuropsychobiology, 42, 187–191.

Gurman, A. & Kniskern, D. (Eds) (1981). Handbook of Family Therapy. New York: Brunner/Mazell.

Hage, Sally (2006). Profiles of women survivors: The development of agency in abusive relationships. Journal of Counseling and Development, 84, 83–94.

Hammack, Phillip (2005). The life course development of human sexual orientation: An integrative paradigm. Human Development, 48, 267–290.

Harmon-Jones, Eddie (2003). Clarifying the emotive function of asymmetrical frontal cortical activity. Psychophysiology, 40, 838–848.

Harmon-Jones, E., Abramson, L., Sigelman, J., Bohlig, A., Hogan, M. & Harmon-Jones, C. (2002). Proneness to hypomania/mania symptoms or depression symptoms and asymmetrical frontal cortical responses to an anger evoking event. Journal of Personality and Social Psychology, 4, 610–618.

Hawthorne, Gerald (2003). The presence and the power: The significance of the Holy Spirit in the life and ministry of Jesus. Eugene, Or: Wipf and Stock Publishers.

Herlihy, B. & Corey, G. (1996). ACA ethical standards casebook. Fifth edition. Alexandria, VA: American Counseling Association.

Heyman, G. Dweck, C. & Cain, K. (1992). Young children's vulnerability to self-blame in borderline personality disorder. American Journal of Psychiatry, 146, 490–495.

Hildebrandt, H., Brokate, B., Eling, P. & Lanz, M. (2004). Response shifting and inhibition, but not working memory, are impaired after long-term heavy alcohol consumption. Neuropsychology, 18, 203–211.

Howell, Don (1997). Confidence in the Spirit as the governing ethos of the Pauline mission (pp 36–64). C. Douglas McConnell (Ed) In the Holy Spirit and mission dynamics: William Carey library. Pasadena, Ca: Evangelical Missiological Society.

Hund, A. & Espelage, D. (2005). Childhood sexual abuse, disordered eating, alexithymia, and general distress: A mediation model. Journal of Counseling Psychology, 52, 559–573.

Hunt, C., Keogh, E., & French, C. (2006). Anxiety Sensitivity: The role of conscious awareness and selective attentional bias to physical threat. Emotion, 6, 418–428.

Johnson, S. (2002). Emotionally focused couple therapy with trauma survivors: Strengthening attachment bonds. New York: The Guilford Press.

Jones, S. L. & Butman, R. E. (1991). Modern psychotherapies. Downer's Grove: InterVarsity Press.

Joyce, P., Luty, S., McKenzie, J., Mulder, R. McIntosh, V., Carter, F., Bulik, C., & Sullivan, P. (2004). Bipolar II disorders: Personality and outcomes in two clinical samples. Australian and New Zealand Journal of Psychiatry, 38, 433–438.

Karkkainen, Veli-Matti (2002). Pneumatology: The Holy Spirit in ecumenical, international and contextual perspective. Grand Rapids: Baker Book House.

Karwoski, L., Garratt, G., & Ilardi, S. (2006). On the integration of cognitive-behavioral therapy for depression and positive psychology. Journal of Cognitive Psychotherapy: An International Quarterly, 20, 159–170.

Kellogg, Scott. (2004). Dialogical encounters: Contemporary perspectives on "chairwork" in psychotherapy. Psychotherapy: Theory, Research, and Practice, 41, 310–320.

Kenny, M. & Selcuk, S. (2006). Parental attachment, self-worth, and depressive symptoms among emerging adults. Journal of Counseling and Development, 84, 61–71.

Lazarus, Arnold (1989). The practice of Multimodal therapy: Systematic, comprehensive and effective psychotherapy. Second Edition. Baltimore: Johns Hopkins University Press.

Leahy, R. (2003). Cognitive therapy techniques: A practitioner's guide. New York: Guilford Press.

Lekander, Mats (2002). Ecological immunology: The role of the immune system in psychology and neuroscience. European Psychologist, 7, 98–115.

Lewis, C. S. (1943/1980). Mere Christianity. Edited by Arthur Owen Barfield. New York: Simon & Schuster.

Liska, Ken (2004). Drugs and the human body with implication for society. Seventh Edition. Upper Saddle River, NJ: Pearson-Prentice Hall.

Lovelace, Richard (1979). Dynamics of spiritual life: An evangelical theology of renewal. Downers Grove, Illinois: InterVarsity Press.

Lundqvist, G., Hansson, K. & Svedin, C. (2004). The influence of childhood sexual abuse factors on women's health. Nordic Journal of Psychiatry, 58, 395–401.

Luycks, K., Goossens, L. & Soenens, B. (2006). A developmental contextual perspective on identity construction in emerging adulthood: Change dynamics in commitment formation and commitment evaluation. Developmental Psychology, 42, 366–380.

Luycks, K., Soenens, B. & Goossens, L. (2006). The personality-identity interplay in emerging adult women: Convergent findings from complementary analyses. European Journal of Personality, 20, 195–215.

Lynch, S., Turkheimer, E., D'Onofrio, B. Mendle, J., Emery, R., Slutske, W. & Martin, N. (2006). A genetically informed study of association between harsh punishment of offspring behavioral problems. Journal of Family Psychology, 20, 190–198.

MacArthur, John (1994). The vanishing conscience: drawing the line in a no-fault, guilt-free world. Dallas, Texas: Word Publishing.

Malony, H. Newton (1995). Win-win relationships. Nashville, Tennessee: Broadman and Holman Publishers.

Mantler, J., Schellenberg, E.G., & Page, J. S. (2003). Attributions for serious illness: Are controllability, responsibility, and blame different constructs? Canadian Journal of Behavioral Science, 35, 142–152.

Markoff, L., Reed, B. G., Fallot, R. & Elliot, D. (2005). Implementing trauma-informed alcohol and other drug and mental health services for women: Lessons learned in a multi-site demonstration project. American Journal of Orthopsychiatry, 75, 525–539.

Markowitz, John (2004). Interpersonal psychotherapy of depression. In Mick Power (Ed) Mood disorders: A handbook of science and practice (pp. 167–182). West Sussex, UK: John Wiley and Sons, Ltd.

Martsolf, Donna & Draucker, Claire (2005). Psychotherapy approaches for adult survivors of childhood sexual abuse: An integrative review of outcomes research. Issues of Mental Health Nursing, 26, 801–825.

Mayne, T. & Ambrose, T. (1999). Research review on anger in psychotherapy. Journal of Clinical Psychology, 55, 353–363.

Measelle, J., & Stice, E. & Springer, D. (2006). A prospective test of the negative affect model of substance abuse: Moderating effects of social support. Psychology of Addictive Behaviors, 20, 225–233.

McCormick, Bruce (2004). What's at stake in current debates over justification? (pp. 81–117). M. Husbands & D. Treier (Eds) In Justification: What at stake in current debates? Downers Grove, Illinois: InterVarsity Press.

McGrath, Alister (2005). Iustitia Dei: A history of the Christian doctrine of justification. Third Edition. Cambridge University Press.

McGraw, K. (1987). Guilt following transgression: An attribution of responsibility approach. Journal of Personality and Social Psychology, 53, 247–256.

McIntyre, R. & Katzman, M. (2003). The role of atypical antipsychotics in bipolar depression and anxiety disorders. Bipolar Disorders, 2, 20–35.

McMinn, Mark R. (1996). Psychology, theology and spirituality. Wheaton, IL: Tyndale House Publishers.

McNally, R.J. & Clancy, S.A. (2005). Sleep paralysis in adults reporting repressed, recovered or continuous memories of childhood sexual abuse. Journal of Anxiety Disorders, 114, 147-152.

Meston, C. M., Rellini, A. & Heiman, J. (2006). Women's history of sexual abuse, their sexuality, and sexual self-schemas. Journal of Consulting and Clinical Psychology, 74, 229–236.

Middelberg, Carol (2001). Projective identification in common couple dances. Journal of Marital and Family Therapy, 27, 341–352.

Middleton, Warwick (2005). Owning the past, claiming the present: Perspectives on the treatment of dissociative patients. Australian Psychiatry, 13, 40–49.

Miller, Michael (Ed.), (2006). Drug treatment of bipolar disorder. Harvard Mental Health Letter, 22, 1–4.

Miller, Michael (Ed.), (2006). Your brain and psychotherapy. Harvard Mental Health Letter, 23, 1–3.

Miller, W., Hertel, P., Saucedo, C. & Hester, R. (1994). Effects of alcohol and expectancy on episodic memory in individuals reporting alcoholic blackouts. Experimental and Clinical Psychopharmacology, 2, 161–166.

Millon, Theodore & Davis, Roger (2000). Personality disorders in modern life. New York: John Wiley & Sons.

Minuchin, Salvador (1974). Families & Family Therapy. Cambridge: Harvard University Press.

Mowrer, O. H. (1980). Integrity group. In R. Herink (Ed). The psychotherapy handbook: The A to Z guide to more than 250 different therapies in use today. (pp. 313–315). New York: Meridian Books.

Murray-Swank, N. & Pargament, K. (2005) God, where are you? Evaluating a spiritually-integrated intervention for sexual abuse. Mental Health, Religion & Culture, 8, 191–203.

Naeem, F., Kingdon, D., & Turkington, D. (2006). Cognitive behavior therapy for schizophrenia: Relationship between anxiety symptoms and therapy. Psychology and Psychotherapy: Research and Practice, 79, 153– 164.

National Institute of Mental Health (1981). Diagnostic interview schedule. Department of Heath and Human Services, Public Health Service, Alcohol, Drug Abuse and Mental Health Administration.

New, A., Buchsbaum, M., Hazlett, E., Goodman, M., Koenigsberg, H. Lo, J. Iskander, L., Newmark, R., Brand, J., O'Flynn, K. & Siever, L. (2004). Fluoxetine increases relative metabolic rate in prefrontal cortex in impulse aggression. Psychopharmacology, 176, 451–458.

Nichols, David (1994). Medical chemistry and structure—activity relationships. In Arthur Cho & David Segal (Eds) *Amphetamine and its analogs*. San Diego: Academic Press.

Nichols, Michael (1984). Family therapy: Concepts and methods. New York: Gardner Press, Inc.

O'Connor, L., Berry, J., & Weiss, J. (1999). Interpersonal guilt, shame, and psychological problems. Journal of Social and Clinical Psychology, 18, 181–203.

Oden, Thomas (1980). Guilt free. Nashville, Tennessee: Abingdon Press.

Oliver, Gary (1997). Promoting change through brief therapy in Christian counseling. Wheaton: Tyndale House.

Packer, J. I. (1973). Knowing God. Downers Grove, Illinois: InterVarsity Press.

Perls, Frederick S. (1959). Gestalt Therapy Verbatim. In John O. Stevens (Ed.) New York: Bantam Books.

Peskin, J. (1992). Ruse and representations: On children's ability to conceal information. Developmental Psychology, 28, 84–89.

Piper, John (1986). Desiring God: Meditations of a Christian hedonist. Portland, Oregon: Multnomah Press.

Plantinga, Cornelius (1997). Sin and Addiction. In Robert C. Roberts & Mark A. Talbot (Eds.), Limning the psyche: explorations in Christian psychology (pp. 245–263). Grand Rapids, Michigan: Wm. B. Eerdmans Publishing Company.

Plantinga, Cornelius (1995). A breviary of sin. Grand Rapids, Michigan: Wm. B. Eerdmans Publishing Company.

Polcin, Douglas (2003). Rethinking confrontation in alcohol and drug treatment: Consideration of the clinical context. Substance Use & Misuse, 38, 165–184.

Pope, K. & Vasquez, M. (2001). Ethics in Psychotherapy and Counseling. Second Edition. San Francisco: Jossey-Bass.

Powell, Douglas (2004). Behavioral Treatment of debilitating test anxiety among medical students. Journal of Clinical Psychology, 60, 853– 865.

Power, Mick (2004). Cognitive behavioral therapy for depression. In Mood disorders: A handbook of science and practice (pp. 167–182). West Sussex, UK: John Wiley and Sons, Ltd.

Powers, M. J. & Schmidt, S. (2004). Emotion-focused treatment of unipolar ad bipolar mood disorders. Clinical Psychology and Psychotherapy, 11, 44–57.

Powlison, David (2001). Questions at the Crossroads. In Mark McMinn & Timothy Phillips (Eds.), Care for the soul: exploring the intersection of psychology and theology (pp. 23–61). Downer's Grove, Illinois: InterVarsity Press.

Preston, J., O'Neal, J., & Talaga, M. (2001). Handbook of Clinical Psychopharmacology for Therapists. Second Edition. New Harbinger Publications, Inc.

Prochaska, J. & Norcross, J. (1994). Systems of psychotherapy: A transtheoretical analysis. Third Edition. Pacific Grove, CA: BrooksCole Publishing Company.

Pugh, John (1993). Patterns of pathology and the child within: A fresh look at the adult victim of child sexual abuse. Doctoral dissertation presented to Walden University.

Rapoport, B. (1980). Depth therapy. In R. Herink (Ed). The psycho-therapy handbook: The A to Z guide to more than 250 different therapies in use today (pp. (pp. 145–148). New York: Meridian Books.

Raskin, N. & Rogers, C. (2000). Person-centered therapy. In Current Psychotherapies. Corsini, R. & Wedding, D. (Eds). Itasca, IL: F.E. Peacock.

Reiker, P. & Carmen. E. (1986). The victim-patient process: The disconfirmation and transformation of abuse. American Journal of Orthopsychiatry, 50, 360–370.

Rettew, David & McKee, Laura (2005). Temperament and its role in developmental psychopathology. Harvard Review of Psychiatry, 13, 14–27.

Rivas-Vazquez, Rafael (2002). Clinical and toxic effects of MDMA ("Ecstasy"). Professional Psychology: Research and Practice, 33, 422–425.

Roberts, Robert (1993). Taking the word to heart: self & other in an age of therapies. Grand Rapids, Michigan: Wm. B. Eerdmans Publishing Company.

Rodriguez, M., Perez, V. & Garcia, Y. (2005) Impact of traumatic experiences and violent acts upon response to treatment of a sample of Columbian women with eating disorders. International Journal of Eating Disorders, 37, 299–306.

Rogers, Carl (1951). Client-centered therapy: Its current practice, implications and theory. Boston: Houghton-Mifflin Company.

Rogers, Carl (1961). On becoming a person: A therapist's view of psychotherapy. Boston: Houghton-Mifflin Company.

Rubenfeld, I. (1980). Gestalt synergy. In R. Herink (Ed). The psychotherapy handbook: The A to Z guide to more than 250 different therapies in use today (pp. 252–256). New York: Meridian Books.

Rychlak, Joseph (1981). Introduction to personality and psychotherapy: a theory construction approach. Second Edition. Boston: Houghton-Mifflin Company.

Saddock, J. & Saddock, V. (1998). Synopsis of psychiatry: Behavioral sciences/ Clinical psychiatry. Ninth edition. Philadelphia: Lippincott, Williams & Wilkins.

Sansone, R., Hendricks, C.M., Gaither, G., & Reddington, A. (2004). Prevalence of anxiety symptoms among a sample of outpatients in an internal medicine clinic: A pilot study. Depression and Anxiety, 19, 133–136.

Saltzman, N. (1980). Bio scream psychotherapy. In R. Herink (Ed). The psychotherapy handbook: The A to Z guide to more than 250 different therapies in use today (pp. 66–68). New York: Meridian Books.

Seigel, S. & Krank, M.D. (1987). Anticipation of pharmacological and non-pharmacological events: Classical conditioning and addictive behavior. Journal of Drug Issues, 17, 83–109.

Shaw, Jon (2004). The legacy of child sex abuse. Psychiatry, 67, 217–221.

Shoptaw, S., Majewska, M., Wilkins, J., Twitchell, G., Yang, X. & Ling, W. (2004). Participants receiving dyhydriepiandrosterone during treatment for cocaine dependence show high rates of cocaine use in a placebo-controlled pilot study. Experimental and Clinical Psychopharmacology, 12, 126–135.

Silverstein, S., Hatashita-Wong, M., Wilkniss, S., Bloch, A., Smith, T., Savitz, A., McCarthy, R., Freidman, M. & Torkelsen, K. Rehabilitation of the "treatment refractory" schizophrenia patient: Conceptual foundations, interventions, and outcome data. Psychological Services, 3, 145–169.

Smith, N. & Smith T. (1980). Psychoanalytic group therapy. In R. Herink (Ed). The psychotherapy handbook: The A to Z guide to more than 250 different therapies in use today (pp. 511–513). New York: Meridian Books.

Sproul, R. C. (1989). Surprised by suffering. Wheaton, Illinois: Tyndale House Publishers.

Stahl, Stephen (2000). Essential psychopharmacology: Neuroscientific basis and practical applications. Second edition. Cambridge: Cambridge University Press.

Stalker, C., Gebotys, R. & Harper, K. (2005). Insecure attachment as a predictor of outcome following inpatient trauma treatment for women survivors of childhood abuse. Bulletin of the Menninger Clinic, 69, 137–156.

Steele, Howard (2003). Unrelenting catastrophic trauma within the family: When every secure base is abusive. Attachment and Human Development, 5, 353–366.

Stein, Edward (1968). Guilt: theory and therapy. Philadelphia, Pennsylvania: Westminster Press.

Stephenson, R. (1980). Guided group interaction. In R. Herink (Ed). The psychotherapy handbook: The A to Z guide to more than 250 different therapies in use today. New York: Meridian Books.

Stevens, J. (1980). Gestalt therapy. In R. Herink (Ed). The psychotherapy handbook: The A to Z guide to more than 250 different therapies in use today (pp. 247–252). New York: Meridian Books.

Stice, E., Burton, E. & Shaw, H. (2004). Prospective relations between bulimic pathology, depression, and substance abuse: Unpacking comorbidity in adolescent girls. Journal of Consulting and Clinical Psychology, 72, 62–71.

Stierlin, H. (1977). Psychoanalysis and family therapy: Selected papers. New York: Jason Aronson, Inc.

Stovall-McClough, K. C. &Cloitre, M. (2006). Unresolved attachment, PTSD, and dissociation in women with childhood abuse histories. Journal of Consulting and Clinical Psychology, 74, 219–228.

Thase, M. & Callan, J. (2006). The role of homework in cognitive behavior therapy of depression. Journal of Psychotherapy Integration, 16, 162–177.

Thyer, B., Parrish, R., Curtis, G., Nease, R. & Cameron, O. (1985). Ages of Onset of DSM-III Anxiety Disorders. Comprehensive Psychiatry, 26, 113–122.

Trask, T. & Goodall, W. (1998). The blessing: Experiencing the power of the Holy Spirit today. Grand Rapids: Zondervan Publishing House.

Tripp, Tedd (1995). Shepherding a child 's heart. Wapwallopen, PA: Shepherd Press.

Truax, C. & Carkhuff, R. (1972). Toward effectiveness of counseling and psychotherapy: training and practice. Chicago: Aldine Publishing Company.

Turner, Max (2000). Power from on high: The Spirit's in Israel 's restoration and witness. Sheffield, GB: Sheffield Academic Press.

Vanderbeeken, R. & Weber, E. (2002). Dispositional Explanations of Behavior. Behavior and Philosophy, 30, 43–59.

Van Der Bosch, L., Verhuel, R. & Van Der Brink, W. (2003). Trauma, dissociation, and posttraumatic stress disorder in female borderline patients with and without substance abuse problems. Australian and New Zealand Journal of Psychiatry, 37, 549–555.

Van Goozen, S., Frijda, N. & Van de Poll, N. (1994). Anger and aggression in women: Influence of sports choice and testosterone administration. Aggressive Behavior, 20, 213–222.

Vassilopoulos, Stephanos (2005). Social anxiety and the effects of engaging in mental imagery. Cognitive Therapy and Research, 29, 261–277.

Veleber, D. & Templer, D. (1984). Effects of caffeine on anxiety and depression. Journal of Abnormal Psychology, 93, 120–122.

Victorson, D., Farmer, Burnett, K., Ouellette, A., & Barocas, J. (2004). Maladaptive coping strategies and injury-related distress following traumatic physical injury. Rehabilitation Psychology, 50, 408–425.

Wakefield, Jerome (2006). Are there relational disorders? A harmful dysfunction perspective: Comment on the special section. Journal of Family Psychology, 20, 423–427.

Walvoord, John (1958). The Holy Spirit: A comprehensive study of the person and work of the Holy Spirit. Grand Rapids: The Zondervan Publishing House.

Weekes, Claire (1977). Simple, effective treatment of agoraphobia. American Journal of Psychotherapy, 32 , 357–369.

Welch, Edward (1998). Blame it on the brain. Phillipsburg, NJ: Presbyterian & Reformed Publishing.

Welch, Edward (1997). When people are big and God is small. Phillipsburg, NJ: Presbyterian & Reformed Publishing.

Westermeyer, Robert (1994). Harm reduction and moderation as an alternative to heavy drinking. http://www.habitsmart.com/cntrldnk.html.

Wilson, Earl D. (1987). Counseling and guilt. In Gary Collins (Ed.), Resources for Christian Counseling, Volume Eight. Waco, Texas: Word Books.

Wolpe, Joseph (1973). The practice of behavior therapy. New York: Pergamon Press.

Wright, Pearce (1996). Nitric Oxide: From menace to marvel of the decade. Retrieved on November 19, 2006 http://www.absw.org. uk/briefings/nitric%200xide.htm.

Yablonsky, L. (1980). Psychodrama. In R. Herink (Ed). The psycho-therapy handbook: The A to Z guide to more than 250 different therapies in use today (pp. 517–522). New York: Meridian Books.

Yalom, I. (1995). The theory and practice of group psychotherapy. Fourth edition. New York: Basic Books.

Yen, S., Shea, T., Pagano, M., Sanislow, C., Grilo, C. McGlashan, T., Skodol, A., Bender, D., Zanarini, M. Gunderson, J. & Morey, L. (2003). Axis I and Axis II disorders as predictors of prospective suicide attempts: Findings from the collaborative longitudinal personality disorders study. Journal of Abnormal Psychology, 112, 375–381.

Yong, Amos (2003). Beyond the impasse: Toward a pneumatological theology of religion. Grand Rapids: Baker Book House.

Zacharias, Ravi (1998). Cries of the heart: Bringing God near when he feels so far. Nashville: Word Publishing.